The American Metropolis

Leonard E. Goodall
University of Illinois at Chicago Circle

Charles E. Merrill Publishing Company
A Bell & Howell Company

Library of Congress Catalog Number: 68-12791

1 2 3 4 5 6 7 8 9 10 11 12 13—75 74 73 72 71 70 69 68 67

Printed in the United States of America

Preface

There was a time when the citizen interested in learning about the government and politics of our cities read a book or took a course on "Municipal Government." It was appropriate for him to do so for most of the activities involved in governing our cities were the responsibility of municipal governments, with possibly some occasional help (or hindrance) from the state. A study of municipal government will still tell one much about the governing of our cities, but increasingly it is only a part of the picture. One of the two general themes which I have tried to emphasize in this book is that the governing of our major cities and metropolitan areas is essentially an intergovernmental or multi-governmental process. It involves governments at all levels—local, county, state and national—and the developing patterns of cooperation and conflict among these governments are one of the most important facets of the governmental process in metropolitan areas.

The second general theme I have attempted to stress is that the process of governing urban areas is a political process, and at several points in the work some discussion is devoted to what is meant by the term "political process." I have defined politics here as conflict over public policy. One of the political characteristics of local government has been the continual attempt to "depoliticize" the local political process through such means as nonpartisan elections and the council-manager plan. Many times these reforms have made a most beneficial effect, but the point made throughout the book is that while such reforms may change the form of the local political process they do not eliminate politics from the process.

It is hoped that those in courses in municipal and metropolitan government, urban politics, and state and local government will find the book particularly useful. In addition, students of urban sociology, city planning and related areas, as well as interested citizens and members of civic organizations like the League of Women Voters, may find the book helpful in getting a compact, comprehensive look at government and politics in the metropolitan area.

I am indebted to many people that have influenced the content of the book. Professor Charles M. Kneier has influenced my thinking about local politics more than any other one person. Two colleagues, Bruce B. Mason and Dwight Carpenter, read parts of the manuscript and provided valuable commentary. I am very indebted to the many appointed and elected officials with whom I have had extended conversations about the concepts discussed here. In particular, I would mention two elected officials, Mayor Milton H. Graham and Councilwoman Sophia Kruglick of Phoenix, several members of the city management profession—Robert Coop, Mark Keane, Lee Kraft, Gale Christy, William Donnaldson and Richard Malcolm—and Jack DeBolske, Executive Director of the League of Arizona Cities and Towns. Extended informal conversations with these people have sharpened and often altered my own views about how local politics operates. Marion Hargreaves typed much of the manuscript and her help is appreciated. Finally I express my appreciation to my wife, Lois, for her encouragement and patience (in addition to her typing and proofreading) throughout the writing process.

For the ideas and concepts as well as the errors that finally found their way into print the author as usual accepts full responsibility.

Leonard E. Goodall

Table of Contents

chapter 1

Urbanization in America

If you live in the United States, the chances are about two-to-one that you live in one of the nation's metropolitan areas. If your income places you in the "middle class" category or higher and if you are not a Negro or a member of some other minority group, it is very likely that you live in one of the suburbs of your metropolitan area rather than in the central city. Your family's move to the suburbs, however, has probably taken place since World War II. Although you may have moved to the suburbs, it is probable that you still work in the central city and that you battle rush hour traffic each day driving to and from work on what you consider to be totally inadequate streets or freeways.

Increasingly, the average American is dwelling not just in urban areas but in those vast urban complexes we call metropolitan areas. An ever-increasing percentage of our population is living in the very small percentage of land area occupied by our metropolitan areas. This transition from a rural to an urban to a metropolitan nation is discussed below.

THE DEVELOPMENT OF AN URBAN NATION

The nation founded by the leaders of the American revolution and the writers of the constitution was a predominantly rural nation. At the time of the nation's first decennial census in 1790, only 5 per cent of the population lived in urban areas. Philadelphia, with 42,000 inhabitants, was the country's largest city while New York had only 33,000. Thomas Jefferson extolled the virtues of the rural society and once suggested that the "mobs of great cities" impede the achievement of good government, but his ideal was soon to pass out of existence. By 1850, New York had a population of over 500,000, and five other cities (Baltimore, Boston, Philadelphia, New Orleans, and Cincinnati) had over 100,000 inhabitants each. On the other hand, it is interesting to note that the population of Chicago was less than 30,000 at that time. By 1880, New York City's population had passed the million mark, and by 1890, the population figures for Philadelphia and Chicago (having experienced very rapid growth) also exceeded that level.

The decade of 1910-20 was a most significant one in the urbanization process of the country, for it was during that period that the nation became predominantly urban. The census of 1920 was the first to show a majority, 51.2 per cent, of the population living in urban areas. By 1940, 56.5 per cent of the population was urban, and there were five cities of over one million population. Since World War II the urban trend has continued unabated, and the 1960 census showed about 70 per cent of the population living in urban areas.

It is important to note that urban growth has not been uniform. Many smaller cities and villages are actually losing population or are growing at a slower rate than the population generally, and some of our largest cities, such as New York and Chicago, are also not holding their own. From 1950 to 1960 the population of the nation increased 18.5 per cent, but during that same period New York City had a 1.4 per cent decline in population, Chicago declined by 1.9 per cent, and Cleveland by 4.2 per cent. The major population gains are taking place in the fringe areas around the larger cities.

The term "metropolitan area" is one that must be understood in order to appreciate the degree of urbanization taking place in the country. The U. S. Bureau of the Budget has defined a standard metropolitan statistical area (SMSA) as a central city (or cities) of 50,000 or more inhabitants, the county or counties in which the central city is located, and other contiguous territory which is economically and socially integrated with the central city. In determining whether contiguous territory outside the central county is to be part of the metropolitan area, the Bureau of the Budget takes into consideration such factors as degree of population density and per cent of population engaged in nonagricultural activities.[1] The San Francisco-Oakland SMSA includes six counties and there are also six counties in the Chicago SMSA.

Metropolitan areas may extend across state boundaries. For example, the Washington, D. C. SMSA includes areas in Maryland and Virginia as well as the District of Columbia. The St. Louis metropolitan area

---

[1] For the complete definition of "metropolitan area" see U.S. Bureau of the Budget, *Standard Metropolitan Statistic Areas*, (Washington: U.S. Government Printing Office, 1961).

includes parts of both Missouri and Illinois, and the Kansas City area covers parts of Kansas as well as Missouri. Although there are no legal definitions covering such areas, it is obvious that some metropolitan areas are in reality international in scope. It is hard to think about the Detroit area without thinking also of Windsor, Ontario, and the same would be true of San Diego and Tijuana or El Paso and Juarez.

In 1960, 112.9 million people, or 62.8 per cent of the population, lived in the nation's 212 metropolitan areas. Between 1950 and 1960, 85 per cent of the total population increase of the country took place in metropolitan areas. In the 1950-60 decade the population of metropolitan areas increased by over 28 million, which is roughly the equivalent of adding to the nation eight cities the size of Chicago! The extent to which we are becoming a metropolitan nation is pointed up by the fact that the 62.8 per cent of our population who live in metropolitan areas occupy only 8.7 per cent of the country's land area. About 10.7 million people live in the New York City metropolitan area, more people than the combined population of fourteen states, Alaska, Arizona, Delaware, Hawaii, Idaho, Maine, Montana, New Hampshire, New Mexico, North Dakota, South Dakota, Vermont, Rhode Island, and Wyoming.

In recent years a new word has entered the vocabulary of those who study the problems of metropolitan areas: "megalopolis." The term is broader than "metropolitan area" and refers to an extended area of contiguous urban and suburban territory. Such an area may include several metropolitan areas. Professor Gottman has referred to the megalopolis along the northeastern seaboard as "an almost continuous stretch of urban and suburban areas from southern New Hampshire to northern Virginia and from the Atlantic shore to the Appalachian foothills."[2] In this area live over 38 million people, about one-fifth of the total population. But this is not the only megalopolis. Other megalopolises are developing around the southern shores of the Great Lakes, along the Gulf of Mexico, and on the West Coast. Not just Metropolis but Megalopolis is becoming the center of population, industry and employment.

There is no reason to believe that the urbanization trend is coming to an end. The census of 1970 is almost certain to show an increase in the percentage of the population living in metropolitan areas, and we are probably not very far from the time when three-fourths of the people will reside in such areas.

_____

[2] Jean Gottman, *Megalopolis: The Urbanized Northeastern Seaboard of the United States* (New York: Twentieth Century Fund, 1962).

REASONS FOR THE URBAN TREND

Why has the dramatic move to the city taken place? What has been behind the trend that shows more of the population becoming "city folks" with each decennial census? Some of the more important reasons for the trend are discussed below.

Improvements in Agriculture

There have been many contributing factors to the trend toward urbanization, but basic to everything else has been the "agricultural revolution" which freed man from the soil. So long as men had to spend nearly all of their time tilling the earth in order to grow food for themselves and their families, there was little chance or reason for them to congregate into common living areas and develop cities. As improvements were made in agricultural methods, a smaller percentage of the population could produce the food necessary to feed the nation, and many formerly engaged in farming made their way to the city in search of other types of employment. In 1800, 71.9 per cent of the inhabitants of the United States were employed in agriculture. In 1900 the figure had fallen to 36.8 per cent. Every decade finds fewer people providing the necessary food supply for the nation, and in 1960 only 6.7 per cent of the population were employed in agriculture. Though he may regret it, the American farmer today is generally unable to keep his children "down on the farm." The opportunities there are too limited and the attractions of the city too great.

Employment Opportunities

If the agricultural revolution made it possible for man to leave the soil, the industrial and commercial activities of the city gave him a motive for leaving. The opportunity for employment (real or imagined) has long been the magnet that draws people to the city. One need not look far to see the impact of industry and commerce on urbanization. The economy of the Detroit area is closely tied to the automobile industry, the steel mills have an important influence on the Pittsburgh area, and Chicago, with its huge stockyards serving the midwestern states, early gained a reputation as "hog butcher to the world." Not all cities, of course, have huge manufacturing plants with tall smoke stacks and sprawling parking lots. In some communities the local "industry" may be something quite different. Cambridge, Massachusetts, and Berkeley,

California, are well-known centers of the education "industry." The same would be true on a smaller scale for Iowa City, Iowa, or Champaign-Urbana, Illinois, and the Chamber of Commerce of Columbia, Missouri, advertises that "Education is Columbia's leading enterprise." Government employment is a major factor in the economy of Washington, D. C. and of many state capitols. For cities like Miami, Phoenix, and Atlantic City, the tourist trade provides many employment opportunities and is an important stimulant to the local economy.

The extent to which employment opportunities are the attraction that bring people to the city is well illustrated by the fact that the urbanization trend is much more pronounced in times of prosperity than in times of recession. For example, the decade of 1860-70 saw the urban population grow from 19.8 per cent to 25.7 per cent of the total population, but during the following decade, which included the financial panic of 1873, the rate or urbanization slowed, and the urban proportion of the total population only increased from 25.7 per cent to 28.2 per cent. In the 1880's as the nation pulled out of recession and moved again into prosperous times, the urban population rose to 35.1 per cent of the total. The pattern for the depression of the 1930's was similar. While the urban population grew rapidly during the 1920's and again in the 1940's, the urban trend came almost to a standstill during the 1930's as the percentage of inhabitants living in urban areas increased only from 56.2 per cent to 56.5 per cent during that decade. It appears that prosperous times accelerate the trend to urbanization while an economic slowdown will tend to have the opposite effect. A current example of the move to the city in search of employment is the migration of southern Negroes to northern cities such as Chicago, Cleveland, and Cincinnati. Unfortunately, the job opportunities they are seeking are often more hoped for than real, and many of them find themselves in a strange city without a job or much chance of getting one.

Improvements in Transportation

The development of cities as large industrial and commercial centers was made possible by improvements in the available means of transportation. When poor transportation facilities made it necessary for goods to be produced near the consumers who would use them, each town had its small factories and family operated stores that served primarily the people living in the immediate area. It was only as improvements were made in the means of transportation that cities could become large production centers serving consumers living hundreds and later thousands of miles away. The opening of the Erie Canal in 1821 led rapidly to the development of commercial centers throughout the state of New York, as communities like Buffalo, Rochester, and Syracuse grew from small villages into busy cities. Every American history book points out the importance of the extension of the railroad in the western movement of the frontier. As the railroad was built across the western frontier, finally spanning the continent in 1869, new cities sprang up out of barren plains, and those who populated these new cities were encouraged by the knowledge that some of the luxuries to be found in the older cities in the East would now be available to them, thanks to the "iron horse." In the twentieth century, air transportation has further expanded the markets of any given area. Today, it is possible to buy freshly grown orchids from Hawaii in Chicago flower shops, and investors in Honolulu may get the current Wall Street Journal which is flown daily from the mainland. Expanded markets made possible by improved transportation facilities have played a major role in the growth of our large cities.

Geographical Factors

Geography has been another key factor in the growth of cities. One would be hard pressed to name a major city in the world in which geography has not played an important part in its location. It was no accident that cities like Paris, London, St. Louis, and New Orleans were located on major rivers nor is it any surprise that they grew and prospered during those periods when water routes were the major means of transportation. The cities of New York and San Francisco owe much of their prosperity to the fact that their strategic locations enabled them to become major ports for foreign shipping and commerce. Chicago's location at the southern tip of Lake Michigan and Cleveland's position on the shore of Lake Erie are evidence that lakes as well as rivers and oceans can lead to significant commercial development.

In some cases, the proximity of power or raw materials necessary for industry has been significant in the location and growth of major urban areas. The growth of Pittsburgh has been due in part to the nearness of large coal deposits. Tulsa and Dallas are in the midst of the oil producing areas of the southwest. Cities have grown up along rivers not only because the river provides a transportation route, but also because it provides the power necessary for the operation of industrial plants. In the midwest, the growth of Kansas City and Chicago has been due in part to their location near the major agricultural regions of the country, making them natural centers of processing and marketing for agricultural products.

Immigration

A final factor which should not be overlooked in discussing the reasons for the trend to urbanization is immigration from abroad. The latter part of the nineteenth century and the early part of the twentieth century saw thousands of immigrants enter the United States, primarily from Europe. A few of these people moved to agricultural areas and followed their former profession of farming, a fact which is still evident by the large number of Scandinavian names to be found in the agricultural areas of Wisconsin, Minnesota, and the Dakotas. Most of these newcomers, however, located in cities. The German sections of Milwaukee and St. Louis, San Francisco's Chinatown, and the numerous ghettos representing various nations and cultures in New York and Chicago testify to the importance of immigration in the growth of our cities.

LIFE IN THE CITY

Higher (And More Expensive) Living Standards

The urbanization of the nation has brought about a number of basic changes in the living patterns of Americans. One significant change has been the rise in the standard of living which has accompanied the urban trend. The city dweller may complain about poor streets and crowded highways, but these are still improvements over the unpaved roads that were (and in many places, still are) characteristic of much of rural America. The city dweller will lament the passing of the family doctor in favor of a multitude of specialists, but he will be pleased that the hospital and medical personnel are now only blocks, rather than miles, away. At the turn of the century the average housewife, living on a farm, made the traditional Saturday afternoon trip to town to get groceries and supplies to last through the next week, and during the winter months the trips were usually much more than a week apart. Today the average housewife lives only blocks from the shopping center, and it is easy for her to make a trip there every few days. Not only is the shopping center closer, but it also offers an infinitely wider variety of goods and services than those available a half century ago. Finally, cultural opportunities tend to increase as an area becomes more urbanized. It stands to reason that a densely populated area can support a wider variety of libraries, musical and theatrical presentations, fine restaurants, and the like than can a more sparsely populated area.

The advantages of urban living do not come cheaply, however. The urban resident generally finds that living in the city brings not only a higher, but also a more expensive, standard of living. Wages and salaries are usually higher in the city, and these costs will be reflected in the prices which must be paid for goods and services produced there. Labor unions have been most successful in organizing workers in urban industrial areas, and this factor, among others, will tend to bring about the somewhat higher labor costs found in urban areas. Indeed, some small towns have sought to lure industry away from the cities by promising an escape from the high labor costs of the city.

Another contributing factor to the high costs of urban living is the high cost of land. It is obvious that in densely populated areas the demand for land is great and the supply is limited. Because of this, the long trend has been a steep rise in the cost of urban land and it is reasonable to expect that this will continue. High land costs will, of course, be reflected in the costs of owning or renting a home. Business establishments in such areas will have to pay high rents, a cost which they must include in the prices they charge for their merchandise.

Taxes also are often higher in large cities than in smaller communities. As cities grow, the city government is called upon to provide more services, and the demand for certain types of services, such as welfare services and police protection, is likely to grow much more rapidly than the availability of municipal revenues to provide them. In some areas, city taxes rise because the people demand not only more but also better municipal services. As their standard of living rises and people can afford a nicer home, they also want better schools and parks. As they can afford a nicer automobile, they expect better roads.

Finally, it is only fair to point out that one reason living costs are higher in urban areas is because, as we have said, living standards are higher there. The problem, it might be said, is not so much the "higher cost of living" as it is the "cost of higher living." When theatres and professional baseball, night clubs and French restaurants are available only a few minutes' drive from home, people are going to patronize them more often than if it took several hours or days to reach them. As was just pointed out, when the citizens are able to afford better private goods and services, they will expect better services from their government. It would be foolish to think that better services could be provided without higher costs.

Increasing Economic Interdependence

Another consequence of urbanization is an increase in the economic interdependence of individuals and organizations in society. The American farmer has long maintained (rightly or wrongly) with great pride that living on the land gives him a large degree of economic independence. On the other hand, urban living in the twentieth century involves a considerable sacrifice of economic independence. Today's urban dweller is probably not self-employed, so major decisions concerning his compensation, job security, etc., are made by people other than himself. His economic situation will be affected by the general state of the economy. During periods of economic prosperity he may live well, but a downturn in economic activity may cause him to be laid off temporarily or even to lose his job. Certain welfare measures such as unemployment compensation may cushion the effects of economic crisis on the city dweller, but he is still going to feel the "pinch" of economic conditions over which he has no control. This problem may be especially acute in cities whose economy depends greatly on a single industry. A slowdown in the sale of automobiles, for example, will have serious effects on the economy of Detroit. Not only will those who work in the automobile plants suffer, but as they cut back their spending, supermarkets, clothing stores, and other stores at which the auto workers shop will feel the effects.

The well being of those living in a given city may be affected by decisions made thousands of miles away. Those who work in defense plants in San Diego, for example, may be placed on overtime or lose their jobs depending on decisions made in the Pentagon in Washington, and the Pentagon decisions in turn may be based on the military situation in Berlin or Southeast Asia. Figures mentioned above show that in the past, such as during the financial crises of the 1870's and 1930's, many people who had gone to the city in search of work returned to their families on the farm when they were no longer able to get employment. Today, however, that is no longer a possibility for most city dwellers. Fortunately or unfortunately, depending on how one looks at it, they are part of a vast interdependent economic society over which they as individuals have little control.

The Political Machine

One of the earliest consequences of urbanization, dating back to the nineteenth century, was the rise of the political machine. In the nineteenth century the American system of local government was heavily influenced by the principles of Jacksonian democracy. Most city governments utilized the long ballot, dividing administrative power among a number of elected officials and placing only very limited powers in the office of mayor. Under such a system, no one official has the necessary authority to bring about coordination among various municipal officials or the prestige and power to provide strong policy leadership for the community. As cities began to grow, the need for coordination and policy leadership became more acute, and the inability of the existing governments to meet these needs became more apparent. One of the major reasons for the rise of political machines was that they were able through informal methods to meet these needs which the formal governmental structure could not meet. Since the machine gained control of the dominant political party (machines could work through either party, depending on which was the majority party in that area), its support was necessary for election to office. This being the case, the machine could force a certain amount of coordination and cooperation among office holders.

Another reason for the rise of the machine was that it provided services desired by certain segments of the newly developing urban society. The machine was much like a business in that it provided certain services for which it expected certain types of payment. The machine, usually directed by a small group of people or by a single "boss," had workers throughout the city, but these workers tended to be especially active in the residential areas inhabited by foreign born, minority and low income groups. It was the responsibility of these workers to know and "take care of" the people in their ward or precinct, and the people came to expect certain things of the machine. They knew that the machine's man could cut through the red tape when they needed some form of public welfare and that he was the man to see about getting a job at city hall. They looked forward to the Fourth of July picnic, the Thanksgiving food basket, and the children's party at Christmas, all of which were provided by the machine. In return for these services, the machine expected the people to vote as it directed and the people were usually willing to so do.

The machine also provided services for the business community. The coal dealer who wanted to sell coal to city hall, the transit company that wanted to operate a street car system in the city, and the contractor who wanted the job of repairing the fire station knew the value of being on good terms with the machine. For the business man, being on good terms with the machine generally meant financial contributions. The illegitimate businessman—the operator of the gambling casino or the house of ill repute—needed assurance that the police would not crack down, and it was possible to get this assurance from the machine for a price. The politician who wanted to get elected to office knew that machine support was essential to election. Thus, he would seek the support of the machine in return for his assurance that on matters of importance to the machine he would make the "right" decisions.

The question of the morality of the machine was seldom raised prior to the days of the muckrakers. It was simply a business operation, selling services and favors in return for votes, granting contracts or police protection in return for financial help, and offering political support in return for the loyalty of those elected to office. The machine was certainly not all bad. In most places it provided adequate city government. One must remember, after all, that the machine could do nothing if its candidates were not elected to office, and the number of votes that could be delivered by the precinct workers was often not sufficient to win elections. The machine, therefore, had to provide good enough government to win some voters to its cause.[3]

On the other hand, the excesses of corruption and favoritism characteristic of many machine organizations brought a reaction against machine rule about the time of the turn of the century. Demands to "throw the rascals out" and movements to reorganize city government slowly led to the demise of the big city machine. Today relatively strong political organizations exist in some major cities, such as New York and Chicago, but their operations are much different from those of the machines of earlier years. During the latter part of the nineteenth century and the early part of the twentieth century, nevertheless, the city machine was not only a result of but also an important influence on the nature of urban life.

The Sociological Revolution

Another consequence of urbanization has been what might be called a sociological revolution. As discussed above, the process of urbanization takes away from the individual much of his economic independence, but at the same time it gives him more social independence. The anonymity of urban living means that the city dweller can do pretty much as he pleases without fear of social retribution. He need not fear the curious eye of neighbors or the fast working tongue of the backyard gossip often associated with rural or small town living. The average city dweller may not even know the names of his neighbors, and if he does, it is still probable that they have little knowledge of and little interest

---

[3] Works on the political machine include Lincoln Steffens, *Shame of the Cities* (New York: McClure, Phillips and Co., 1904); C. W. Van Devander, *The Big Bosses* (New York: Howell, Soskin Co., 1944); W. M. Reddig, *Tom's Town: Kansas City and the Pendergast Legend* (Philadelphia: J. B. Lippincott Co., 1947); a good discussion on the latent functions of the machine is found in Robert K. Merton, *Social Theory and Social Structure* (New York: Free Press, 1957), pp. 71–82.

in his personal life. This social freedom that characterizes urban living was unknown in a predominately rural society.

This freedom, however, is not an unmixed blessing. It exists only because of what sociologists refer to as a substitution of secondary for primary relationships. Rather than having a small group of very close friends, the individual who lives and works in the city is more likely to have a large, but less intimate, group of friends and acquaintances. These will be people he knows at work or perhaps at church or in clubs, but they are often not what could be called close, intimate friendships. Certain aspects of this situation may be attractive, but other aspects of it present problems for city life. Not only do one's acquaintances in the city not impose social sanctions, but they also do not give him recognition and acclaim for his achievements or assurances of loyalty when he needs it. In short, it seems to the individual that in the city no one really cares.

David Riesman and his co-authors in *The Lonely Crowd*[4] suggest that this dilemma has brought into being the "other directed man." Prior to recent times, according to this theory, individuals sought security through conformity to the values of their parents, especially their father. These values were impressed upon them through the authority relationships that existed between parent and offspring. Today this situation has changed. The living patterns of an urban industrial society have broken the close family ties characteristic of an earlier time, and the individual now looks to other sources for cues for his behavior patterns. He finds security in conforming to the values of his business and professional associates, his neighbors in suburbia, and others whom he knows mainly in secondary rather than primary relationships.

A particular type of "other directed man" is the "organization man," a concept developed by William H. Whyte in the book of that title.[5] The organization man seeks security through the organization that employs him, most commonly the large corporation. He attempts to adopt the organization's values and the behavior patterns of others in the organization. In return he hopes to acquire security of social position in the form of acceptance by his associates and security of economic position in the form of a good salary and liberal fringe benefits from the organization.

In various ways, the "other directed man" and the "organization man" seek to trade conformity for security. The stories of suburban subdivisions where all the men are corporation vice presidents, wear dark suits,

---

[4] David Riesman *et al., The Lonely Crowd* (New Haven: Yale University Press, 1950).

[5] William H. Whyte, *The Organization Man* (New York: Simon and Schuster, 1956).

live in ranch style homes of the same design and color, and belong to the same clubs are undoubtedly exaggerated, but there is enough truth in them to indicate the importance of the sociological revolution in urban America and of man's attempt to adjust to it.

Demands for Social and Economic Change

A final consequence of urbanization has been increasing demands for social and economic change. Historically, cities have been the centers of movements for reform while rural areas have been more reluctant to accept the new proposals. This has manifested itself in American national politics in several ways. First, the President, who must rely heavily on the votes of urban areas to get elected, is generally somewhat more liberal than is the Congress, which is more representative of rural areas. Also, within the Congress, the more liberal members in both parties will tend to come mainly from the nation's major urban areas. In state governments, this problem has resulted in what has come to be known as "the urban-rural conflict," a situation aggravated by malapportioned legislatures in which the rural legislators will comprise a majority of the members of the legislature, or at least of one house, even though they represent only a minority of the state's population. This has often led to serious conflict when the rural legislators refused to consider solutions to the critical problems facing urban areas. Recent decisions by the United States Supreme Court[6] requiring that state legislatures be apportioned strictly on the basis of population may alleviate this problem, but the contrasting views on political issues between rural and urban elements of the population will probably continue. The metropolitanization of the nation is likely to raise new issues in this area. Suburban legislators are not likely to view the problems of the metropolitan area in the same way as legislators from the central city. In several states there are now three geographical groupings in state politics—rural, urban, and suburban—and it remains to be seen just what long-range effects this tripartite political grouping will have on governmental functions.

POLITICS IN THE CITY

At this point, you may be tempted to ask, "So what?" It is true that we are becoming an urban nation and that this has brought about pro-

---

[6] See Baker v. Carr, 369 U. S. 186 (1962); Westberry v. Sanders, 84 S.Ct. 526 (1964); Gray v. Sanders, 83 S.Ct. 801 (1963); Reynolds v. Simms, 84 S.Ct. 1362 (1964).

found changes in our living patterns, but the question remains whether this has much to do with the study of politics. It might be suggested that the problems of urbanization are primarily problems for city planners, tax experts, civil engineers, and landscape architects. Reformers often urge us to "take local government out of politics," and to "run our city like we would run a business." We have been told that "there is no Democratic way to pave a street and no Republican way to repair a sewer." The implication in such statements is that the governing of urban and metropolitan areas is not basically a political function.

In order to determine whether this is a valid position, one must have some idea of what is meant by the term "politics." There is no single definition of the word that everyone would accept, but many political scientists would agree that a simple working definition of "politics" is that it is conflict over public policy. There may be no Democratic way to pave a street, but there will be disagreement over which streets to pave with the money that is available this year and which must wait until next year. We like to think that we keep education out of politics, but the decision of where to build the new high school is likely to provoke much conflict. Should the city accept federal funds for its urban renewal program? Should those who live in the suburbs be taxed to help pay for central city services? Should the school district build a new grade school or add new wings to two of the old ones? These are questions on which there will be conflict among the populace; thus, they are political questions. Perhaps one difficulty in seeing urban problems as political ones is that we are used to thinking of politics as conflict between Democrats and Republicans. As a matter of fact, urban politics is often exactly that. But it may be something else. The fact that an issue such as which streets to pave when may evoke conflict between those who live on Brown Street and those who live on Green Street rather than between Democrats and Republicans does not mean that it is not a political question. It merely shows that conflict over public policy can divide the people along many different lines. To suggest that we can take city government out of politics is to suggest that we can get everyone to agree on what the city ought to do and how it ought to do it.

THE METROPOLITAN AREA PROBLEM

Students of local government today often refer to the "metropolitan area problem." What is meant by this term? Would it not be more reasonable to use the term in its plural form for are there not many metropolitan area problems—transportation, housing, smog, education, social welfare, etc.? It is true, of course, that these are the substantive problems of most urban areas regardless of whether they are metropolitan areas. The term "metropolitan area problem" is generally used to refer to the fact that in metropolitan areas the entire area is economically and socially integrated to a large degree, but politically divided into many separate governmental units. To put it another way, a common cliché is that the metropolitan area problem is one of the "big problems and little governments."

It was pointed out above that nearly 11 million people live in the New York metropolitan area, but this fact alone does not suggest unique problems for governing that urban complex. It is only when we know that this area is governed by over 1000 separate governmental units that we see this is an extreme example of the metropolitan area problem. In many ways the area is economically and socially integrated. People who live in the suburbs go into the city to work, attend theatrical presentations or visit the museums, while those who live in the city go to the suburbs for a picnic or a hike. The people travel back and forth throughout the area in search of work, knowledge or pleasure, hardly noticing state borders, county lines, or city limits. Yet there is no government that recognizes this as a single area. Rather, the 1000 governments of the area—states, counties, cities, school districts, special districts, authorities, etc.—each with their own particular functions and limited responsibilities perform their duties, often with little or no coordination with other governments. The Chicago metropolitan area, with about 1000 governments, and the St. Louis and San Francisco metropolitan areas, with about 400 governments each, would be other examples of the problem.

To say that having 400 to 1000 separate governments in a given area is a problem does not necessarily imply that getting rid of the governments is the solution to that problem. There are some who would advocate abolishing most of the individual governments in a given area and establishing a single area-wide government as a means of solving the metropolitan area problem. This is only one approach, however, and most research that has been done indicates that this type of approach. is not popular with most people. In some cases the solution may be abolishing some of the existing governments; in others it may be creating new governmental units; in still others the solution may be devising schemes for bringing about more effective cooperation among existing governments. There is no reason to believe that there is one best approach which will work in all areas or which will be popular with the people in all areas. Different areas will seek different solutions. It is to the subject of how best to govern metropolitan areas in order to minimize what we have called the metropolitan area problem that the remainder of this book is primarily directed.

Suggested Readings

Adrian, Charles R. *Governing Urban America,* 2d ed. (New York: McGraw-Hill Book Company, 1961).

Banfield, Edward C., and James Q. Wilson, *City Politics* (Cambridge: Harvard University Press, 1963).

Gottman, Jean, *Megalopolis: The Urbanized Northeastern Seaboard of the United States* (New York: Twentieth Century Fund, 1962).

Kneier, Charles M., *City Government in the United States,* 3d ed. (New York: Harper & Row, Publishers, 1957).

Mumford, Lewis, *The City in History* (New York: Harcourt, Brace & World, Inc., 1961).

Syed, Anwar, *The Political Theory of American Local Government* (New York: Random House, Inc., 1966).

chapter 2

Suburbanization

THE MOVE TO THE SUBURBS

Professor George S. Blair has suggested that the United
States has experienced three major changes in its living
patterns in the past century.[1] The first change was that
from a rural to an urban society; the second was the
shift from an urban to a metropolitan society; the third
has been the movement from the central city to the suburbs of the metropolitan areas. The term "suburb" has
never been precisely defined, but it generally refers to
the densely populated areas on the fringes, but beyond
the city limits, of our large cities. These areas are often
separate incorporated cities; but there are also unincorporated communities around the fringes of some large
cities, and it would be hard to say that the characteristics of these unincorporated communities are essentially different from those of the
incorporated cities.

In recent years most of the growth in our standard metropolitan statistical areas (SMSA's) has occurred in the suburbs. From 1950-1960
central cities in the nation's metropolitan areas grew at a rate of 10.7 per
cent while the suburban areas around them grew at a rate of 48.6 per
cent. If it had not been for the fact that several cities annexed large areas
during the 1950's, the population growth of central cities would have
been even smaller. In 120 SMSA's, the central cities actually lost population during the decade of the 1950's. In the Philadelphia SMSA, for
example, the central city population declined by 3.3 per cent, but the
suburban population increased sufficiently to give the entire metropolitan
area a population increase of 18.3 per cent for the decade. During the
same period the Washington, D. C. SMSA increased in population by

---

[1] George S. Blair, *American Local Government* (New York: Harper and Row
Publishers, 1964), pp. 527–28.

36.7 per cent while the central city population was declining by 4.8 per cent.

In many SMSA's, well over half of the population now live outside the central city, and that figure is continually rising. In the St. Louis area only 36.4 per cent of the population lived in the central city in 1960 whereas 49.8 per cent had lived there in 1950. In the Cleveland area the central city accounted for 48.8 per cent of the population in 1960; ten years earlier the figure had been 62.4 per cent. Metropolitan areas in the western part of the country tend to have a higher proportion of their population residing in the central city than do areas in eastern states. The city of Houston, for example, includes 75.5 per cent of the people living in the Houston SMSA. Phoenix accounts for 66.2 per cent, Dallas for 62.7 per cent, and San Diego for 55.5 per cent of the populations of their respective metropolitan areas. One reason this is true is that western cities are newer and incorporated suburbs have not yet been created to hem them in on all sides. Thus large cities may extend their boundaries through annexation, bringing many of those in the SMSA into the central city. Also western cities, being newer, are not yet as intensely developed as the older cities in the East, and there is still much vacant land available for the building of new homes and apartments. Another factor is that annexation laws are more liberal in most western and southwestern states, making it easier to bring adjacent land within their borders. In older cities such as New York and Chicago, in contrast, land in the central city is virtually all developed, and the city is surrounded by incorporated suburbs; any significant population increase which takes place must of necessity occur in the suburbs.

To many people the typical suburb consists of such characteristics as split-level homes, station wagons, outdoor barbecues, and PTA meetings. In reality, there is no typical suburb. They come in all shapes and sizes. There are some suburbs, such as Grosse Point Woods near Detroit or Shaker Heights near Cleveland, where most of the residents are quite wealthy, while others, such as Gary, Indiana, are the homes of factory workers and union members. In spite of these differences, there are a few general statements that can be made about suburban areas.

As a rule, suburban dwellers have higher incomes than their neighbors in the central city. Figures for 1960 show that the median family income in the 25 largest cities in the nation was $5935 at that time; for the suburban areas around those cities the figure was $7082. This should not be surprising since it is widely recognized that the general movement pattern is for many who live in the central city to move to the suburbs as soon as they climb high enough on the economic ladder to enable them to do so.

Suburbanites are also generally white. We sometimes hear the term "lily-white suburbs" used to refer to the fact that very few nonwhite residents are to be found in suburban communities. The central city, on the other hand, is likely to have a much higher proportion of nonwhite citizens. Figures for the nation's 212 SMSA's show that in 1960 17.8 per cent of the population of the central cities was nonwhite compared with only 5.2 per cent in the suburbs. In many cities the proportion of nonwhite population is even higher than these averages would indicate. In St. Louis the nonwhite population accounted for 28.8 per cent of the total in 1960. In the St. Louis suburbs, in contrast, it accounted for only 6.2 per cent of the total. In the nation's capital, well over half (54.8 per cent) of the population was nonwhite in 1960. Since World War II, the central cities have been getting darker and the suburbs lighter. In 1940 the central cities of our metropolitan areas had a population in which the nonwhite residents accounted for only 10.1 per cent of the total; as shown above, this group accounted for 17.8 per cent in 1960. These changing racial patterns may be obscured by the population statistics. The fact that the populations of cities like New York and Chicago changed little from 1950 to 1960 does not mean that no population movement was occurring there during that time. What was happening was that many white residents of the central cities were moving to the suburbs and were being replaced in the cities by Negroes from the South and by other minority groups who were moving in. There has been little change in the composition of the suburbs, but what change has occurred has been in the direction of more "lily-whiteness." Whereas 5.2 per cent of the suburbanites were nonwhite in 1960, this figure had been 6 per cent in 1940. This does not mean, of course, that no nonwhite citizens are moving to the suburbs, but they are not moving there as rapidly as are their white neighbors.

Another general statement which can be made about suburban residents is that they are usually family people. The 1960 census statistics showed that in the nation's metropolitan areas, 52.4 per cent of the families living in the central cities had children under the age of 18 while 61.6 per cent of the families in the suburbs had children in that age group. The belief that "It's a good place to rear children" seems to be a significant influence in causing people to move to the suburbs. The belief is strong that the suburbs offer a better school system, less crime, cleaner air, and more open space. Dad believes this type of environment is "better for the family," and he is willing to make the sacrifice of having to drive several miles farther to work every day in order to be able to live in such an area. On the other hand, the fact that suburban life is so family centered tends to make it unattractive to other groups. The young married person, the widow, the divorcee, and the older couple whose children have grown often find the city more appealing than the child-oriented society in suburbia.

THE ATTRACTIONS OF SUBURBIA

The Rural Tradition

In the *Ethics,* Aristotle wrote that when a city reaches a population of one hundred thousand "it is a city no longer." We noted in the first chapter that Thomas Jefferson wrote of the superiority of the rural society, spoke harshly about the "mobs of great cities," and hoped that the nation which he had helped to establish would retain its rural characteristics. These attitudes reflect an age-old belief in the virtues of a rural society, a belief that is still very much a part of the value system of many Americans. It was long relied upon to help justify the overrepresentation of rural areas in state legislatures. The fact that we get a good laugh out of stories about the "country bumpkin" putting one over on the "city slicker" reflects this attitude. It is very probable that one of the attractions of suburbia for many people, whether they realize it or not, is that in suburbia there is a chance to recapture some of the virtues of rural life which seem to be beyond the grasp of the city dweller. It was pointed out that suburbia is considered to be a desirable place for families with children, and the bit of rural life that one can get there is one of the reasons. In terms of geography and population, the suburban community is like the rural society in that it is a small town (at least it is smaller than the city). Because the community is relatively new and there are few families with roots there, it will have trouble conveying a small town atmosphere, but it tries nevertheless. The green grass in suburbia is reminiscent of the farm, and it looks very attractive to the family whose front yard for years has been the sidewalks of the city. There is the feeling that suburbia, like the small town, comes closer to the ideal of "grass roots democracy" than does the city. The city councilmen may live on the next block, the mayor or city manager is willing to listen to complaints by all who want to phone, and government generally seems closer to the people.

The Escape From the City

Closely related to the rural tradition in attracting people to the suburbs is another factor—the desire to escape from the city. For some people the suburbs are attractive not because they like what they find there, but because they dislike what they have found in the city. The city is a place of continuous hustle and bustle, of crowds and hurrying, and of sirens at midnight these people have discovered, and to them suburbia may actually be a little boring but it will at least be quiet.

Another characteristic of the city that many want to escape is "big city politics." Although the city political machine has been dead for some time, some remnants of it remain and its image is still very present in the minds of many people. Although they cannot quite prove it, many people are still pretty sure that the politics of the city is crooked, that city hall is corrupt, and that everyone on the city payroll is a political hack. Of course, there is still a bit of truth in such charges, and from time to time a scandal will erupt to confirm their suspicions. Suburbia, on the other hand, appears to be free of such vices, and government there seems to be much more "nonpolitical."

There is also the matter of crime. The city seems to have more crime than the suburbs, and in many places it is no longer safe to walk alone down city streets or in city parks. The serenity of the suburbs appears to offer a welcome contrast to this situation.

Finally, many people flee the city in an attempt to escape the ever higher taxes that are being levied there. As the slum problem becomes more acute, as the need for better transportation facilities becomes more serious, and as many businesses and families leave the city, thereby decreasing its taxable base, the tax rate goes up and up. The rising tax rate then begins a vicious circle, for as higher taxes help drive people from the city, the tax base is further eroded and taxes must be raised again. The paradox in all of this is that the individual who leaves the city partly in reaction to the tax spiral is going to be in for a shock when he gets to suburbia, for taxes are also going up and up there. In fact, even though suburban tax rates are often lower than those in the city, at the present time they are in many cases rising at a faster rate. The building of one housing development after another in suburban areas creates the need for new sewer lines, new streets, and additional police and fire protection, and these facilities must be paid for by taxes. In particular, the need for new schools puts a strain on the taxable resources of the community. The question of schools brings us to another of the attractions of suburbia.

The Search for Better Schools

There is little doubt that one of the main reasons that families move to the suburbs is in an attempt to find better educational facilities for their children. After the decision has been made to move to suburbia, the question of where the best school system is to be found will often be important in deciding in which suburb to live. There are a number of reasons why the suburban schools appear attractive. In the first place, they are newer in most cases than the schools of the city. While they may have some space problems, they are usually not as crowded as the city schools. The average middle class parent has high hopes that his children will go on to college, and the suburban school system tends to offer a college preparatory curriculum while the city schools, in contrast, may be somewhat more oriented toward vocational training. There is another characteristic of the suburban school which, although he won't talk about it, the suburban dweller finds very attractive. The school, like the community, is "lily-white." There are few, if any, children from Negro or other minority group families there. The parent will tell himself that this is desirable because such children tend to "hold back the progress" of the others in the class. It would be very unfair to suggest that all suburban parents take this attitude. Indeed, there are many parents who honestly feel that the school could offer a more well rounded education if the student body were less homogeneous, but there are still those who consider the absence of minority groups to be an advantage.

The desire for good schools often presents the suburbanite with a conflict. On the one hand, he may have moved to the suburbs partly to escape the high taxes of the city. On the other hand, the superior schools that he wants cost a great deal of money. The suburban dweller often resolves this conflict by being generally "tax conscious," but at the same time being much less tax-conscious on questions of schools than on other matters. It is common in suburban communities to find that bond issues for new sewers, fire stations, or city halls have much more difficulty in getting the approval of the voters than do bond issues for new schools.

The Desire for Home Ownership

Some families are attracted to the suburbs because they want to own their own home. The desire for home ownership ranks very high in the value systems of many Americans. It is a symbol of prestige, a sign of economic security. Not only do many people want to own a home, the fact is that more and more of them are becoming *financially able* to do so. If the old rule-of-thumb that a family can afford to spend two-and-one-half times its income on a home, then those families in the $7000-$9000 a year category can afford homes costing between $18,000 and $23,000. In most metropolitan areas, there are adequate homes available in this price range in suburban areas. The availability of homes through low down payments and long term loans adds to the number of families who can own a home.

If one wants to own his home today, the opportunities to do so are often much greater in the suburbs than in the central city. There is little land available in the city, and what is available is so expensive that it is beyond the reach of middle income families. Thus, the new housing developments that are being built are located in suburban areas, and those wanting to purchase a home have little choice but to go there even if they prefer to live elsewhere.

The Role of the Federal Government

In several ways programs of the federal government have helped make suburban living more attractive. Those who want to buy a home find that it is much easier to do because of certain government programs. The Federal Housing Administration insures loans on residential dwelling, making it possible to borrow money at a lower interest rate and to get loans for as long as 30 years. The Veterans Administration makes it possible for veterans who meet certain qualifications to purchase homes under even more favorable conditions, often without the necessity of even making a down payment. Federal income tax laws also encourage home ownership. The interest payments which one makes on money he has borrowed are deductible on his federal income tax. In the early years of repaying a home loan, a large percentage of the monthly payments go for interest, meaning that that portion of the payment is tax deductible. On the other hand, no part of rent payments are tax deductible.

The federal government has also given impetus to the move to the suburbs through its highway construction program, a point discussed below.

Improvements in Transportation

A move to the suburbs offers many attractions, but it also has disadvantages, one of which is a longer trip to work for those who continue to work in the central city. This problem has been alleviated in several ways in recent years. The freeway, which allows the suburbanite to drive at a rather rapid rate of speed from his home to the downtown area of the city, is becoming common in many urban areas. The federal government has provided valuable assistance here also by providing most of the funds for freeway construction when freeways are built in conjunction with the federal interstate highway system. The number of two-car families is continually increasing, meaning that Dad can drive to work without leaving the family stranded at home.

Public transportation—buses, streetcars, subways, commuter trains—has had harder going in recent years. The suburbanite has largely abandoned it in favor of the automobile, and many urban transportation systems are losing money in spite of having curtailed service and raised rates, the deficit being financed out of tax resources. Publicly owned transit systems are often operated at a loss in hopes of encouraging increased use of them. In addition some state and local governments are now subsidizing the private transportation systems in their areas through tax exemptions and monetary payments, and the federal government is now entering the picture with grants to urban transportation systems.

In spite of the problems of the urban transportation systems and certain other difficulties (such as where to park his car after he drives into the city), the suburban dweller still finds that he can get to work in a reasonable amount of time, reasonable enough anyway that he is willing to endure the problems of commuting in return for what he considers to be the advantages of suburban living.

Changes in Employment Patterns

A relatively short work week would seem to be an impetus in the move to the suburbs. With a 40 hour work week, and pressure in some fields to reduce this still further, the individual employed in the central city gets away from his job about 4:30 or 5:00. This means that even if he spends an hour or more commuting, he is still home in time to have dinner with the family, mow the lawn, and enjoy his favorite TV show.

While such mid-twentieth century developments as freeways and a relatively short work week lighten the burdens of living in the suburbs and working in the city, it should be remembered that many who are attracted to the suburbs do not face this problem at all because they do not work in the city. The fact is that not only have the suburbs grown rapidly in population, but they have also grown in terms of employment opportunities. The neighborhood shopping center not only serves suburbanites, it also employs a great many of them. Many office buildings and light industries are now being located in the suburbs. Wilfred Owen has pointed out that in the eight years immediately following World War II, the number of jobs in New York City increased by 3 per cent, but the total number in the remainder of the metropolitan area increased by 28 per cent.[2] For an increasing number of people, living in suburbia means being nearer, not farther, from their employment.

The Lack of Alternatives

We have been talking about the reasons why the average American has been attracted in large numbers to the suburbs in recent years. One rea-

---

[2] Wilfred Owen, *The Metropolitan Transportation Problem* (Washington: The Brookings Institution, 1956), p. 19.

son that is seldom discussed but which seems to be quite important is that he has not been offered many alternatives to suburban living. Let us take as an example an average young American couple living in a large city. He is employed in the downtown section of the city, and they live in a small apartment not far from his work. As time passes, they have one or two children, and the apartment becomes too small for their needs. At the same time his salary has been increasing until they are in a position to afford something more than their small apartment. Where can they go?

They have surveyed suburbia in terms of their own needs and desires and found it wanting. They are aware of the attractions of suburbia, but they also discover that there are definite disadvantages. Since they cannot yet afford a second car, commuting to work would mean leaving the family at home without transportation. In addition, some people just do not like the tensions of rush hour commuting. For them, suburban living is just not worth it. Our young couple also enjoy the cultural activities to be found primarily in the city—good restaurants, theatres, museums, art galleries, the symphony—and this means driving to the city not only to work but also driving back again at night whenever they want to go out for an evening's entertainment. The young wife prefers to do her shopping in the large downtown department stores which offer much more variety than the suburban shopping centers. They are not especially attracted by the suburban school system because they believe there would be advantages in having their children grow up in a cosmopolitan atmosphere, developing friendships with persons of various social, religious and racial backgrounds. In short, they have decided the suburbs are not for them.

Unfortunately, they will find in many metropolitan areas that living in the city is very difficult for a middle income family. In looking for a larger apartment, they find that there are few two and three bedroom apartments available, and those that are are in the "luxury" category considerably beyond their economic limits. If possible, they would prefer buying to renting since that would enable them to build up an equity, but they run up against the same problem here. There are residences available in the "silk stocking" section of the city, but other than that most of the homes for sale are very old (probably being sold by a family moving to the suburbs!) and likely to be located near the expanding slum areas of the city. Faced with this unhappy situation, our young couple is likely to pack up and, somewhat reluctantly, take the freeway to a split-level home in suburbia. This failure of the nation's large cities to make urban living possible for those who would really prefer it has certainly added to the post-World War II movement away from the city.

THE CONSEQUENCES OF SUBURBANIZATION

Local Taxation Problems

The move to the suburbs has created or aggravated a number of governmental problems, one of the most severe of which has been the loss of the tax base in the central city. When the middle and upper classes move out of the city, they diminish the tax base of the city considerably for they are the people most able to pay taxes. What were once the large homes of wealthy families have often become apartment houses, and streets that once could claim the elite of the city in many cases are now the homes of lower middle class and minority families. These changes in the living patterns of the city lead to a constant lowering of property valuations and thus of taxable resources.

These are not the only ways in which the tax base has been eroded. One constantly hears discussion of the need for more parks and playgrounds and for more open grassy areas to provide needed air and sunshine. There is little doubt of the need for such facilities, but since such properties are publicly owned they remove even more wealth from the tax rolls. The critical need for more parking area in the central city is often met through the construction of municipal parking lots, but here again valuable property is removed from the tax rolls, and such parking lots do well if they pay their own way much less provide any additional funds for the city.

The effect of eroding the tax base of the city is to accentuate the unequal tax distribution in terms of need and availability. At the same time that those most able to pay taxes are moving to the suburbs, they are being replaced by people who are able to pay little, if any, taxes. To add to the problem these people not only are unable to pay taxes, but they require more city services than the wealthier individuals whom they replaced, so that at the same time that the city's available resources are diminishing the demands on it for services are increasing. Those who live in or near slum areas, for example, require relatively large expenditures for police protection because the crime rates in such areas tend to be high. Because slum housing is old and often in poor repair the costs of fire protection are high there. The increasing numbers of low income families in the city lead to increased expenditures for social welfare activities.

Another factor in the financial woes of the city is the paradoxical fact that it must subsidize suburban dwellers and suburban governments in several ways. Since many of those who live in the suburbs continue to work in the city, they drive to work each day on streets that must be built and maintained by the city government. The policemen who try to keep the city orderly during the day and those who direct traffic during the morning and evening rush hours are rendering services that benefit not only those who live in the city but also the suburban dweller who only comes into work. Since the suburbanite does some buying in the central city he will contribute something to the city treasury in the form of municipal sales, cigarette, gas or amusement taxes, and some cities are now levying a municipal earnings tax which must be paid by all who work in the city regardless of their place of residence. In most cases, though, the suburbanite is beyond the reach of the city tax collector.

The central city will sometimes subsidize the suburban areas around it through providing them with various types of municipal services at low cost. Chicago, which provides water to many of the suburban communities in the area, is prohibited by the state legislature from charging suburban communities more for water than it charges its own inhabitants even though losses which might occur in the city could be made up through other city taxes. The suburban governments, in turn, often sell the water to their own residents at a substantial profit, which means that the city of Chicago is actually subsidizing the treasuries of many of its suburbs. This situation or others similar is not uncommon in other metropolitan areas across the country.

One way in which some central cities subsidize suburban areas is through its citizens paying large sums of tax money to the county for which they receive few services.[3] City dwellers, like those who live outside the city, must pay county taxes, but the county performs most of its services beyond the borders of the central city. The county sheriff provides protection primarily for those areas that are not within the limits of any city or town. The county roads department is primarily responsible for road construction and maintenance in the county's rural areas and does little, if any, work on streets in the city, thus pinching still further the purse strings of the central city.

On the other hand, the central city is not alone in facing new financial problems because of the rapid move to suburbia. Suburban communities are faced with the necessity of providing municipal services to more and more people each year, and their costs are increasing accordingly. Many suburban communities have literally sprung up where nothing but open fields existed only a few years ago, and this has meant that they have had

---

[3] This would not be true in New England because of the nature of county government there, or in areas where the central city has been consolidated with or separated from the county.

to start from scratch in providing sewers, streets, and other urban services. Adding to these costs is the fact that population density is usually lower in suburban areas than in the city, making it more costly to provide a given number of people with the necessary services. It costs much more to provide sewer facilities to 500 people spread out along suburban streets three or four to a house than it does to provide such facilities to the same number of people living in a single apartment building. The per capita costs of building a street are considerably higher when the street is lined with single family dwellings on large lots rather than with duplexes and apartment houses built as closely together as possible. The continually expanding need for schools, as has already been pointed out, is another major contributor to the rising costs of government in suburbia.

The Loss of Civic Leadership

When middle and upper income groups move to the suburbs the central city not only loses access to much of their taxable resources, but also loses the benefit of their interest and leadership in the city's civic life. It is on people such as these that a community depends for many of its civic and cultural activities. The more prominent among them will be on the board of the Chamber of Commerce and the Civic Art Gallery; they will be the leaders in the various fund drives, and some of them will be on the Mayor's Citizens Committee to Study This or That. When people such as these move *en masse* to the suburbs, the city is likely to feel the effects of the leadership vacuum. The business or professional man whose business interests are in the city will continue to participate in some city affairs even after moving away. He may remain as a member of the city Rotary Club since he is in the city at noon when its luncheons are held, and if his company expects it, he will continue to be active in the Chamber of Commerce. His vital interest in the civic affairs of the city and in making the city a desirable place to live, nevertheless, will be much diminished after he has moved his family to the suburbs. At least one writer has warned the upper income suburbanite that he should seriously consider the long run consequences of turning the city over by default to the leadership of lower income groups when he continues to own business property and earn a livelihood there and when he still looks on the city as the center of cultural, entertainment, and educational activities.[4] The consequences of this possibility for all groups in society deserve much thought.

---

[4] See Norton E. Long, "The Corporation, Its Satellites and The Local Community," in Edward S. Mason (ed.), *The Corporation in Modern Society* (Cambridge: Harvard University Press, 1959), pp. 202–17.

If the city's loss were the suburb's gain, we might at least be able to say that the advantages and disadvantages offset each other, but this is not the case. When the city family moves to the suburbs, the wife may join the local League of Women Voters and help with the Red Cross drive. Her husband, in contrast, will find it more difficult to participate in community life. He is absent from the community during the working day and his acquaintance with local business and professional people is likely to be very limited. As Professor Norton Long has said:[5]

> The executive tends to be neither an active citizen in his suburban dormitory, nor more than a chamber-of-commerce ceremonial citizen of the central city where his office lies. The suburban politico and small businessman is likely to look on him as a resident alien and a spokesman for the big-town chamber of commerce, rather than for the local interests. In the central city, lack of residence and vote has a crippling effect on a more than ceremonial or check-writing role.

Professor Long has pointed out another factor in the loss of civic leadership: the changing character of the corporate executive. With more of the nation's corporations becoming national in scope, today's executive is a transient. He lives in the suburbs and works in the city, but he has no real interest in either because he doesn't really think of the area as "home." The branch manager of a plant or office in Cincinnati, Kansas City, or Denver will engage in civic activities to the extent that his corporation demands of him, but to him his current position is just a temporary stop on the way to a vice-presidency at the home office in Chicago or New York.

Problems for Downtown

One of the most universal problems with which our major cities are faced in the wake of the move to the suburbs is the deteriorating condition of the downtown business districts. The suburban housewife finds that it is a long drive downtown, and she is doing more of her shopping in the nearby shopping center, making only occasional trips to the downtown area. This has meant a serious loss of business for the merchants in the central business district. Since the business district is now often surrounded by residential areas housing low income families, those who can conveniently do their shopping there are looking for much less expensive merchandise than downtown department stores have been accustomed to offering. Some stores have attempted to adjust their stock to this new market, but the profit margin on inexpensive merchandise is usually much

---

[5] *Ibid.*, p. 212.

lower than on higher quality products, a fact that makes store managers reluctant to make the shift. Some stores resist the shift for reasons other than economic. Many department stores have long standing reputations as centers of high quality merchandise, and they are anxious to maintain their reputations if at all possible. It would be difficult to think of Marshall Field's in Chicago or The Emporium in San Francisco becoming "cut rate" stores.

The plight of the businessman in the central business district is further complicated in that while his business may be declining his costs are not. Land costs, and therefore rental costs, remain very high in the center of the city. Also, as taxable resources are moved to the suburbs, the wealth remaining in the city must carry more of the tax load, so the businesses in the downtown area find themelves carrying a heavy city tax burden. With shrinking markets, diminishing profits, and higher taxes, the storeowner in the central business district is often reluctant to spend large sums of money to modernize. Thus, the downtown area takes on a drab and unattractive look, the suburban shopper is more reluctant than ever to go downtown to shop, and the vicious circle of problems for the central business district continues.

Government Fragmentation

We pointed out in Chapter 1 that one of the problems in governing metropolitan areas is that there are often dozens or even hundreds of separate governments operating in the area. The move to the suburbs has done much to intensify this problem. As people move beyond the limits of the city, they take with them the need for urban services. If they move into a suburban community with an existing government, they look to it for services. In unincorporated communities, the movement of people into the area may increase pressures for incorporation or perhaps for establishment of special districts to provide services. The fear of annexation by the central city also often leads suburban areas to incorporate. This in turn complicates the governmental structure and provides the target for the reformer who points out with alarm that "our area has ninety separate municipalities, each with its own police, fire, street and other departments." The maze of central cities and suburbs has led to a situation in which some suburbs have become completely surrounded by the central city as the city has expanded its boundaries through annexation. For example, the cities of Hamtramck and Highland Park, Michigan, are bordered on all sides by Detroit.

In a democratic society it is difficult to argue that having ninety separate municipalities, or whatever the number may be, is wrong if that is the choice of the people. Nevertheless, there is little doubt that such fragmentation of government presents numerous problems. A city may wish to annex land which, on the basis of the growth pattern of the city, should become a residential area, but which has been zoned for commercial use by the county while it was outside the city limits. Worse yet, a county or neighboring community may have either no zoning laws at all or else very weak ones, and cities find that the property around their fringes has been allowed to develop and grow "like Topsy." To cite another example, there have been cases where firemen have had to stand and watch a building burn to the ground because it was located just across a city boundary in the neighboring municipality. Government fragmentation, along with the lack of coordination or the presence of actual conflict resulting therefrom, is one of the key problems in the governing of metropolitan areas.

THE FUNCTIONS OF SUBURBS

The image of suburbia that we have presented is primarily that of the *residential suburb* or, as it is sometimes called, the *dormitory suburb*. They are so called because they are living areas for those who work elsewhere, either in the central city or elsewhere in the metropolitan area. Residential suburbs exist in various forms. There are the high income suburbs where the houses are large, the lots consist of several acres each, and the quiet, winding streets are well landscaped and well maintained. There are the suburbs consisting primarily of tract homes for the middle classes where the yards are smaller, the streets are rougher, and where house, yard, and street are all likely to be full of children playing while mother busily prepares to leave for the PTA meeting. There are working class suburbs where the houses all look like square boxes painted different colors to provide some much needed variety, the lots are little larger than the houses, and the street is likely to be unpaved, or badly in need of repair.

Not all suburbs fit the description of residential suburbs. There are also *industrial suburbs,* where there are residential areas but where there is also a significant amount of industry. Gary, Indiana, near Chicago, and Granite City, Illinois, across the river from St. Louis would be in this category. There are suburbs which provide special services, such as Evanston, Illinois, which is known as an education center because of Northwestern University being located there. Berkeley, California would be in a similar situation.

Some communities become known as *recreational suburbs,* because they are known for being "wide open." It is often understood that prostitution and gambling will be allowed to operate with little harrassment from the police in such areas. It is not easy to point out recreational suburbs because periodic clean-up campaigns by local reform minded citizens often force a crackdown on vice, at least temporarily. At various times Cicero has been such a suburb in the Chicago area; Newport, Kentucky has performed this function in the Cincinnati area; and Tijuana, although it is across the border in Mexico, has been known as a recreational suburb of San Diego.

Finally, it should be pointed out that suburbs do not fit neatly into categories. Many suburbs combine the various functions mentioned. Evanston is not only an educational center, it is also the home of many business and professional people whose work is in Chicago. Dearborn, Michigan, is a residential suburb of Detroit, but it is also the location of an important segment of the automobile industry. Likewise, the problems of suburbs and of metropolitan areas generally do not lend themselves well to categorization. Not all metropolitan areas have downtown areas that are deteriorating. Not all local governments are caught in a financial squeeze. Like people, cities have their individual characteristics and problems and must be dealt with in that way.

Suggested Readings

Berger, Bennet M., *Working Class Suburb: A Study of Auto Workers in Suburbia* (Berkeley: University of California Press, 1960). An interesting study showing, among other things, that all suburban communities do not fit the usual middle class, white collar image.

Dobriner, William (ed.), *The Suburban Community* (New York: G. P. Putnam's Sons, 1958).

Long, Norton, *The Corporation, Its Satellites and the Local Community,* in Edward S. Mason (ed.), *The Corporation in Modern Society* (Cambridge: Harvard University Press, 1959).

Riesman, David, *et al., The Lonely Crowd* (New Haven: Yale University Press, 1950).

Seeley, John R., *et al., Crestwood Heights: The Culture of Suburban Life* (New York: Basic Books, 1956).

Whyte, William H., *The Organization Man* (New York: Simon and Schuster, 1956).

Wood, Robert C., *Suburbia: Its People and their Politics* (Boston: Houghton Mifflin Co., 1959). This book remains as the best general study of suburban politics.

chapter **3**

Governing the
Central City

THE STRONG MAYOR

In Chapter 4 we shall discuss in some detail the development of the reform movement in American local
government. Briefly, the reform movement included demands for such structural changes as nonpartisan elections, at-large (rather than ward) elections, small city
councils of five or seven members, municipal civil service systems, and the council-manager form of government. At this point it is sufficient to recognize that the
reform movement, thought of in these terms, never
caught on in most of America's largest cities. To be sure,
there are large cities in which some of these characteristics are to be found. Also, many cities have had what
have been called "reform" campaigns. In cities such as New York, Philadelphia, and St. Louis, the old political machines were thrown out of
office by candidates running on a reform platform, and men like Richardson Dilworth and De Lesseps Morrison gained reputations as reform
mayors. In these instances, however, the word "reform" referred to getting
rid of corruption and providing higher levels of integrity in government
and was not meant to include the specific reforms mentioned.

There are important reasons why our major cities have not been attracted to these reforms. One reason is that reforms of this type tend to
minimize the importance of conflict in government, and while this may
be possible in smaller communities, it cannot be done in major cities. The
reasoning behind at-large elections, for example, is that councilmen so
elected can view the interests of the city "as a whole" and not be bound
to protect geographical interests. Such a plan may work in a city where
the population is homogeneous and most citizens tend to view the problems of the city from a similar perspective. It is much less likely to work

in a large city where the downtown businessman, the Negro in the slums, and the Italian in the ghetto see their own problems and the problems of the city "as a whole" from totally different points of view. Similar reasoning, tending to minimize the role of conflict in society, supports other reforms, such as nonpartisan elections, small councils, and the council-manager form of government.

Perhaps the most significant reason why such reforms have not been widely used in major cities is their failure to provide for one of the city's major needs, strong policy leadership. If a modern city is to attempt to solve the massive problems facing it, it must have dynamic leadership. There must be someone who is contantly pointing out the major problems, seeking solutions, and providing the driving force for putting those solutions into effect. Unfortunately, reform government seldom meets this need. The council-manager plan, which is usually the foundation on which a local reform movement is built, is not well adapted to providing for policy leadership. In council-manager cities, the mayor is often not popularly elected. Rather, the council chooses one of its members to serve as mayor, his duties being limited primarily to presiding at council meetings and representing the city at ceremonial functions. Even in cities where he is popularly elected, his duties are generally the same. The city manager, on the other hand, is hired by the council and is responsible for the administrative activities of the city. He can involve himself in policy to some extent by making recommendations to the council, but he also is in no position to provide strong leadership on controversial issues.

The desire to provide for policy leadership has been a major reason for the establishment of the strong mayor-council form of government in large cities. Under this form of government, the mayor is directly elected by the people, often in a partisan election. He usually appoints department heads, directs preparation of the city budget, and supervises the administrative activities of the city. He usually presides over council meetings and often has a veto over council action. A mayor with these powers is in a position to provide policy direction if he so desires. There is no doubt that he is the number one man in the city, since there is no city manager involved and he is not "just another councilman" as is sometimes the case under other forms of government. His views about city problems will make the local radio and television newscasts and the front page of the daily paper, and he is always a welcome speaker at the luncheon clubs. No other local personality can compete with him in commanding the attention of the public for the purpose of airing his views of local problems. As administrative head of the city he can "knock heads together" or do whatever else is necessary to see to it that policies are carried out as he desires. As a leader in his political party, he can often use the party to get support for his programs although, as we shall discuss below, there is great variation in the amount of control or influence that modern day mayors have over party organizations.

All of the nation's cities with over one million population operate under some form of the strong mayor-council plan of government, and over three-fourths of all the cities of over one-half million operates under this plan. Cincinnati is one relatively large city where the council-manager plan has operated with much success, but even former Mayor Charles B. Taft of that city has called attention to the limitations of that plan for large cities.[1] In 1949, a group of Philadelphia citizens who were writing a charter for their city visited Mayor Taft to discuss the operation of the council-manager plan in Cincinnati. They were surprised when Taft, after commenting favorably on the operation of the manager plan in his city, said frankly that he would not recommend its adoption for a city the size of Philadelphia. Freedgood quotes one of the Philadelphians as saying, "When the Lord himself said he didn't want those ten commandments spread elsewhere, that was the death knell." Philadelphia later adopted a charter providing for a strong mayor.

On the other hand, some rather large cities, including Kansas City, San Diego, Dallas, and Phoenix in addition to Cincinnati, do operate under the council-manager plan, and most observers agree that these cities have been very well governed. Some of them have also had mayors who provided effective leadership in spite of the apparent limitations on the office. Murray Seasongood, an attorney and law professor, showed during his years as mayor in Cincinnati that a mayor can provide dynamic policy leadership in a council-manager city without coming into conflict with the manager or involving himself unduly in the administrative affairs of the city. The powers of the office of mayor, like those of the President, depend far more on the characteristics of the person holding the office than on the legal structure of the office itself; however, other things being equal a capable mayor will have a better chance of providing strong policy leadership under the strong mayor-council system than under the council-manager plan.

THE MAYOR AND THE MACHINE

We mentioned previously that one of the major characteristics of urban politics during the last quarter of the nineteenth century was the political machine, that informal organization which dominated the ma-

---

[1] Seymour Freedgood, "New Strength in City Hall," in Editors of Fortune, *The Exploding Metropolis* (Garden City, New York: Doubleday & Co., Inc., 1958), pp. 76–77.

jority party of a city, controlled city hall, and thereby traded favors of
various types for the money and votes it needed to maintain its position.
One should also understand that with all its shortcomings and misdeeds
which writers like Lincoln Steffens depicted so graphically, the machine
had certain advantages for the period in which it thrived. In the first
place, the machine provided through informal means for the centralization of power necessary for the city administration to govern effectively
when the formal governmental-structure provided for decentralization of
power and responsibility. Many cities of that era found that the weak
mayor-council system of government, under which power was dispersed
among a host of elected officials, was difficult to adapt to the needs of a
fast growing city, because the difficulties involved in getting the various
officials to cooperate in unified assault on the city's increasingly complex
problems often seemed virtually insurmountable. To some extent the
centralization of power in the machine facilitated coordination and alleviated this problem. Also, the machine provided representation at city
hall for interest groups whose voices might not have been heard under
other more "pure" forms of government. In an era when business dominated both the economic and political spheres of activity, the machine
served as a channel through which the voices of immigrants, minority
groups, and the generally poorer segments of society were heard by
those in positions of authority. The machine, with its free load of coal
in winter and its food basket at Christmas, also acted as a sort of public
welfare agency for the city's unfortunates, a not inconsequential function
in the years before social security, old age pensions, and unemployment
compensation.

Another point, one which may seem repugnant to the ardent democrat (small "d"), is that the machine, with its efficient organization, protected the city from the possibly undesirable effects of direct control
of the city government by either a single interest group on the one hand
or an uninformed and possibly misled public on the other. Myerson
and Banfield consider this point especially important in their study of
politics of public housing in Chicago. Although they are dealing with a
recent period of Chicago politics, their point applies well to machine
organizations generally:[2]

> But it was also an advantage of the Chicago system that, while
> keeping control over local matters within the voter's reach, it
> interposed the party between the voters and the most important
> city-wide (as well as state- and nation-wide) decisions. The heads
> of the machine could not ignore the voters on all issues, but they

---

[2] Martin Meyerson and Edward C. Banfield, *Politics, Planning and the Public
Interest* (Glencoe, Illinois: Free Press, 1955), p. 291.

could ignore them on many issues and on almost any particular issue. The advantages of this were great. Chicago was not governed, as are some cities in which strong machines do not stand between the voter and the issue, by the pull and haul of a few irresponsible pressure groups which get the voter's ear at election time; instead, there were only two important political organizations, the Democratic and Republican parties, both of which had to accept some responsibility for not one or a few interests but for all of the many conflicting interests that were important in the life of the city.

Strange though it may seem, the machine may on occasion be an instrument for achieving, rather than obstructing, democracy in local government.

Granted that the machine had its good as well as its seamy side, the fact remains that the old style political machine is of declining importance in most American cities, and in many cases the powers and prerogatives which the machine is losing are being gained by the mayor. One reason for this is that most reorganizations of large city governments in recent years have tended to strengthen the office of mayor. In many cities his term of office has been lengthened from two to four years, his appointing power has been broadened, and his control over the budget has been strengthened. The mayor feels more independent of the machine today than he did fifty years ago because he knows that the machine can no longer make or break him by itself. The rise of the middle class and the development of government welfare programs have severely limited the number of people susceptible to control by the machine, the result of which is that there are no longer enough "deliverable" wards to swing city elections at the will of the machine. In order to get elected in most large cities today, a mayor must therefore seek to build up support beyond the limits of the old political organization. He will try to appeal to the so-called "newspaper" wards, those outlying areas of the city which are inhabited by the middle classes who are unattracted by what the traditional machine had to offer, who are civic minded and desirous of "clean, honest government," and who take careful note of what the news columns and editorial pages of the metropolitan daily says about the goings-on at city hall. A good current example of this is Mayor Richard Daley of Chicago, a man whom many considered to be a typical spoils politician but who, upon assuming the office of mayor, instituted a number of reforms to improve the operations of city hall. The efforts of Mayor Daley to maintain his strength among the old line machine politicians of the city while at the same time attempting to woo the business community, civic leaders, and reformers is a good commentary on the type of tightrope balancing act that a modern mayor must perform if he is to be a success.

The machine has been further weakened by the fact that the major interest groups of the city now work directly with city hall rather than going through the machine. Business leaders interested in zoning or Chamber of Commerce officials working to bring new industry to the city want to discuss their problems directly with the mayor or with the department heads involved. The municipal employees union is now more interested in a merit system and a good retirement plan than in the patronage that was formerly available mainly for party workers. The ever present eyes of the reformer and the reporter make it difficult, if not impossible, for city hall to sell protection to the underworld today in the manner that was once common. The gambler or dope peddler may be able to get an occasional policeman on the beat to look the other way, but he can no longer secure a guarantee of city-wide protection from the machine, so he is forced to work around, rather than with, city hall. When a business no longer has good products to sell (even when the products are favors, votes or protection), the business will suffer or possibly die. Such has been the fate of the city machine.

Although it would be hard to document, there is another likely reason for the decline of the machine: the rise in the calibre of person now found in city government. As the mayor's office has become more powerful and the problems facing cities more challenging, municipal office has become more attractive to high quality individuals. Cities are now finding that men like Hubert Humphrey in Minneapolis and Raymond Tucker in St. Louis are willing to accept the responsibilities of city business. The result of this, it seems logical to assume, is that such men are not likely to be willing to serve as stooges for a political boss or to take orders from a smoke-filled room. The mayor in turn must search for qualified men rather than good party workers (of course, a person may be both) to serve with him in the city government. It is more important to the mayor that his director of public health have an M.D. and his director of streets have a degree in civil engineering than that they be able to deliver their wards on election day.

THE MAYOR AND INTEREST GROUPS

As the role of the machine has declined in urban politics, the role of interest groups has become more important. Interest groups, or "lobbies," tend to operate in about the same manner at the local level as they do at the national and state levels. They attempt to influence decision-makers to accept their point of view concerning what the government ought or ought not to do. There is a seemingly endless list of interests that attempt to influence the policies of the city government from time to time, but Professor Adrian has called attention to a very pertinent point when he suggests that "the political activity of any group is proportionate to its stake in the marginal definition of legality and of law-enforcement levels."[3] He means by this that those people who live completely within the limits of the law, such as the junior executive or the blue collar worker, are unlikely to attempt to influence government actions because such actions are not likely to affect his personal well being. Likewise, the bank robber is so far beyond the limits of the law that he is unlikely to try to influence government action because there is no possibility of getting public acceptance for his activities. On the other hand, the liquor or race track interests will be much involved in such matters because the actions of government directly affect the operations of their businesses. Real estate interests, which are vitally concerned with local tax rates, and utility companies, which must secure franchises and which are subject to rate regulation, will also actively seek to look after their interests at city hall.

In most communities, various businesses will be powerful interest groups. In addition to those businesses just mentioned, certain others will be very concerned about actions taken at city hall because of the effects on their business. Taxi companies, for example, are interested in limiting the number of taxi licenses issued in a city, since the result of such action is limited competition. It is no accident that some of the most reasonable taxi rates in the nation are to be found in Washington, D. C., where Congress is the "city council" since Congressmen are more susceptible to pressure from the "folks back home" than from the local cab companies. Downtown businesses will be interested in getting action at city hall on freeways to bring the shoppers conveniently into the city while businesses located in neighborhood shopping centers will more than likely oppose the freeways and the added tax burden necessitated by them. In a general sense, groups such as bankers and real estate people are always interested in the level of business activity in the city, and they will urge the city government to do what it can to "create a good business climate" in order to attract new industry and commerce to the city. In addition to business, certain other groups such as race relations organizations (NAACP, CORE, etc.), veterans groups, unions, "good government" groups (League of Women Voters), and religious organizations will often be found at city hall urging the council to support or oppose various causes.

---

[3] Charles R. Adrian, *Governing Urban America* (New York: McGraw-Hill Book Company, Inc., 1961), p. 123.

The role of the mayor in this maze of interest group activity is often that of negotiator, of compromiser. It becomes his job to bring the various interests together and to attempt to persuade them to accept compromise proposals which, while being completely satisfactory to no single group, provide all with "half a loaf." Sometimes the mayor's role becomes that of an implementor, merely putting into effect a proposal on which those interest groups primarily affected have come to agreement. Interest groups are usually sufficiently powerful on really crucial issues that the mayor dare not ignore them or even choose between them, deliberately favoring the position of one interest and opposing that of another. Rather he must take the road of negotiation, seeking to salvage something for everyone and trying to alienate completely no one. An example of this is found in the fact that the typical modern large city mayor who is a Democrat, elected with the help of the traditional source of Democratic support including union labor and minority groups, finds it very important to make peace and to work closely with the business leaders of the community once in office. Many of them have been quite successful in doing so.

One reason for the powerful role of interest groups in urban politics is that as a general rule the influence of interest groups on specific issues increases as the interest and awareness of the general public decreases. To cite an example at the federal level, bills to lower taxes or to extend the draft law will provoke much public interest and discussion while a bill concerning the application of anti-trust laws to the electric industry will not arouse public interest in most cases. In the latter case, the lack of concern on the part of the public will give the interests directly involved much more leverage in making their influence felt on the bill. Transferring this to the local level, few issues of urban politics evoke great public interest. Most local issues are frankly not exciting, and even on matters such as zoning or urban renewal, the debates may be vigorous, but they will usually involve only those few people or interests that feel directly and immediately affected by the issue. Thus the part played by interest groups in the resolution of conflict in urban politics is a crucial one. As Banfield has pointed out, the mayor "will ratify almost any proposal upon which the principally affected interests agree, and (he) will postpone as long as (he) can a decision upon any proposal about which they are not agreed."[4]

On the other hand, the ability of the interest groups to influence policy is also limited by several factors. First, there will obviously be disagree-

---

[4] Edward C. Banfield, *Political Influence* (New York: Free Press, 1961), pp. 271–72.

ment among various interests on what actions the city ought to take. The proposals of downtown businessmen will be opposed by neighborhood businessmen, and labor union spokesman may be opposed to both groups. The National Association for the Advancement of Colored People will want public housing to be integrated while neighborhood improvement associations may oppose this position. The ability of a mayor to impose his own solution in a conflict is strengthened when the battling between affected interests ends in a "dead heat." Second, the power of interest groups is limited simply by the time factor. A busy individual just cannot become involved in every decision that may have some peripheral effect on him. The owner of a store in a neighborhood shopping center may wish that the city council would deny zoning requests to establish other competing shopping centers, but if he appeared at city hall to testify at every zoning hearing held by the council he would get little else done. Influential people are also usually busy people, and how busy they are will determine to some extent how free they are to use their influence. Third, at some point in the process of settling a conflict, the usually apathetic and unorganized general public may become sufficiently aroused to bring their influence to bear on an issue, thereby limiting the ability of interest groups to dictate a decision. A quiet neighborhood with little interest in government or politics may become suddenly alive with political activity, petitions, and appearances at city hall if it is learned that the city government is considering locating a busy freeway, a smoke producing factory, or an integrated housing project in the neighborhood. Factors such as these limit the extent to which interest groups may have their own way in urban politics.

The point was made that the need in the mayor's office today is for an individual who can be a strong policy leader; however, the most important limiting factor on the mayor's ability to perform that function is the powerful role of interest groups, which often cause the mayor to be more of a negotiator than a strong leader.

THE "HEMMED IN" MAYOR

Seymour Freedgood has suggested that today's mayor is "hemmed in" in a number of ways that limit his freedom of action and his ability to provide dynamic leadership for his city.[5] In addition to being hemmed in by interest groups in the manner just described, Freedgood suggests that he is also hemmed in by the municipal bureaucracy, by public

---

[5] Freedgood, *op. cit.,* pp. 65–86.

authorities and special districts, by the state legislature, and by the suburbs.

The mayor is hemmed in, in the first place, by the municipal bureaucracy. Most large cities have replaced the old patronage system of employment with a local civil service system; there is general agreement that this has raised the quality of municipal employees, but the civil service idea is not without its problems. The mayor is finding in some cases that he is unable to control his own administration because of the protection given to employees by the civil service rules. Although he is usually free to appoint his department heads, the number two and three men in departments are now likely to hold civil service status and be beyond his control even though their duties and responsibilities place them in a position to influence policy.

The historical reason for this goes back to the turn of the century when the political machine in control of city hall passed out city jobs on the basis of service and loyalty to the party. The reaction against this led reformers to insist that city employees be protected to the fullest extent possible from the political officials of the city. Members of the civil service commission were given longer terms than the mayor and could not be removed from office by him; hiring based on merit was required, and rules stating that employees could be fired only for specified reasons were established. The systems often included only limited numbers of employees when they were created, but they have been continually expanded so that now they include nearly all of the city's employees, even some who are in positions of influence on policy. There is difference of opinion about how far merit systems of employment should go in providing job security for the employee, but most students of the subject agree that those in positions involving policy making should be subject to appointment and removal by the political head of the government. There is no doubt that there was great need to protect city employees from the corrupt patronage practices of the machine in many cities at the turn of the century; however, it seems probable that for most cities today there is less danger of getting a corrupt mayor than of getting one whose powers are so restricted that he cannot carry out his programs for the city.

A second factor which tends to limit the mayor is the existence of a multitude of special districts and authorities in the city. A district or authority is a separate unit of government performing functions in or near the city. The Port of New York Authority, the Chicago Park District, and the Southern California Metropolitan Water District are examples. In one sense these governments aid the city in that they perform functions which the city might otherwise have to undertake. Special districts and authorities perform such varied functions as provision of water, sewers, and parks, maintenance of ports and airports, the building of bridges, and the operation of subways. The problem with units of government such as these is that, while they often operate within the limits of a given city, they are usually completely independent of the city government. They levy taxes or charge fees for their services, borrow money, and perform services with little or no coordination with the city. The conflicts between the Port of New York Authority and other governments in the metropolitan area are widely known and illustrate well the problems involved. A mayor, trying to view broadly the problems of his area, is obviously limited in his attempts to encourage a coordinated approach to those problems by the existence of numerous governments and districts, all independent of city hall and of each other.

The state legislature is a third restricting force on the mayor and the city government's freedom of action. The city government is legally a "child of the state," and the courts of nearly every state in the union interpret the powers of local governments very strictly. Cities may levy only those taxes authorized by the legislature, they may borrow only in accordance with state established procedures, and in most states they are limited in the amounts they may collect in taxes or borrow by state statutes or the state constitution. Unless the city has its own "home rule" charter, such matters as the term of office of the mayor, the number of members on the city council, and the administrative organization of the city will be established by the state. In the past, the rurally dominated state legislatures have often kept a skeptical eye on the big cities, granting them only the barest of powers and keeping them generally in a legislative straitjacket. It may be that recent Supreme Court decisions requiring legislative districts to be based more specifically on population will produce legislatures more sympathetic to urban problems.

Finally, the mayor is hemmed in, both geographically and legally, by the suburbs. He finds that the problems of his city extend beyond the city boundaries, but he knows that the city can no longer annex new territory because it is already surrounded by incorporated municipalities. He discovers that such matters as transportation, smog, and water supply must be considered on an area-wide basis even though they may currently seem crucial only to the central city. If he is lucky he may find that officials of the county and the suburban communities are willing to work seriously with him on such problems; too often he is not that lucky.

HELP FOR THE MAYOR: THE CAO

Giving the mayor sufficient power to fight his way through this maze of restrictions is a major goal of those involved with the organization of large city governments. One approach that a number of our largest cities have adopted is the creation of a new administrative position, the Chief Administrative Officer (CAO). Although the role of this official varies from city to city, he is usually appointed by the mayor and may be removed by the mayor, although in a few cities the council must approve either appointment or removal. His title also varies from city to city. It may be chief administrative officer, director of administrative services, managing director, city administrative officer, or city administrator.

The CAO usually serves as a general supervisor of administrative activities. Mayor Wagner referred to New York's city administrator as an "executive vice president in charge of operations." The CAO often has authority to appoint some, though usually not all, department heads. In San Francisco, for example, he is primarily responsible for those departments dealing with public works. In New Orleans and Philadelphia the CAO's appointing authority is broader, but he must have the approval of the mayor for his appointments. The CAO, working under the general direction of the mayor, usually directs the administrative affairs of the city, leaving the mayor free to spend more time on broad policy matters. Mayor Joseph S. Clark of Philadelphia, for example, remarked that the heads of the ten line departments of the city dealt almost exclusively with the managing director and that he seldom saw them except at the quarterly staff meetings.

The CAO concept was developed in an attempt to have the best of both worlds, the policy leadership of the strong mayor-council form of government and the administrative efficiency of the council-manager form of government. Many large cities have also been attracted to it because it is a convenient compromise. Political and civic leaders of major cities, recognizing the need for improving the administrative operations of their city but being reluctant to make the dramatic departure from local traditions and political patterns involved in establishing the council-manager plan, have found some form of the strong mayor-council plan with a CAO to be the most acceptable proposal. Political parties, which often violently oppose the council-manager plan for reasons which may or may not be valid, are much more willing to accept the strong mayor-CAO concept.[6] The most important feature of this plan for the governing of large cities is that whereas a city manager is "the council's man," the CAO is "the mayor's man." He is responsible to the mayor, and his responsibilities are directed toward relieving the mayor of responsibility for administrative minutia so that the mayor may concentrate his efforts on other matters. He is also an advisor to the mayor on management ques-

---

[6] For a discussion of possible reasons for opposition to the council-manager plan, see Chapter 4.

tions, and in some cities, such as Los Angeles, he has primary responsibility for preparation of the annual budget.

The CAO idea is not without its problems. Since he is the mayor's man, the man in the position of CAO is likely to be replaced with each change in the occupancy of the mayor's office, and such turnover may well have a less than desirable effect on administrative continuity. City managers often retain their positions through many changes in the composition of the city council, but CAO's, being responsible to a single individual, are subject to a higher mortality rate. Strong advocates of "reformism" suggest that the corrupting influences of partisan or machine politics are more likely to creep back into city hall under this plan than under a full fledged council-manager plan. Although the plan has not yet been adopted by a sufficiently large number of cities to make recruitment a problem, the time may come when the question of who should serve as CAO will be a pertinent one. Should CAO's have essentially the same training as city managers? Up to the present time there has been little interchange between those in city manager positions and those serving as CAO's. Should CAO's be local individuals who have proved their management ability in business, and if so, can this type of person be persuaded to take the position? The few cities now operating under the plan have been fortunate for the most part in acquiring outstanding men to serve as CAO. For example, Luther Gulick, one of the nation's leading authorities on public administration, served as the first city administrator of New York City. It remains to be seen whether the quality of those serving as CAO will remain high as the popularity of the plan spreads and the demand for the available talent increases.

THE MAYOR: AN APPRAISAL

There is much to be optimistic about in the development of the office of mayor in our large cities in the last two or three decades. Beginning in some cities as long ago as the reform period of the turn of the century, citizens in one major city after another have strengthened the office of mayor until today it has become a position of considerable power, the center of gravity at city hall. While smaller cities have often downgraded the position of mayor in favor of a city manager, the largest population centers have come to look more and more to that office for leadership in meeting their critical problems.

As the concept of the office has developed, better men have been attracted to it. The list of outstanding men who have recently sat in the mayor's office is impressive, and the list of relatively unknown but nevertheless conscientious and capable mayors is even longer. Today's big city mayor is seldom a machine politician, but neither could he be described as nonpolitical. He is likely to be active in his party, he is probably a Democrat, and he is very often associated with the reform or anti-machine faction of that party. As in the cases of DeLesseps Morrison, Hubert Humphrey, and Joseph Clark, he may step from the mayor's office to a higher political position. Interestingly enough, the mayor's office is becoming sufficiently attractive in some cities to win the attention of those in other offices. Mayor John F. Shelley of San Francisco, for example, gave up his seat in Congress to seek the position of chief executive of that city in 1963. To quote Freedgood again:[7]

> Today the big city must rank as one of the most skillfully managed of American organizations—indeed, considering the problems it has to face, it is better managed than many U.S. corporations.
> . . . Since the 1930's, and at an accelerating rate after the second world war, the electorate in city after city has put into office as competent, hard-driving, and skillful a chief executive as ever sat in the high-backed chair behind the broad mahogany desk.

There is, of course, the other side of the coin. In many cases the mayor still finds himself "hemmed in" and frustrated by lack of authority, and the image of the machine politician in the mayor's office which still lingers in the minds of many undoubtedly still deters many able men from seeking the position. Nevertheless, recent history offers hope for the future, and it appears that the incumbent at city hall is becoming more and more deserving of the title "His Honor."

THE CITY COUNCIL

Council Structure and Powers

While the powers of the mayor have been significantly expanded, the city council continues to be the supreme legislative body of the city. Even in strong mayor cities, and especially so in cities under other forms, the policies of the city government are set by the council. The council also controls the financial affairs of the city. How much money the city shall spend next year, what taxes will be levied, and what borrowing shall be undertaken are questions which must receive council action. On financial questions the council often finds that it, like the mayor, is "hemmed in" by the state legislature. The legislature determines which taxes cities may and *may not* levy, but it also often requires certain expenditures by cities

---

[7] *Ibid.,* pp. 62–63.

such as by establishing minimum salaries for policemen and firemen which cities are required to pay. State action forcing particular expenditures upon cities while at the same time limiting their sources of income places many cities in a financial straitjacket. Moreover, in some cities the council may not appropriate funds unless the appropriations have been recommended by the executive responsible for budget preparation (mayor or manager). It is also sometimes the case that the council may not increase or add items to the amounts recommended by the executive. Still, within limits such as these, it is the council that establishes the financial policies of the city.

The council often has important appointive powers. In council-manager cities the council is responsible for choosing the city manager. In most cities there are many appointments to be made to various boards and commissions—park board, library board, planning and zoning commission, personnel board, etc., and these appointments are usually made either by the council or by the mayor with council approval. Even where the council has no authority to remove board members once appointed, the initial decisions concerning who is to receive these appointments may well affect the approach the city will take to various problems.

A very important power which in most cities is vested in the city council is the authority to make the final decision concerning planning and zoning matters. Decisions involving planning and zoning affect the physical growth patterns of the city and influence something of vital importance to many property values. A study of fifty-one city councils in the Los Angeles area showed that zoning questions are more likely to cause conflict among councilmen than any other issue.

The average city council today consists of either five or seven members, although there is a tendency for larger cities to have larger councils. For cities with over 500,000 population the median number of councilmen is fifteen. Chicago, with a city council of fifty members, has the largest council of any major city. Four years is the most common term of office of councilmen. About one-half of all cities of over 5,000 and over two-thirds of all cities with more than 500,000 inhabitants have a four year term. About 60 per cent of all cities have overlapping terms for councilmen, insuring that there will always be some experienced men on the council. Overlapping terms are less likely to be found in our largest cities than elsewhere for only 33 per cent of those cities over 500,000 provide for them. One reason for this is that overlapping terms are used most often in cities operating under the council-manager form of government, a form used in only a few major cities. Virtually all cities today have unicameral councils. The nearest that any large city would come to having a bicameral council would be in New York City, where the Board of Estimate operates in some ways as an "upper house," although its functions in this regard have been diminished by recent charter revisions.

As with the office of mayor, the quality of those sitting on city councils seems to have risen in recent decades. A story prevalent at the turn of the century was that one could empty the council chamber in Chicago by running into the chamber and shouting "Mr. Councilman, your tavern is on fire!" It is safe to say that few city councils today consist primarily of tavern owners or bartenders. The Huckshorn and Young study of councils in the Los Angeles area found that many representatives of professional groups, such as attorneys, engineers, and scientists, were elected to the council. Others often elected included owners of small businesses and real estate and insurance salesmen. On the other hand, very few were elected from the ranks of white collar workers or skilled and unskilled labor. Most of those elected were men, and over two-thirds were Republican although Los Angeles County's voter registration is predominantly Democratic.[8]

Council Elections

Some of the most heated debates about city councils are over how they should be elected. Should elections be partisan or nonpartisan? Should councilmen be elected at-large or from wards? Although 65 per cent of all cities with over 500,000 population today have nonpartisan elections, this figure is very misleading. A nonpartisan election merely means that on election day there are no party designations printed on the ballot. It does not necessarily mean that the political parties play no part in who gets elected. As we shall discuss in the following chapter, political parties often abstain from participation in local elections in smaller communities, but they seldom do so in large cities. Chicago, for example, has legally nonpartisan elections but anyone familiar with Chicago politics knows that the parties play the key role in determining who gets elected to city offices there. Critics of nonpartisan elections argue that in large cities the voter needs the party label to give him some guidance in identifying candidates. According to this line of reasoning, the average voter may know little about the individuals running for council, but he will know which party usually nominates candidates sympathetic to his own point of view. This line of reasoning is valid only in strong two-party cities. If one party dominates city elections, then the real election takes

[8] R. J. Huckshorn and C. E. Young, "A Study of Voting Splits on City Councils in Los Angeles County," *Western Political Quarterly*, Vol. 13, No. 2 (June, 1960), pp. 479–97.

place in the primary of the dominant party, and the voter is again forced to choose between individuals without the guidance of a party label because all of those in the primary are obviously members of the same party.

Critics of nonpartisan elections also contend that they weaken the parties and allow special interest groups, in particular the business community, to influence unduly local elections. In those cities where local elections have been dominated by reform groups or local parties, such as the Charter Party in Cincinnati, the Citizens Association in Kansas City, or the Charter Government Committee in Phoenix, there is little doubt that the influence of the business community has been very great in proportion to its numbers. Critics also suggest that nonpartisanship tends to work in favor of the minority party. Supporters of the system, rather than denying this, consider it an advantage in that capable members of the minority party have a chance of election under nonpartisanship which they might not have otherwise. Advocates suggest that removing the party name from the ballot encourages the voter to vote on the basis of local rather than national issues and to choose between men rather than between parties.

There is little doubt that nonpartisan elections have weakened the role of national parties in local elections in many cities. This has been the case in Detroit, for example. In spite of this, it should be recognized that the parties have done a rather good job of overcoming this handicap, and they are usually among the most important participant groups in local elections in large cities. Perhaps one of the most valid arguments against nonpartisan elections in major cities is that true nonpartisanship is almost an impossible goal to attain there. Regardless of the form of the ballot, the major parties will participate in local elections either openly or under cover if they so desire, and it is better to have their participation open and above board. It appears that even in cities where the political parties formerly played little part in local elections, their role increases as the size of the city increases. This has happened in both Phoenix and San Diego, where for years the parties showed little interest in local elections, but as these cities passed the half million population mark, the role of the parties became more influential even though it was an informal behind-the-scenes role. It may be that as cities grow larger and the stakes in local politics become higher, the parties will no longer be willing to abstain from participation.

While over 60 per cent of all cities of over 5,000 elect all of their city councilmen at-large, the ward system of election continues to be popular in large cities. Over 55 per cent of the cities with over 500,000 population elect all or some of their councilmen from wards. Detroit and

Boston are examples of cities which elect all councilmen at-large; Chicago and Los Angeles elect all councilmen from wards; Oakland, California, and Tuscon, Arizona, are examples of cities which nominate candidates from wards, but elect at-large.

The at-large system of election became popular at the time of the reform movement. Advocates of at-large elections believed that doing away with wards would discourage factionalism among council members and also help eliminate the "you-scratch-my-back-I'll-scratch-yours" approach to local problems. It was believed that councilmen elected at-large would have to take a broader view of the city's problems rather than limiting their outlook to the problems and interests of a single ward. Critics contend that the practical effect of at-large elections is to enlarge the voice of the upper economic classes in local affairs. They argue that those individuals who are known throughout the city (or who can afford to make themselves known through a good campaign) have the best chance of getting elected. It is also suggested that at-large elections tend to keep members of minority groups from getting elected to the council. In fact, the positions of both the advocates and opponents of the plan are generally valid. Councilmen elected at-large do take a view of city problems that is not limited to a single geographic section of the community, but this gain sometimes comes by trading a bit of local democracy for rule by those at the top of the economic ladder.

A few cities, such as Oakland and Tucson, have attempted to combine the systems by nominating candidates in each ward but electing them at-large. The purpose in this arrangement is to insure representation to various areas of the city but at the same time to encourage councilmen to take a broad view of city problems by providing that they be elected by the voters of the entire city. Other cities, such as Houston, attempt to accomplish these ends by electing some councilmen from wards and others at-large.

THE URBAN POWER STRUCTURE AND DECISION-MAKING

The Power Structure Literature

For the past ten or fifteen years students of local government and politics have devoted much time and effort to the study of what has come to be called the "community power structure." The power structure literature attempts to discover who actually rules and how decisions actually get made in local politics. It begins with the assumption that influence on public policy in local government is not limited to those who hold official government positions. Rather it is believed that certain other community leaders—perhaps bankers, corporation executives, newspapermen, political bosses, or others—exercise much power over local policy decisions, and it is the goal of the students of community power to discover who these people are and in what ways they make their influence felt. Two of the more well-known community power studies are those of Atlanta and New Haven.

Power in Atlanta. Floyd Hunter's study of Regional City (Atlanta) was one of the earliest and remains one of the most widely known of the community power studies.[9] Hunter suggested that the power structure of Atlanta is shaped like a pyramid with the important decisions in the city being made by a small "elite" group of very powerful individuals at the top of the pyramid. This group consists of the owners or top executives of the city's major banks, utilities, and industrial and commercial establishments. When an important matter faces the community this group will confer informally and after deciding on a course of action will pass the word down so that it can be carried out by those on the next levels of the pyramid, bank vice-presidents, public-relations men, corporation attorneys, and sometimes the professional executives of civic and service organizations. According to Hunter, the membership of the "elite" was very stable, and its power extended to all areas of community activity.

Power in New Haven. Robert Dahl's study of community power in New Haven found a much different type of power structure from that described by Hunter for Atlanta.[10] He discovered no all powerful elite there. The power structure is pluralistic rather than elitist, with a number of groups having the power to influence public policy. To be sure, New Haven has its "economic notables" as Dahl calls them, and they are an influential force in local decision-making, but they are only one of several such groups. Also, each of the various group's leaders exercises influence over decisions in only a few issue areas instead of having broad encompassing influence as Hunter found in Atlanta.

Why the Differences? A logical question to ask is why the researchers in these two communities came up with such widely varying findings? A number of answers are possible. One answer is that each of them is right, that there really is a power elite in Atlanta while the political environment in New Haven is more pluralistic. Another possible answer is that the research methods they used influenced the type of conclusions to which they came. Hunter in studying Atlanta used a form of the method

---

[9] Floyd Hunter, *Community Power Structure* (Chapel Hill: University of North Carolina Press, 1963).

[10] Robert A. Dahl, *Who Governs?* (New Haven: Yale University Press, 1962).

known as "reputational analysis," in which selected individuals are asked to identify those in the community who are influential in key decisions. Those so identified are then interviewed and asked similar questions, and in this manner the elite is discovered. Dahl in studying New Haven focused on particular issues and studied the processes through which public policy decisions are made. Rather than looking directly for an elite he sought to determine how decisions get made and then to project from that the role of various groups in the decision process. Is it possible that if Hunter's research methods had been used in New Haven and Dahl's in Atlanta that different conclusions would have been forthcoming? Perhaps, Banfield's study of Chicago also focused on a series of important issues in that city and, like Dahl, his findings emphasized the role of competing groups in the political process. In spite of years of research and writing, there is still much that we do not know about community power. It is probably safe to say that the research methods that one employs and the questions that one asks will have some effect (we do not know how much) on the answers that he will get. It can also be said that each of the various approaches to the study of community power has been subject to attack, although most students in recent years have been most critical of the various forms of reputational analysis and also of the idea that most cities are ruled by a monolithic power elite.

Community Power: Some General Observations

While the community power debate continues and definitive statements about how the political process operates at the local level are yet to be made, it does appear to be possible to make a few general, though tentative, statements on the subject.

(1) Many cities may have a potential power elite that could rule if it chose to do so, which it usually does not. Certainly there are a relatively few people in most cities who control a sufficient amount of the city's financial and economic resources to bring their power to bear decisively on public policy matters. If this is true, why do they choose not to do so? One reason undoubtedly is that the stakes are often not high enough to make it worth their while. Relatively few of the local decisions that make the front page and appear significant to the average observer of local affairs have a substantial effect on the members of the potential power elite, and like the rest of us these people devote their attention to those things that seem to matter. Several writers have also pointed out the importance of the time element here. The members of

the elite indeed might rule if only they had time to get together, but almost by definition these are extremely busy people. Banfield points out, perhaps with tongue in cheek, that even if there were "four young men" with the power to run Chicago, as one of his informants suggested, there would still be the formidable problem of getting them together for lunch so that they could perform their kingly duties. Long makes the same point with relation to the Cleveland Fifty Club, which is supposedly made up of the "fifty most important men in Cleveland." According to Long, the lead time required just to get the members together has been an important reason why it has not functioned effectively as a power elite. Finally, the concept of a power elite ruling the city assumes that the members of the elite will agree on vital issues, an assumption that will often be invalid.

(2) If the point above is true, then the key decision-makers (as opposed to the potential decision-makers) in a city are unlikely to take the form of a static pyramid. It seems more probable that the key influentials will tend to be different on different isuues. On taxation issues, for example, certain persons may be able to exert decisive influence, while on matters involving education or urban renewal entirely different individuals may play crucial roles. There may well be cities such as Atlanta where the pyramid image correctly describes the local power structure, but it is probably not valid for most cities.

(3) Where pyramid shaped elites do hold and make use of real power today, it is likely that they exercise partial rather than complete power. They may have the power to block any action that they so desire but not the power to initiate any action to their liking. There may be rather well understood limits beyond which the public will not tolerate action, and in such cases the elite realizes that its power must be exercised within these limits. The elite's power may be limited to certain issue areas with competing groups demanding a voice in the determination of policy in other areas.

(4) To the extent that the power structure of the city is pluralistic, with several groups competing with each other for a voice in policy matters, the role of the city government and especially of the mayor in the policy process seems to be enhanced, for one of the major functions of the mayor in our major cities today is to act as a negotiator among various groups interested in public policy.

(5) Finally, whether or not a city actually has a power elite, it is very likely that the average citizen believes there is one. Long's point is well made that the public finds it convenient to believe that there is a "they" in the city. If taxes are too high, "they" are to blame because "they" are feathering their own nest. If a worthwhile project bogs down, "they" are blocking it for one reason or another. On the other hand, "they" are not always bad. One can assure himself that if the parking problems or the slum conditions or the tax rates get bad enough, "they" will eventually do something about it. One can partially excuse his own lack of involvement in such matters by telling himself that he could do no good anyway because there is a "they" who really control such matters.

Suggested Readings

Agger, Robert E., Daniel Goldrich and Bert E. Swanson, *The Rulers and the Ruled* (New York: John Wiley & Sons, Inc., 1964). An analysis of the political process in four small cities in the southern and western parts of the nation.

Banfield, Edward C., *Big City Politics* (New York: Random House, Inc., 1965). A comparative study of the political systems of nine major cities.

Banfield, Edward C., *Political Influence* (New York: Free Press of Glencoe, 1961). A discussion of urban politics, based primarily on case studies taken from the Chicago area and placed in a theoretical framework.

Buckley, Wm. F., *The Unmaking of a Mayor* (New York: Viking Press, 1966). The author's interesting and amusing analysis of his unsuccessful race for the office of mayor of New York City.

Dahl, Robert A., *Who Governs?* (New Haven: Yale University Press, 1961). An empirical study of decision-making in New Haven, in which Dahl questions some of the methodology and conclusions of Floyd Hunter's study.

Editors of Fortune, *The Exploding Metropolis* (Garden City, New York: Doubleday & Company, Inc., 1958). Chapter III is particularly significant.

Goodall, Leonard E., (ed.), *Urban Politics in the Southwest* (Tempe, Arizona: Arizona State University, Institute of Public Administration, 1967). A comparative study of the political systems of eleven southwestern cities.

Hunter, Floyd, *Community Power Structure* (Chapel Hill: University of North Carolina Press, 1953). The book that started the debate of the 1950's and early 1960's over the question of whether power structures exist and how they operate.

Lowi, Theodore J., *At the Pleasure of the Mayor* (New York: Free Press of Glencoe, 1964). A study of appointive officials in the city government of New York City.

Presthus, Robert, *Men at the Top* (New York: Oxford University Press, 1964). A study of decision-making in two small counties in New York. A significant contribution to county power and decision-making theory.

Sayre, Wallace S., and Herbert Kaufman, *Governing New York City* (New York: Russell Sage Foundation, 1960). The most thorough analysis yet done of government and politics in New York City.

chapter 4

Governing the Suburbs

In the not-too-distant future, a majority of the residents of metropolitan areas will live beyond the boundaries of the central city, and for many of those who remain in the city, a home in the suburbs will be a highly desired goal. The task of providing adequate governments for the rapidly growing suburbs promises to be one of the most challenging goals facing this highly urbanized— and suburbanized—nation in the coming decades. It is a task that cannot be accomplished by a governmental organization based on the old stereotype of a local government consisting of a volunteer fire department, a few policemen, and an ancient city hall inhabited by an elderly city clerk and two or three faithful but mediocre secretaries. The residents of many suburban communities have taken quite seriously the problem of how best to govern themselves, and through study committees, research reports, public hearings, and other devices of democracy they have come up with some answers. While the suggestions for governing suburbia represent a broad range of political thought, if one had to describe the predominant influence behind the organization and structure of suburban governments today in a single word, that word would be "reform."

THE SUBURBAN POLITICAL ETHIC: REFORM

The years from 1880 to 1920 were years when the spirit of reform manifested itself in many spheres of American life. The federal civil service system was born with the passage of the Pendleton Act in 1883, and the years following saw the federal government begin to assume a responsibility for the nation's economy with the establishment of the Interstate Commerce Commission in 1887, the enactment of the Sherman Anti-

Trust Act in 1890, and the creation of the Food and Drug Administration in 1906. The doctrine of social reform was preached with emotion by such diverse elements of society as the muckrakers, the suffragettes, and the prohibitionists. During this period the Constitution was amended to provide for the federal income tax, the direct election of United States Senators, woman's suffrage, and prohibition.

It was in this era also that the reform movement in local government had its beginning. Shocked by the corrupt practices of political machines and swept up by the prevalent spirit of reform, businessmen, journalists, educators, clergymen, and interested citizens from many other backgrounds turned their attention to "cleaning up city hall." In 1904 Lincoln Steffens published his famous work, *The Shame of the Cities,* in which he exposed the corruption he had discovered in city government in several large cities which he had visited. Steffens was especially critical of the buying and selling of municipal franchises for streetcar companies, electrical systems, and other utilities, which he claimed went to the firm which offered the council the most in bribes without reference to which company could offer the public the best services. In 1906, the Bureau of Municipal Research, an organization dedicated to promoting honest and more efficient local government was established in New York City, and civic minded citizens in other cities soon established similar research bureaus. The National Muncipal League had been established even earlier, in 1894, and it soon became a leader in the fight for better local government, a position which it still holds today.

Although the emphasis of the reform movement varied from one city to another, the reformers tended to focus their attention on a few basic goals. They generally sought to bring to their communities: (1) either the commission or the council-manager form of government; (2) nonpartisan elections; (3) at-large elections; (4) proportional representation; (5) a small city council (five to seven members); (6) a local civil service system; (7) direct democracy in the form of the initiative, referendum, and recall; (8) municipal home rule. Some of these reforms, such as proportional representation, had largely faded from the picture by the middle of the twentieth century, but most remain quite popular, especially in the metropolitan suburb.

Commission and Council-Manager Government

Two new forms of government structure were born during the first decade of the century. In 1900, a hurricane and flood devastated the city of Galveston, Texas, creating a crisis with which the local government, operating under a weak mayor-council system, was unable to cope. A reorganization of the city's government brought into being the commission form of government, under which five elected commissioners served both as the legislative and executive heads of the city. The commissioners sat collectively as the city's legislative body and established the basic policies of the community. They also served individually as department heads for the various operating departments of the city government. The success of Galveston's commission plan in guiding the city to recovery after its crisis popularized the plan and led to its adoption in a number of cities throughout the country, including Des Moines, Iowa. As more cities gained experience with the plan, certain shortcomings began to appear. This system of government assumed that the commissioners would have both the general knowledge of their communities necessary to make basic policy decisions and the technical knowledge necessary to direct the operations of a major city department such as the sewer, streets, or fire department. Even under ideal conditions it was difficult to find citizens who were both highly competent and willing to serve. Under this plan there was also the temptation for the commissioners to adopt a mutual "hands off" policy toward each other. The typical attitude would be "I won't try to tell you how to run your department and you don't interfere in how I run mine." The principle of legislative checks on administrative activities obviously breaks down in such a situation. The commission plan enjoyed its greatest popularity prior to 1920, but it was never used in more than a small minority of the nation's cities at any given time. In 1965, it was being used in 7.9 per cent of the cities with more than 5,000 population.[1]

One reason that commission government never got more than a foot in the door of American local government is that soon after it was first established in Galveston the interest of the reformers turned to another new form of local government, the council-manager plan. This plan is based on the theory that the city will be governed by a relatively small number of citizens elected to the city council and that these will usually be the only elected officials of the city. The council will be the policy-making body of the city, and administrative activities will be directed by a professional city manager who is to be appointed by, and subject to removal by, the council. The manager is responsible for appointing and removing department heads, directing and coordinating city activities, and preparing the annual city budget for the consideration of the council. In the early years of the plan, much attention was given to making a distinction between "policy" which was the responsibility of the council and "administration" which was the responsibilty of the manager. Each was warned by professors and practitioners of government to be careful not

---

[1] *Municipal Year Book: 1966* (Chicago: International City Managers Association, 1966), p. 90.

to interfere with the responsibilities of the other. In more recent years, it has come to be recognized that the distinction between these two functions is at best a fuzzy one and that the two will often overlap. The decisions made by the city manager in preparing the annual budget are certain to have policy implications and because the manager is familiar with the day-to-day operations of the city, the city council will often ask his recommendation on how best to handle some problem facing the city. Likewise, policy decisions made by the council will often affect the manner in which the manager directs the administrative affairs of the city.

The cities of Staunton, Virginia, and Sumter, South Carolina, vie for the honor of having been the first council-manager city. In 1908, the Staunton city council appointed a "general manager" to oversee the administrative affairs of the city, but the city retained the long ballot, and the powers of the manager were very limited. The idea of placing the city's administrative matters in the hands of a professional executive soon spread, and other cities experimented with the idea. Richard S. Childs, who was then secretary of the National Short Ballot Organization and later became an active leader in the National Municipal League, refined the theory by suggesting combining the appointment of a city manager with adoption of the short ballot. The first city to adopt a true council-manager plan as we know it today was Sumter, which began to operate under this form of government in 1912. In 1914, Dayton, Ohio, became the first relatively large city to adopt the plan.

Council-manager government quickly captured the imagination of the leaders of the reform movement because it appeared to be a means of achieving many of the goals of the reformers. The idea, associated with the plan from the beginning, that the council should be small and should be elected on a nonpartisan ballot coincided with the reformer's desire to remove local government from the domination of party machines and politicians. The concept of having administrative activities directed by a professional manager found support in the reform ideal of government employment on the basis of ability rather than party loyalty. Advocates of the council-manager plan pointed out that good management practices would bring about increased economy and efficiency, goals that were valued very highly by those fighting the graft and inefficiency of machine government.

The popularity of the plan has grown continually since its inception. In 1965, 40 per cent of all cities with more than 5,000 inhabitants operated under the plan.[2] The plan was especially popular in cities in the middle population ranges, with over half of the cities of between 25,000

---

[2] *Ibid.*

and 250,000 population operating under this form of government. The plan has been very popular in metropolitan suburbs as can readily be seen by noting the predominance of this form of government in communities around such major cities as New York, Chicago, St. Louis, and Los Angeles.

The plan appealed to the suburbanite of the 1960's for many of the same reasons that it had appealed to the reformer of a period fifty years earlier. Its association with nonpartisanship appealed to the suburbanite's desire to "take local government out of politics" in so far as possible. As the suburban dweller is often a white collar or middle management worker, he is attracted to the council-manager plan's emphasis on professionalism in management and on efficiency and economy in government.[3] In the last two decades or so the plan has also broadened its base of support by changing its image somewhat. At least until the time of World War II certain groups, laborers and minority racial groups in particular, considered the plan to be primarily an instrument for imposing the values of the business and management classes on the community. One reason for the early development of these sources of opposition was that most of the first managers came to their positions from a background in engineering or business. They had little education in the social sciences or humanities, and the value systems which they brought to the city management profession were such that they often alienated members of racial minorities, ethnic groups, and the lower economic classes.

The educational preparation of the city manager has changed significantly in recent years, and the trend is toward a degree in the social sciences, especially public administration or political science. In 1964, 54 per cent of those with a college degree who were holding manager positions had majored in public administration, political science or some other social science, and 30 per cent held degrees in some field of engineering. Among the younger managers the trend is very pronounced. For managers 29 and under, 61 per cent had majored in public administration or political science, 13 per cent majored in other social sciences, and 17 per cent held degrees in some field of engineering, mostly civil engineering. In addition, 39 per cent of the managers in the 29-and-under category held masters degrees in public administration.[4] This trend toward managers with a degree in the social sciences has tended

---

[3] On the attraction of the plan for those in business and professional positions, see Edgar L. Sherbenou, "Class Participation and the Council-Manager Plan," *Public Administration Review,* Vol. XXI, No. 3 (Summer, 1961), pp. 131–35.

[4] *Municipal Year Book: 1965* (Chicago: International City Managers Association, 1965), pp. 513–15.

Form of Government in Cities over 5,000 Population

Population Group	Total Number of Cities	Total Number of Cities in Table	Mayor-Council		Commission		Council-Manager	
			Number	Per Cent	Number	Per Cent	Number	Per Cent
Over 500,000............	27	26	20	76.9	1	3.8	5	19.2
250,000 to 500,000.....	27	27	11	40.7	3	11.1	13	48.1
100,000 to 250,000.....	96	96	34	35.4	12	12.5	50	52.0
50,000 to 100,000	232	227	84	37.0	22	9.7	121	53.3
25,000 to 50,000	476	462	167	36.1	50	10.8	244	52.8
10,000 to 25,000	1,165	1,105	538	48.7	99	9.0	468	42.4
5,000 to 10,000	1,171	1,146	746	65.1	58	4.9	344	30.0
All cities over 5,000....	3,189	3,089[1]	1,600	51.8	243	7.9	1,245	40.3

[1] Not included in this table are Washington, D.C., 40 cities with town meeting government, 26 with representative town meeting government, and 33 other cities for which no information was received.

Source: International City Managers Association, *Municipal Year Book: 1966*

to lessen the fear of these opposition groups that a city manager will necessarily hold values incompatible with their own.

The council-manager plan has also been criticized for placing too much emphasis on organizational structure and administrative techniques. Council-manager plan advocates are accused of being more interested in organization charts and neat administrative procedures than in the substantive problems facing their communities. In particular, city managers are often accused of being unresponsive to social problems. Critics suggest that even when the manager deals with substantive issues he is likely to be more interested in questions concerning streets or sewers than in such matters as unemployment, slum problems, or civil rights. Many city managers, aware that they have been criticized for being unresponsive to the problems of racial and low-income groups, have worked hard to overcome this criticism. Wayne Thompson, former city manager of Oakland, California, a city with a population that is one-fourth Negro, became nationally known for his leadership in dealing with that city's social problems. In general, while council-manager advocates have not won the strong support of these groups, they have succeeded in alleviating many of their greatest fears and in changing the attitudes of such groups to one of neutrality or "wait-and-see" rather than open opposition.

A problem faced by many council-manager cities is that the structure of the plan fails to provide for strong policy leadership. The fact that often neither the mayor nor the city manager is in a position to provide dynamic policy leadership for the community was discussed in Chapter 3. This tends to be a relatively minor problem in small or middle-sized communities where the main problems are those of good housekeeping in municipal departments, and questions demanding major policy decisions seldom arise. In larger council-manager cities, on the other hand, this is a continuing source of difficulty, often leading to conflict between the manager and the mayor or council. L. P. Cookingham, city manager of Kansas City for nearly twenty years, was a forceful leader on policy questions, and this was one of the factors which eventually cost him his position in 1959. Samuel E. Vickers, city manager of Phoenix, was fired in 1963 because of a conflict between him and the mayor about the proper role of the two offices. In both Kansas City and Phoenix, this conflict did not become acute so long as the incumbent mayor was not interested in exercising strong leadership himself, but when a mayor was elected who was interested in developing the policy leadership potential of the mayor's office to the fullest extent possible (Roe Bartle in Kansas City and Milton Graham in Phoenix), conflict arose between mayor and manager. On the other hand, one of the criticisms made by the commissioners of Dade County, Florida, against O. W. Campbell when he was removed from the office of county manager was that he did not provide strong leadership for the county. The pattern has been that as council-manager cities grow larger, the problems and conflicts related to the matter of policy leadership become more acute.

This discussion should suggest why the council-manager plan has been especially popular in the middle-class metropolitan suburb. Its association with professional management practices, efficiency and economy, and non-partisanship make it very attractive there. In addition, the problems most often associated with the plan, such as the opposition of low-income groups and racial minorities and the potential conflict over the question of policy leadership, are problems that are uncommon to this type of suburban community. It should be remembered, however, as was pointed out earlier, that there are many types of suburbs, and while the plan has been well accepted in what we have described as the typical middle-class suburb, there will be other suburban areas where the characteristics of the community will make the plan less workable.

Nonpartisanship

The concept of nonpartisanship is both popular and ambiguous. Because politics has gained an unfortunate reputation of association with graft and smoke filled rooms, many citizens are attracted by the idea of making local government nonpolitical or nonpartisan. We discussed earlier the fact that one cannot remove city governments from politics so long as there is conflict over how local problems should be solved. Nevertheless, many cities have attempted to disassociate their government from partisan political activity through non-partisan elections. It is important to understand that, *legally and formally,* non-partisanship means nothing more than removal of the party labels from the ballot. It is well recognized that this action alone will not prevent active partisan participation in local elections. Charles R. Adrian has suggested that nonpartisan elections fall into four general categories:[5]

(1) Elections where the only candidates who normally have any chance of getting elected are those supported by major political party organizations. In other words, the only difference between partisan and this type of nonpartisan elections is that in the latter the party names do not appear on the ballot. Chicago city elections would be

---

[5] Charles R. Adrian, "A Typology for Nonpartisan Elections," *Western Political Quarterly,* Vol. XII, No. 2 (June, 1959), pp. 449–58.

an example of this pattern, and Adrian suggests that Jersey City under the Hague machine probably fit this category also.

(2) Elections where slates of candidates are supported by various groups including both political party and other types of organizations. An example would be Cincinnati, where the locally organized Charter Party often competes against the regular Republican organization. Adrian would also place Omaha, Albuquerque and Seattle here.

(3) Elections where slates of candidates are supported by various interest groups and political party organizations normally play no important part in campaigns. The political affiliation of candidates in these cities would be either unknown or considered unimportant by the electorate. The major political organization in local campaigns in such cities often comes from a reform group or a business organization, such as the Chamber of Commerce. Denver, Dallas and Phoenix would fit this classification.

(4) Elections where neither political parties nor slates of candidates are important. Every man tends to run on his own, with the support of his friends and neighbors and perhaps an ad hoc organization formed just for that particular elction. Eugene C. Lee refers to this pattern as the "politics of acquaintance." This pattern is most common in cities in the middle and smaller population categories, especially in cities under 5,000 population.

The majority of local elections in metropolitan suburbs which have relatively homogeneous populations probably fall in the third and fourth categories. The idea of partisan activity is often frowned on, and it is common in such communities for "the office to seek the man" rather than vice versa. A local good government, reform, or civic improvement organization is commonly formed to seek out the "best" candidates and urge them to run for office. In this sense "best" usually means candidates who fit the mold of middle class values. Lee's study of councilmen elected in nonpartisan elections in California found that the average councilman[6]

> ... is a man of 45 to 50 years of age, engaged in some professional, managerial, or sales activity and living in the "better" part of town. He belongs to a service club, is probably a Mason, a member of a veterans group and of the chamber of commerce. He is a Protestant but not necessarily affiliated with any church. He had no previous official city experience, although he was active in Com-

---

[6] Eugene C. Lee, *The Politics of Nonpartisanship* (Berkeley and Los Angeles: University of California Press, 1960), p. 50.

munity Chest, Red Cross, or related activities. He is a registered
Republican, but has not taken a very extensive part in partisan
politics. He has lived in the city for a considerable length of time.

A study of mayors and councilmen in Los Angeles County in 1957 presented a similar profile.[7]

Although it would be impossible to fit all cities neatly into one of
Adrian's categories, statistics show that nonpartisanship, at least in form
if not always in fact, is widely used in American cities. In 1964, 64 per
cent of all cities of more than 5,000 population elected officials on a
nonpartisan ballot. The figure is highest among council-manager cities,
84 per cent of which have nonpartisan elections. For mayor-council
cities, the figure is 48 per cent. There is not a great amount of variation
on the basis of population. The lowest usage of nonpartisan elections,
62 per cent, is found among cities of 5,000 to 10,000 population; the
highest, 80 per cent, is in cities with from 250,000 to 500,000 inhabitants. If we can assume that most suburban communities fall in the
middle population categories from 25,000 to 250,000 we find a higher
than average utilization of this form of election, with 69 per cent of the
cities in this range having nonpartisan elections.[8]

Adrian has reported on several general characteristics of non-partisan
elections suggested by his research.[9] First, he says, nonpartisanship tends
to segregate partisan and nonpartisan political activities. There is a tendency for political leaders to be divided into the two areas with little
moving from one to the other. There are exceptions, such as Hubert
Humphrey, who was elected mayor of Minneapolis in a nonpartisan election even though he was a known and active Democrat, but the general
trend is in the opposite direction. It is not uncommon, in fact, for a
partisan political activist almost to be ruled out of participation in city
elections, for if he chooses to run for municipal office, he is immediately
attacked by civic leaders and the local press for attempting to introduce
"politics" into their nonpartisan local government. This segregation applies to campaign funds as well as candidates, with political party organizations usually playing little role in fund raising for local candidates.

---

[7] Robert J. Huckshorn, "Spotlight on City Councilmen," *BGR Observer* (November, 1957).

[8] *Municipal Year Book: 1965* (Chicago: International City Managers Association,
1965), p. 118.

[9] Charles R. Adrian, "Some General Characteristics of Nonpartisan Electons,"
American Political Science Review, Vol. XLVI, No. 3 (September, 1952), pp.
766–76.

The regular political parties may be weakened by reducing their role at the local level, thereby providing less motivation for party members to be actively involved in party affairs at the grass roots level. Since strong organization at the local level is of vital importance to the health of a political party, it may be seriously hampered by the apparent abolishing of its *raison d'etre* in local politics.

Nonpartisanship may attract some candidates for local office who would not otherwise be interested. Since many citizens accept the view that the regular political parties are a bit tainted, some may be willing to run for city council or school board where the elections are nonpartisan who would not run for the same office if the election were on a partisan basis.

Another characteristic is that nonpartisan elections tend to work in favor of incumbents. Because there is no party affiliation or other organization with which to label the candidates, familiarity with individual names is of crucial importance in voter identification. The incumbent usually has an advantage here over newcomers to the local political scene. The result of this is that councils are often oriented toward conservatism since their membership may consist of members who have served several terms and who form a type of in-group into which it is hard for the non-incumbent newcomer to break. This situation is related to other characteristics. Since voting for individuals rather than slates is emphasized, there is usually an avoidance of issues in campaigns. The candidate finds it advantageous to depend on the "politics of acquaintance" to get elected and usually avoids taking firm stands on issues. The whole question of what the key issues are may never be articulated in a campaign for city office.

Finally, there is no collective responsibility on a council elected through nonpartisan elections. Since each man was elected on his own, the public cannot place responsibility for policy on an identifiable majority block as can be done when Democrats or Republicans (or others) as a group form the majority in a legislative body. This characteristic would not apply where local parties or civic groups nominate and elect slates of candidates, but it is true where slate-making does not take place and to some extent where slating occurs only for the purpose of the campaign. A result of this is a tendency for protest voting to be frustrated. When candidates are not grouped together so that collective responsibility can be assigned, it is very difficult for voters who want to "throw the rascals out" to identify the proper rascals.

In spite of criticism of nonpartisan elections by many political party activists and political scientists, the principle appears to be strongly supported by most citizens so far as local elections are concerned, and there is no evidence that any trend away from it is likely to develop.

Small Councils, At-Large Elections

Two related reforms concerning the city council pertain to size and method of election. The present trend is for councils to be relatively small, with a membership of between five and nine. Except for cities of over 500,000, the size of councils varies little, the average falling within the five-to-nine range in all population categories. The reason for having such small councils (in relationship to other legislative bodies such as Congress and the state legislatures) relates to the function which is perceived for it. In general, the average citizen seems to consider that the council functions more like a corporate board of directors, setting long-range goals and making broad policy decisions, than like other legislative bodies which are characterized by give-and-take and compromise among competing interest groups. Whether this contrast is valid is debatable, but the citizen, relying again on his philosophy of a non-political local government, believes that it should be. One problem with the small council is that it limits representativeness; each councilman must represent a larger segment of the population in cities where district or ward elections are used.

Closely related to questions about the size and representatives of councils is the issue of whether councilmen should be elected at-large or by wards. This question was discussed in Chapter 3, and it was pointed out that at-large elections tend to be less popular in large cities than in those in middle population categories. About 65 per cent of the cities of between 25,000 and 250,000 population use at-large elections compared with only 40 per cent among cities of 500,000 or more. Use of at-large elections is closely associated with use of the council-manager plan. Over three-fourths of all council-manager cities elect councilmen at-large while less than one-half of the mayor-council cities do so.[10]

Most of the arguments pro and con concerning the use of at-large elections in large cities also apply to smaller communities although with varying degrees of similarity. Certainly one reason that many have supported at-large elections is that they have felt that it would minimize political "horse trading" among councilmen. They felt that electing councilmen by a vote of the entire city would encourage them to have a more encompassing view of the public interest than is the case where

---

[10] *Municipal Year Book: 1965* (Chicago: International City Managers Association, 1965), p. 118.

each councilman is responsible only to the electorate in his own ward. The criticism that at-large election tends to work in favor of those in the upper economic classes appears to be true in many cases. If we assume that homogeneity is often a chaacteristic of the metropolitan suburb, however, this will be less of a problem there than in the large city which has much social, economic, and ethnic heterogeneity.

Civil Service

Another innovation of the reform era which continues to play an important role in local governments is civil service reform. Throughout the nineteenth century employment practices at all levels of government were based mainly on patronage. "To the victor belongs the spoils" was fact as well as slogan in most jurisdictions. Throughout the second half of the century pressure built up for the establishment of public personnel systems based on merit and impartiality, and in 1883 Congress passed the Pendleton Act establishing a merit system of employees of the federal government. Although the Pendleton Act originally covered only about 10 per cent of all federal employees, it was the beginning of a movement that was soon followed by other levels of government. Although merit system reform has moved somewhat slowly at the state level and even more so among counties, it has made considerable progress in city government. In 1884, only a year after the adoption of the Pendleton Act, a merit system was established for cities in the state of New York by state statute. The merit system concept for cities received a strong boost after the turn of the century through its close association with the commission and council-manager forms of government, and most cities adopting these governmental forms instituted personnel reforms also.

Originally municipal civil service systems were usually administered by an independent civil service commisson of three or five members who were appointed by the mayor or council and who served staggered terms. It was almost always required that both of the major political parties be represented on the commission. This organizational structure was designed to give the commission the maximum possible independence from the regular elected city officials who were believed in many cases to be more interested in patronage and political influence than in good personnel practices. The system was by no means foolproof, for the commissioners were appointed by the elected officials, and if the mayor and his associates wanted to make the commission an instrument for patronage rather than a protection against it, they could do so. A civil service commissioner in Chicago is said to have remarked once, "Sure, I believe in civil service, but I think the Democrats should get the jobs."[11] On the whole, however, the independent commission has been successful in insulating the personnel system from the political officials.

The question is currently being raised whether this independent status is any longer a desirable organizational arrangement. While such separation may have had a purpose when patronage and corruption were commonplace at city hall, there is strong feeling among students of administration that this structure is not conducive to the best management practices today. Although some questionable personnel practices undoubtedly are still to be found in city government, the days of the "boss" and the flagrant misuse of patronage are over, and the major problem facing city officials today is not how to prevent corruption but rather how to have a well managed, well coordinated organization with which to meet urban problems. With this in mind many observers today are recommending that the personnel function should be placed under a director who is appointed by and responsible to the city's chief executive (mayor or manager). For example, the Municipal Manpower Commission, a group of distinguished citizens who undertook an in-depth study of city personnel problems, recommended that the independent civil service commission be abolished or limited to an advisory function and that personnel administration be placed within the responsibility of the chief executive.[12] This recognizes personnel administration as an integral part of the management function and encourages confidence and close cooperation between the director and the chief executive.

In many cases where reorganization of this type has occurred, the commission has not been abolished, but its function has been changed to that of advisor and evaluator of personnel policies. In some cities the commission also serves as a review or appeal board for city employees who believe they have been unfairly treated. There is disagreement about whether the commission should continue to exist at all. The Municipal Manpower Commission concluded that the local civil service commission "has outlived its usefulness as an instrument of personnel management," although it agreed that it might still serve a purpose if it were used only for the purpose of reviewing and reporting on personnel practices. The Public Personnel Association has taken the view that no one form of personnel organization can be considered best for all jurisdictions and each city should decide for itself which organizational structure best fits its own situation.

---

[11] Quoted in Leonard D. White, *Introduction to the Study of Public Administration,* Fourth Edition (New York: The Macmillan Company, 1954), p. 315.

[12] For the complete report see Municipal Manpower Commission, *Governmental Manpower for Tomorrow's Cities* (New York: McGraw-Hill Book Company, 1962).

Another change in merit system operation has been a shift from a negative to a positive attitude toward the whole field of public personnel management. The purpose for which civil service systems were originally established was a distinctly negative one—to keep the political hacks and incompetents off the public payroll. The result of such an approach often turned out to be the recruitment of a group of honest but mediocre public employees. Administrators gradually came to realize that this philosophy was not sufficient to provide the type of people needed to meet the challenges of an urbanizing society, and there has been a marked shift in general approach in recent years. It is accepted now that the goal of a good municipal civil service system should be not just to keep the worst people out of public employment but also to bring some of the best people in. Many larger cities (along with states and the federal government) now send recruiters to college campuses just as major corporation do. In addition to written examinations, public jurisdictions are making broader use of oral examinations, which allow the interviewers to get an idea of the applicant's ability to think quickly, express himself well, and converse personably with others. Internships, in-service training programs, and encouragement and support for employees who want to take advanced university courses are other innovations now in use in many cities. Better salaries, promotion policies, and retirement systems are helping cities attract better employees.

While most cities still find it difficult to compete with private employers and other public employers in what it can offer in salaries and fringe benefits, their most serious recruitment problem is that the image of city employment is still very poor. It is safe to say that the average college student today gives less consideration to the possibility of a career in local government than in national or international agencies. He is still likely to view city hall as a rather drab place filled with clerks with eyeshades and to feel that there is nothing for him there. Good people in fields such as public administration, accounting, civil engineering, and planning are much needed by city governments. The sharp improvement in municipal personnel systems has done much to help get them, but there is still a long way to go.

Municipal Home Rule

Home rule, broadly defined, means granting to local governments the right to frame and adopt their own charters. The movement for home rule had its origins in the nineteenth century. Missouri in 1875 became the first state to adopt constitutional home rule, granting it to cities with a population of 100,000 or more, and three other states, California

(1879), Washington (1889), and Minnesota (1896), had adopted constitutional home rule provisions by the turn of the century. A few states, beginning with Iowa in 1858, have attempted to grant home rule through legislative act, although this approach runs into the problems of instability and uncertainty associated with being subject to constant revision or revocation by the legislature. A major impetus for the campaign to get home rule for cities was the desire to free them from excessively restrictive control by state legislatures. In the late 1800's and early 1900's state legislatures, like politicians, were in bad repute, and many citizens believed that local government could be improved by removing it as far as possible from influence by the legislature. Another factor was the tendency of the courts to follow Dillon's Law, a judicial ruling which interpreted the powers of local goverments very narrowly, in determining the distribution of powers between state and local governments.

Today about one-half of the states provide for some type of local home rule, most of them through constitutional rather than statutory provisions. It is common for states to authorize only those municipalities over an established population figure to take advantage of home rule provisions. Arizona, for instance, allows cities and towns with a population of 3,500 or more to frame and adopt home rule charters. Missouri, which originally extended home rule powers only to cities of more than 100,000, now offers them to all cities of 10,000 and over.

In practice, home rule is less than the panacea that many early supporters hoped for. A major problem arises from the fact that in most states home rule has not been precisely defined, either by legislative or judicial action. While most home rule provisions state that municipalities shall have authority to manage "municipal affairs" or "matters of local concern" without state interference, there is no concensus on which affairs are local in nature and which are of statewide concern. In most home rule states the powers granted to local governments are very limited, especially in the area of finance. In New York, for example, the constitution is so worded that no doubt is left that legislative acts are supreme when they conflict with home rule charter provisions. The state statutes in Minnesota provide that all municipalities shall be subject to the statutory debt limits "notwithstanding any home rule charter provision or charter law." On the other hand a few states, examples of which would be California and Colorado, give relatively broad powers to their home rule municipalities.

Generally speaking, home rule provisions have been most successful in giving municipalities power to determine their own organizational structure. Home rule cities are usually free to decide on their form of government, number of councilmen, length of terms, method of selecting administrative officials, internal administrative structure, and similar matters. Home rule provisions have been generally unsuccessful in broadening the powers of municipalities where matters concerning finances are involved.

THE ASSUMPTIONS OF THE REFORM MOVEMENT

Implicit in the goals of the reform movement are certain assumptions about how the political process operates. The first such assumption is that local government can be, and should be, taken out of politics. There is the strong belief even today that politics is corrupt, politicians either inept or dishonest or both, and that local government should be removed from this atmosphere. One needs only reflect on the specific changes recommended by the reformers to be aware of the pervasive influence of the assumption that local government and politics should be separated. The council-manager plan was advocated as a means for substituting businesslike management practices for political manipulation. Nonpartisan elections were to lead to an elimination of the influence of partisanship at city hall. At-large elections were designed to do away with the political horse trading and mutual back scratching associated with councilmen who had to protect the interests of their own ward. It was hoped that civil service systems would replace political loyalty with competence as a criterion for public employment. Home rule charters were advocated in an effort to free municipalities from control by politically oriented state legislatures.

Inherent in this assumption is the belief that local government is somehow different from state and national governments, for one seldom hears reference to taking these levels of government out of politics. If, as we have discussed previously, the concept of politics involves the management of conflict, then local government as surely as any other level of government is involved in politics. What the reform movement may have done was change the rules by which the game of politics is played and thereby change the odds for winning. Many students of government, while applauding the obvious improvements in administrative techniques brought about through reform efforts, believe that another effect of reform has been an enlargement of the voice of middle and upper socio-economic classes in city affairs at the expense of minority groups and the poor. Our discussion of the council-manager plan indicates why this may be true where that reform is in use. Adrian's comments on nonpartisanship suggest that this criticism may also be valid where party labels are removed from the ballot. At-large elections, which give the best chance of winning to the candidate who is known or who can afford to make himself known throughout the community, may have this effect. The validity of this type of criticism is related to the heterogeneity of the community. The undesirable consequences of these reforms will be minimized in highly homogeneous communities. Even in larger communities with more heterogeneous populations, citizens may determine that the administrative and organizational advantages of these reforms more than offset the representational and other disadvantages.

A second, closely related, assumption of the reformers is that there should be "one best way" of reaching a given goal. There is a tendency to believe that if those involved in a dispute are sufficiently intelligent, patient, and public spirited, then they should be able to sit down around a conference table and work out their problems. The danger in this assumption is the temptation to consider conflict as something abnormal or undesirable and to believe that any conflict should be soluble with sufficient effort. This attitude fails to recognize that there may be deep and virtually insoluble differences among various groups in society. It may well be that there will be such strong and lasting disagreements on some issues that no amount of good will and discussion will bring about solutions acceptable to all. In decisions of this type, which often involve either/or answers, the government cannot arrive at a convenient compromise that gives everyone a little of what he wants. Because conflict is in the nature of society, the political process will be affected by reforms which minimize its importance, and this is what many of the goals of the reformers do. A good example would be at-large elections, advocates of which assume that there is some organic good for the entire community which councilmen should seek in their deliberations. They deny the possibility that there may be deep conflict between different elements of the community which can never be properly reflected by councilmen all of whom are expected to represent the interests of the "city as a whole."

These assumptions about the operation of the political process were without doubt products of the environment of the reform movement at the turn of the century. This was the period of the political machine, of widespread corruption at both state and local levels, and of a generally low esteem for public office and public officials. It was from this background that the muckrakers emerged with their broad attack on both politics and politicians. It was this background that produced the municipal reformers with their hopes and techniques for establishing nonpolitical local governments. Whether depoliticized city governments which minimize the role of conflict can effectively deal with the problems of the technological urbanized society of the second half of the twentieth century remains an open question.

THE PRIZES OF SUBURBAN POLITICS

What motivates the suburban dweller to participate in local politics? What does he see of value that is to be gained from participation? First, it is clear from voting statistics and other research that many suburbanites, like many others, do not participate at all or at most participate only to the extent of voting occasionally. The press of business, family, commuting, recreation, and other activities leave little time for political affairs. Interest tends to be low also because suburban politics is often characterized by a lack of important issues (or at least a lack of community recognition of important issues). The major decisions at city hall are housekeeping duties and seldom evoke widespread interest and discussion by the citizens. Of those who do participate some do so not for any potential substantive gains but merely for the satisfaction associated with doing one's part as a good citizen. Nevertheless, the motivations that lead citizens to political participation in suburban communities tend to follow rather consistent patterns.

If there is a single issue in which the citizen of suburbia is likely to be interested, that issue is schools. Since the suburbs are in the main the homes of young families, many, if not most, residents will have a direct interest in school policies. The search for good schools is a major incentive in the decision of many to move to a suburban community, and the quality of education is often the single most important factor in deciding in which particular community to locate. Although the homeowner is very tax conscious and will demand strict economy, perhaps even austerity, in expenditures for other public services, he will be more inclined to look sympathetically on proposals for expenditures for the schools. In balancing his desire for low taxes against his desire for better public services, education is the area in which public services are most likely to win out.

Next to education, and in some communities equal or above it, the interest of the citizen is in issues concerned with the preservation of property values. Issues on this subject take several forms, one of the most common of which is a stern eye on the property tax rate. The typical chamber of commerce advertises that "taxes are low in Elm Tree Heights," and the candidate for city council must promise that he will "lower taxes through better management in city government" or at least that he will "hold the line" on the property tax rate. The particular pattern varies with the type of community. A prosperous area with many residents who are executives and professional people may want high quality services and be willing and able to pay for them. The community with a population of wage earners and heavily mortgaged tract homes will be more inclined to accept a lower level of services as the price of keeping the tax rate down.

The preservation of land values is also involved in zoning policy. What kind of business and industry to allow in the city becomes a key question. From the standpoint of beauty and esthetics, many suburban communities would prefer to be exclusively residential, letting the industry which provides jobs locate in the central city or elsewhere in the metropolitan area. Unfortunately, this policy works at cross purposes with the desire to keep taxes down, for business establishments and industrial plants pay taxes far in excess of their demands for municipal services. Thus cities cannot afford to exclude completely such enterprises, and they must decide instead what kind of industry to let in and where to allow it to locate. Few issues will bring masses of irate citizens to a city council meeting like the threat of some unwanted business locating near where they live. If the business must come to town at all, they are sure a better location for it is in someone else's neighborhood.

Another element involving land values is race. With a few notable exceptions, suburbia is "lily-white," and while the average citizen prefers not to have to admit it, he desperately hopes that it will stay that way. There is the widespread belief that an influx of even a few Negro families will cause propery values to drop sharply. Even though the available evidence seems to deny the truth of this belief, if enough people are convinced that it is true, it can become a self-fulfilling prophecy. In some cases open violence, such as rock throwing and window breaking, has resulted when families of a minority race have moved into previously all white neighborhoods. In most areas the attack is more subtle. Realtors and rental agencies happen to have nothing available when the minority family is looking for living accommodations. Strong social pressure can be brought on a family leaving the community not to sell their home to minority buyers. Although there is little in the way of legal restraints that a community can use to control who moves in, the informal sanctions have been most effective up to the present time. Even with the active support of the national government in the area of civil rights it appears that such barriers will crumble slowly.

One other issue in addition to education and property values that is sometimes found in suburban politics is what might be generally defined as community identity or grass roots democracy. The suburban citizen believes that the best government is that which is closest to home. He is also very conscious of his own community, and he is reluctant to have it identified with, or dominated by, the nearby central city. It is often good politics for the candidate for public office to assure the voters he will not allow the community to be pushed around by the big city. This attitude of intense community pride and local independence may have the unhealthy effect of impeding cooperation among various governmental jurisdictions to solve common area-wide problems. On the other hand, if this community consciousness gives the individual a sense of identification, something to cling to in the mass society, it may help make living in suburban society more bearable.

Suggested Readings

Adrian, Charles R., "A Typology for Nonpartisan Elections," *Western Political Quarterly,* Vol. XII, No. 2 (June, 1959), pp. 449–58.

Carver, Humphrey, *Cities in the Suburbs* (Toronto: University of Toronto Press, 1962). Deals primarily with the physical planning aspects of suburbanization.

Dobriner, Wm. (ed.), *The Suburban Community* (New York: G. P. Putnam's Sons, 1958).

East, John Porter, *Council-Manager Government: The Political Thought of Its Founder, Richard S. Chitels* (Chapel Hill: University of North Carolina Press, 1965).

Lee, Eugene C., *The Politics of Nonpartisanship* (Berkeley and Los Angeles: University of California Press, 1960).

Sherbenou, Edgar L., "Class Participation and the Council-Manager Plan," *Public Administration Review,* Vol. XXI, No. 3 (Summer, 1961), pp. 131-35.

Williams, Oliver P. and Charles R. Adrian, *The Insulation of Local Politics under the Nonpartisan Ballot, American Political Science Review,* Vol. 53, No. 4 (December, 1959), pp. 1052-1163.

Wood, Robert C., *Suburbia: Its People and their Politics* (Boston: Houghton Mifflin Co., 1959). The best general study of suburban politics.

chapter **5**

Governing the Metropolitan Area: Some Moderate Approaches

It is an overly simplified view to suggest that the problem of metropolitan areas is one of inadequate governmental structure. Nevertheless, it is a fact that the structure of government tends to be a complicating factor in dealing with any substantive problem, whether it be air pollution, police protection, or anything else. Today's typical metropolitan area is governed by a multiplicity of governments; it may be the 1400 of the New York area or only a few in the case of some of our smaller areas. The city of St. Louis, for example, is surrounded by nearly one hundred incorporated municipalities in St. Louis County, not to mention school districts, special districts, and other units. It is not unusual to see the speedlimit on a single street move up and down every few miles (or blocks!) as one drives from municipality to municipality, and zoning regulations, building codes and tax rates will be equally varied within a single area.

Many different devices have been experimented with in attempting to overcome problems of jurisdictional and structural inadequacy. These various approaches do not fall neatly into categories, and students of urban government are not agreed on any one classification system into which to fit the many attempts to deal with governmental problems in the metropolitan area. For purposes of discussion here we have divided them into two general categories identified simply as moderate approaches and far-reaching approaches.[1] The criterion which we have tried to use in this division is the extent to which the approaches alter the structure of existing governmental units. Those which do not involve structural alterations or do so only to a minimal extent are considered to be moderate approaches; those which do involve such alterations are called far-reaching approaches. This classification is far from perfect, for there is no approach discussed which might not potentially affect structure, and the extent to which this will occur will vary with the existing situation in the area. We have, for example, classified the special district approach as moderate, but the effects of establishing a special district can be quite far-reaching if it is created to undertake a major function or functions previously provided by other governmental units. The terms "moderate" and "far-reaching" are themselves not perfect. Other terms, such as "procedural" and "structural" or "limited" and "radical," might be used. The author prefers the terms used because they seem to be less emotion-packed and more truly descriptive than others.

With this reservation about the validity of classification in mind, we will discuss the moderate approaches in this chapter and the far-reaching ones in the following chapter. Under the moderate label we will look at annexation, extraterritorial jurisdiction, transfer of functions, regional councils, special districts, and contractual arrangements. In the category of far-reaching approaches we will discuss consolidation of similar governmental units, city-county consolidation, city-county separation, and metropolitan federalism. Regional planning, which is included in some discussions of this type, is dealt with in Chapter 10. The use of the urban county as an instrument for solving metropolitan area problems, which some writers have considered as a separate approach, is discussed in this analysis under transfer of functions, for when the transfer approach is used, the county is often the recipient of such transfer.

SOME CRITERIA FOR EVALUATION

Before going into a discussion of how best to cope with governmental problems in metropolis let us establish some criteria on which to base an evaluation of the approaches. We will suggest four: (1) organiza-

---

[1] For other classification systems, see *Alternative Approaches to Governmental Reorganization in Metropolitan Areas* (Washington: Advisory Commission on Intergovernmental Relations, 1962), pp. 19–80; Roscoe C. Martin, "Action in Metropolis: I," *National Civic Review* (June, 1963), pp. 302–07, 17; and "Action in Metropolis: II," *National Civic Review* (July, 1963), pp. 363–67, 71.

tional simplicity, (2) responsiveness to the public, (3) political accept-ability, and (4) comprehensiveness.[2]

Organizational simplicity is obviously desirable because one of the major problems of the metropolitan area is complexity of governmental structure. When we include this as a desirable criterion we mean from the standpoint of both operating efficiency and citizen interest. It is assumed that a service can be provided throughout an entire area more efficiently by a single governmental unit than by a number of units faced with the inevitable problems of coordination. It is also assumed that organizational simplicity is facilitated by having fewer rather than more governments involved in the governing of area. From the standpoint of citizen interest, it is generally believed that organizational simplicity makes it easier for the citizen to understand and therefore to exercise responsible control over, his government. The ultimate example of organizational simplicity would be a single city government, located entirely in one state and one county and undisturbed by intersecting boundaries of suburbs, special districts, or other units, providing all municipal services for the populated region of a given metropolitan area. Because this is an unattainable (and many would say undesirable) goal in most areas, it is recognized that this is merely a general standard against which to evaluate the more common approaches. As an illustration, an-nexation by an existing city would come closer to meeting this criterion than would the establishment of a special district or the incorporation of a new municipality.

Responsiveness to the public is another standard to keep in mind if we expect government in the metropolis to be kept in the democratic tradition. This does not necessarily mean that we should elect more officials; we may need to elect fewer in order to shorten the ballot suffi-ciently that the voter can make more intelligent decisions on those major policy officials that he is called upon to elect. Public responsibility is not necessarily related to size of governmental unit. There is disagreement about whether the small suburb with its nearby city hall and a council made up of neighbors is necessarily more responsive than larger govern-ments. Questions about method of choosing officials, length of term, and voting qualifications are apt to be more pertinent. Citizen respon-sibility is probably also enhanced by relying as much as possible on the traditional familiar units of local government. The citizen has some general idea of what is meant by terms like "city," "county," and "mayor," and he accepts and grants legitimacy to these parts of a

---

[2] For a somewhat different statement of criteria, see *Alternative Approaches*, pp. 11-18.

system of government with which he has some familiarity. On the other hand, he is unlikely to understand something called "metro" or an official called a "county mayor" or "metropolitan mayor," and that which he does not understand he may fear or oppose. At the very least he will be reluctant to participate in a government which seems complex and unfamiliar.

Public responsiveness includes what is referred to in the literature of political science as "access," or the ability to get one's opinions heard and considered by those in positions of authority. Access is a highly valued political goal, and many citizens place it above more obvious goals in their hierarchy of values. For example, the suburbanite who understands the reformer's arguments about the problems caused by proliferation of governments may still be very willing to pay whatever price is involved in keeping his independent suburban government which is run by "folks pretty much like us" rather than becoming part of the central city and losing control to the (real or imagined) big city machine. Likewise, the central city Negro is likely to prefer ward to at-large elections in spite of any arguments for the latter for the same reason; he feels his access is better protected by ward elections.

From a realistic point of view political acceptability is one of the most important criteria involved in evaluating means of metropolitan cooperation. Regardless of how logical or efficient a given approach may seem, it will not work if it is not acceptable to those directly involved, and nearly every possible approach will appear threatening to someone. City officials may feel threatened by a plan to strengthen the county. Suburban mayors and councilmen will see a challenge to their position and prestige in any plan to consolidate with the central city or establish a system of metropolitan federalism. City employees often fear that a consolidation of functions may cost them their jobs. In some cases formal approval of the electorate must be obtained, as when a referendum is required before implementation of the proposed plan. Annexation, for example, often requires a vote of those in the area to be annexed. Plans for city-county cooperation often must receive separate majority votes from both county and city voters. Unless a proposed reform first meets the standards of political acceptability, it will never get a chance to prove its value in other ways.

Finally, any proposal for metropolitan reform should meet the criterion of comprehensiveness; that is, it should be large enough to encompass the people and the problem (or problems) involved. In some areas where the central city has not been surrounded by suburban incorporations, annexation will enable the city to meet this requirement. Tucson, Arizona, thanks to rigid state laws which discourage fringe incorporations, is such a city. All too often, the problems cut across not only city boundaries but county and state lines as well, making it extremely difficult to devise a sufficiently comprehensive scheme. This criterion should take financial resources into consideration by requiring that jurisdictions be sufficiently large to insure that taxable resources of the area are available to support the needed governmental services. On this basis, the incorporation of a tiny municipality to serve as a tax haven for industry would be considered undesirable, as would any plan which artifically separates taxable wealth from the major service need areas of a metropolitan area. The principle of comprehensiveness must also be considered to include the concept of flexibility. As problems change and populations move and expand, it should be possible to alter the governing system in such a way as to maintain the desired comprehensive characteristic. Annexation is a good example of flexibility in this sense, and voluntary associations also have this advantage in that they are able to add new member governments as the need arises.

It should be obvious that these criteria are subjective and their respective values will be weighed differently in different situations. There will also be times when they will conflict with one another. Some will say, for example, that the more comprehensive a government becomes the less responsive it is to the public, and it is apparent that suggesting the combining of all existing governments into one in order to achieve organizational simplicity will often conflict with the goal of political acceptability. The criteria are at best general guidelines and not objective standards of measurement.

SOME MODERATE APPROACHES

Annexation

One of the oldest, and in many ways the simplest, approaches to metropolitan reform is annexation, the extension of the city limits to bring more area within the municipality. State laws vary on the procedure for annexation, but a majority require some form of popular referendum in either the annexing city or the area to be annexed or both.[3] In Iowa the decision is made by the voters of the existing city, while Michigan is a state which requires the consent of a majority of the voters in the area to be annexed. A few states, such as Arizona, allow annexation to

---

[3] A thorough discussion of alternative annexation methods is found in Frank S. Sengstock, *Annexation: A Solution to the Metropolitan Area Problem* (Ann Arbor: University of Michigan Law School, 1960).

occur without referendum on the basis of council action of the annexing city. In Virginia annexations are made by judicial action. In that state, either the city or the residents in the area concerned may petition the special three-man annexation court to initiate action on the annexation. The court must base its decision on the urban character of the area involved and on the general interests of the entire urban area rather than on the particular interests of the city or the residents of the area in question. Until recent years the court usually ruled in favor of the annexation. In the past few years the courts have often held that the county government was providing the necessary urban services and that fringe area residents were therefore not in need of municipal government.

Annexation would rank high on criteria of organizational simplicity and citizen responsibility. No new governments are added, and no structural changes in existing governments are involved. The only change takes place within the traditional and familiar local governmental structure. It may be that there is some point at which cities get "too big" to be responsive to the public, and if so annexation after that size is reached would be disadvantageous. There is no agreement on where that point is, however, and as we mentioned above, responsiveness is probably much more closely related to other factors than to size. This approach is likely to be relatively more politically acceptable than most other possibilities. While there may be some objections from those living in the area and in some cases their opposition can become quite heated, annexations seldom evoke debate of the intensity associated with consolidation or federal plans.

The major shortcoming of annexation is that it is too late for this method to have any significant effect in many of our largest metropolitan areas. Most state laws make it impossible for one municipality to annex territory that is within the corporate limits of another. Thus, central cities such as Chicago or St. Louis, which are surrounded by incorporated suburbs, are virtually precluded from use of annexation. It is not just by chance that the cities which have followed the most aggressive annexation policies such as Oklahoma City, Dallas, Houston, and Phoenix, are located in the newer areas of the west and southwest where the development of suburbs has not yet surrounded them.

A lack of enabling legislation permitting annexation across county lines in most states along with the impossibility of annexing across state lines also limits the usefulness of annexation as a solution to area-wide problems in many areas.[4] In many cases incorporations of small muni-

---

[4] See James L. Clark and Louis F. Weschler, *Cross-County Annexation by Municipal Corporations in California* (Davis: University of California, Institute of Governmental Affairs, 1965).

cipalities in fringe areas around larger cities occur precisely to head off annexation, a phenomenon that is well illustrated by the patchwork quilt pattern of municipal boundaries found in the populous areas of southern California. There have been other instances where annexation has proceeded on an irrational basis because of competition among cities. In 1960, Tempe, Arizona, annexed a strip of land three feet wide which encircled a large plot of area that the city was not yet ready to annex but which it wanted to prevent neighboring Phoenix from annexing.[5]

Cities are sometimes criticized for overannexing to stop incorporation or annexation by other cities. After annexations totalling 187 square miles by Kansas City in 1960, a picture appeared in the local paper showing a city police car driving down a country road with grazing cattle along the roadside and a farmer on his tractor in the background. For many the implication was obvious—this was territory that did not belong in the city. In defense of such action, it can be pointed out that bringing area into the city before it is built up will assure that it must develop in accordance with the city's planning and zoning laws. Because county planning is often weak, the alternative usually is to wait until an area has developed in willy-nilly fashion before annexing it.

Cities which add large areas through annexation often get criticism from both sides. Residents in the newly annexed area charge that the city will not be able to provide full city services to the area, and at the same time citizens of the city point out that fringe areas often do not pay sufficient taxes to cover the costs of the services they get, thus forcing the taxpayers in the older areas of the city to "subsidize" service costs in the new area. Oregon has attempted to meet this problem by providing, in a law passed in 1959, that cities can make arrangements with residents outside the city limits to provide certain city services in return for payments that cover estimated costs. In order to enter into such an agreement, the area outside the city must agree to become fully annexed to the city within ten years.

Several other states, of which Arizona and California would be typical, have passed laws having a significant effect on annexation procedures. Arizona, in 1961, enacted a law which provided that no new community could incorporate within six miles of the city limits of an existing municipality of 5,000 population or more or within three miles of a municipality of less than 5,000. The result of this has been to stop fringe area incorporations, making it likely that most future urban growth areas will become part of existing communities as those communities exercise their annexation powers.

---

[5] When threatened with court action, the city subsequently repealed this annexation.

California, in 1963, enacted legislation establishing Local Agency Formation Commissions in each county.[6] The commission is empowered to review and approve or disapprove proposed incorporations, creation of new special districts, and annexations. The five member commissions have two members representing the county, two representing existing cities and one "public" member. This innovation has not been without controversy. Those in outlying areas feel that cities are over-represented, while cities feel that the county is over-represented, especially when one of the city representatives comes from a contract city. In spite of such controversy, however, the commissions appear to have had some positive effects. In the long run it is likely that their activities will discourage such practices as strip annexations, fringe incorporations, and the creation of many single purpose special districts. Other states which have recently established review procedures for annexations and incorporations include Alaska, Minnesota, Washington, and Wisconsin.

Use of annexation, which had slowed almost to a halt in the 1920's and 1930's, has increased sharply since World War II. In 1945, 152 cities with a population of over 5,000 annexed additional territory; the figure passed the 500 mark in 1955, and in 1962 a record number of 754 cities in this category used their annexation powers. In 1965, the figure rose to 756. This high interest in annexation in urban areas is likely to continue.

Extraterritorial Powers

Most states authorize municipalities to engage in a variety of activities outside their city limits under certain conditions. These activities generally fall into two broad categories, providing services and imposing regulations. The former, provision of services, is more common and less controversial. Many cities provide water, sewage disposal, and other services to residents of areas beyond their corporate limits, and it is also common for some city owned facilities, such as city dumps (city officials like to call them "sanitary landfills!") and sewage disposal plants, to be located outside the city. The city normally charges fees sufficient to cover the costs of services rendered to residents outside the city, and there are many cases where rates are set higher in these areas than within the city.

The efforts of a municipality to impose regulations beyond its own boundaries will arouse considerably more controversy than the provision of services. Most states grant municipalities some limited jurisdiction,

---

6 For an analysis of the California commissions, see John Goldbach, "Local Formation Commissions: California's Struggle over Municipal Incorporation," *Public Administration Review,* Vol. XXV, No. 3 (Sept. 1965), pp. 213–20.

such as the authority to abate nuisances, in the areas immediately adjacent to the city. Some cities have found it advantageous to establish planning and zoning regulation and subdivision control in areas just beyond their corporate limits, and a few states have authorized cities to enact such regulations within a given distance, usually three to five miles of their boundaries. Cities can be criticized, however, where such regulations are imposed without providing some procedure whereby the residents of the area involved can have a voice in shaping those regulations.

The usefulness of extraterritorial powers in solving the problems of metropolitan areas is extremely limited, but the approach is not entirely without value. It involves little organizational alteration, and it is not likely to upset the local political situation. The willingness of a city to provide services to a nearby area may be of value in heading off the incorporation of a new municipality or creation of a special district to provide services. Perhaps extraterritorial powers are most valuable when used as a step toward annexation. Where cities are authorized to do so, the establishment of planning and zoning regulations for areas which the city plans to annex in the future can insure orderly growth and expansion for the city.

A major problem of this approach is that, like annexation, it offers "too little too late" for these areas which already consist of a multitude of incorporated municipalities. In most states, the state restrictions on this power constitute a serious problem, for the area in which extraterritorial powers can be most useful—planning and zoning—is one of the areas in which cities are most restricted. Cities also face difficulty when, as in some states, they are required by state law to provide services to areas beyond their own limits, sometimes being forbidden to charge any more for services beyond the city limits than they charge their own citizens. This can create a situation where a fringe area cannot be persuaded to annex to the city since it already enjoys the advantages of annexation without being subjected to the disadvantages. On the other hand, this approach may contribute to proliferation of governments if a fringe area is persuaded to incorporate by the threat of having regulations imposed by a nearby city. Where extraterritorial powers can be used as a logical step toward annexation, they will continue to be of value in solving metropolitan area problems; in most other cases the approach will be of limited value in the accomplishment of this goal.

Transfer of Functions

A method which has been used in many area to facilitate area-wide provision of services is the transfer or consolidation of functions. The most common pattern is for functions which have previously been performed by both city and county governments to be transferred entirely to the county. During the 1950's, for example, public health functions were transferred from cities to consolidated county health departments in Maricopa County, Arizona, and Monroe County, New York. In 1952 a broad reallocation of functions was accomplished in Fulton County (Atlanta), Georgia. Transfer of functions appears to have occurred most often in cases involving public health and welfare services, with property assessment and tax collection being other functions which have been consolidated at the county level in many areas. Some functions, examples of which would be air and water pollution control, are of such nature and cover such broad geographical areas that they are being transferred from local and county to state governments in a number of states.

An advantage of transfer of functions is that it contributes to organizational simplicity and efficiency, since overlapping and duplication are eliminated and no new governmental units are created. Because existing governmental units are left intact, this approach is likely to provide less political opposition than would more far-reaching approaches. Since some governmental units will gain functions and some will lose them, however, there is the possibility that some opposition to such proposals will develop. In the effort to transfer public health services from local governments to the county in Monroe County, the strongest opposition came from the town and village health officers, who saw their positions threatened by the move. If the governments involved are controlled by different political parties, as when the city is Democratic and the county Republican, this can further complicate such a change. Perhaps the biggest advantage of this approach is that it can develop one step at a time on a function-by-function basis, thereby approaching area-wide problems on a gradual evolutionary basis which causes less controversy than immediate radical change.

A disadvantage of transfer or consolidation of functions is that the county, which is often involved, is poorly adapted in most cases to meeting the needs of rapidly growing urban areas.[7] With few exceptions, county governments are characterized by long ballots, the absence of a chief executive, and the corresponding lack of an integrated administrative organization. In certain areas, notably Virginia and California,

---

[7] Some discussions of this type include the "urban county" as a separate approach to metropolitan reorganization. The development of an urban county ordinarily occurs through the transfer of functions from other governmental units, and analyses usually point out that the major drawbacks to this at present is the inadequate administrative organization of most counties.

reorganization of some county governments has corrected these problems; unfortunately, these are still the exception to the rule. A serious factor restricting the usefulness of the county in this regard is that over one-third of our metropolitan areas encompass territory in more than a single county, making it impossible for consolidation of functions in any one county really to solve problems on an area-wide basis. Granting these shortcomings, the organizational simplicity and political acceptability of this approach suggest that it will gain somewhat wider usage as time passes.

Voluntary Associations

In about twenty metropolitan areas voluntary associations of local officials have been organized to encourage cooperation on an area-wide base. The earliest such organization, the Supervisors Inter-County Committee (Detroit area), came into being in 1954. Others include the Association of Bay Area Governments (ABAG) in the San Francisco area, Metropolitan Washington (D.C.) Council of Governments, and the Regional Conference of Elected Officials in the Philadelphia area. Names vary from place to place, but most are known as a "committee," "conference," "association," or "council." The organization of the San Francisco area's ABAG would be typical of many. ABAG membership is open to all cities and counties in the area. Its governing body is a general assembly made up of one representative from each member county or local government. When votes are taken, counties and cities vote separately, and a majority vote of each is required. Some associations, such as the Mid-Willamette council (Salem area), include among their membership representatives from the state legislature, and the Washington, D. C. council has representation from two state legislatures and Congress as well as county and local governments in the area.

The functions of associations are quite varied, but usually one of their more important ones is the development of communications channels among governmental agencies. Their meetings provide a forum where officials get together on a regular basis and exchange views, and while this may sound unimportant by itself associations often afford the only opportunity for such interchange. Research is usually an association activity also. Most associations have small research staffs which gather data and prepare reports (and sometimes recommendations) on matters of area-wide concern. The New York area council, as an illustration, has done a study of land needs for recreation in the area and prepared an inventory of water resources and needs for the area. The encouragement of cooperative action is perhaps the underlying *raison d'etre* of the associations, and their communications and research activities are directed toward this end. Several associations have prepared and supported uniform traffic control regulations for their areas, and the encouragement of cooperation among planning agencies in an area is a common function.

The associations are gradually becoming recognized as authoritative "spokesmen" for local governments in their respective areas. If an association can adopt a position on an issue, it can speak as the voice of the governments in the area concerned before the state legislature, Congress, or other groups. ABAG has taken a position on seashore legislation being considered by Congress, and the New York council opposed legislation providing for increased gas rates for its area. If federal legislation moves in the direction of requiring increasing intergovernmental cooperation as a prerequisite for getting federal aid, it is possible that associations may be accepted as evidence of such cooperation. As foundations turn their attention more in the direction of urban problems, associations may well be the organizational mechanisms used for the application for and administration of foundation grants.

The best summary of association activities has been made by the Advisory Commission on Intergovernmental Relations:[8]

> (1) They cut across or embrace several local jurisdictions, and sometimes do not stop at State lines. (2) They are composed of the chief elected officials of the local governments in the area, and sometimes have representation from the State Government. (3) They have no operating functions. Rather, they are forums for discussion, research and recommendation only. Recommendations are made to the constituent governments, or to State legislatures. (4) They are multi-purpose, concerning themselves with many area-wide problems. (5) They employ a full-time staff.

While each association has its individual characteristics which vary from the general description, this is a good composite picture of this type of organization.

This course of action is attractive to many areas because it provides channels of communication and cooperation without disrupting existing governments or official positions. One can point to specific accomplishments of these organizations—the preparation of a study or support for a particular piece of legislation—but in the long run their most important contribution may well be in establishing a regular continuing pattern of communication among officials of the many governments in a given area.

---

8 *Alternative Approaches,* p. 34.

They are relatively easy to establish since no referendum is involved, and they are not hampered by restrictions such as county or state lines. State legislative action authorizing municipalities and other governmental units to spend money to join and support them is usually required.

Their voluntary nature is also their major problem. The fact that member governments cannot be bound by association decisions and may withdraw from membership, or refuse to join in the first place) at their discretion severely limits the effectiveness of associations. Roscoe C. Martin has suggested that voluntary associations are successful only when their proposed solutions involve little controversy, do not challenge the status of member governments, are self-executing, and cost the member governments little or nothing.[9] If these are the conditions of success, their effectiveness is indeed likely to be limited, but this probably assumes that success implies the actual implementation of solutions. If we think of the association as a channel of communication and a catalytic agent for action, the opportunities for success are broadened considerably.

Special Districts

Special districts, unfamiliar though they may be to many, account for well over half of all governmental units in the nation. Of the 91,236 units of government in existence in 1962, 53,001 were special districts (including school districts); and while the total number of school districts has decreased in recent years, the number of other types of special districts is growing rapidly. A special district is an independent, autonomous unit of government which usually has its own taxing and borrowing powers and is created to perform only one or a few functions.[10] The independent school district, which performs the single service of education, is the most common type. Over 70 per cent of all non-educational special districts are outside SMSA's, and many provide services related to agriculture, such as soil conservation, drainage, irrigation, and flood control. When used in urban and metropolitan areas, they often provide such services as sewage disposal, water supply, hospitals, airports, and recreational facilities. Ex-

---

[9] Roscoe C. Martin, *Metropolis in Transition* (Washington: Housing and Home Finance Agency, 1963), pp. 49–50.

[10] On special districts see John C. Bollens, *Special District Governments in the United States* (Berkeley: University of California Press, 1957); and *The Problem of Special Districts in American Government* (Washington: Advisory Commission on Intergovernmental Relations, 1964).

amples would be the Milwaukee Metropolitan Sewerage District, Chicago Sanitary District, Cleveland Metropolitan Park District, and the Metropolitan Water District of Southern California.

Governmental units called "authorities" are almost indistinguishable functionally and legally from special districts. They are somewhat less likely than districts to have the taxing power and are therefore more likely to be engaged primarily in revenue producing activities, such as the operation of toll bridges, tunnels, or public transportation facilities. The Chicago Transit Authority and the Port of New York Authority are illustrative of this type of organization. For purposes of our discussion here, no distinction is made between districts and authorities.

The special district is often used in metropolitan areas because it can overcome the problem of limited jurisdiction which hampers the existing units of government.[11] District boundaries can cut across or encompass those of many other local governments, often including area in more than one county and in a few cases, such as the Port of New York Authority and the Bi-State Development Agency in the St. Louis area, encompassing land in more than one state. This being the case, their boundaries can be adjusted to fit the area affected by a given problem with more flexibility than other governmental units. A proposal to establish a special district to deal with a problem often meets with little political opposition from officials of existing governments for the reason that they do not feel threatened by this action to the extent that they would by proposals for more drastic governmental reorganization. In all likelihood, the district will be providing services which they do not now provide and have no desire to undertake in the future; otherwise, the necessity for establishing the district would not be an issue in the first place. In some cases, the desire to avoid certain state statutory regulations is an incentive in the creation of special districts. This is especially true where cities are bumping up against state imposed tax and debt limitations, since districts have their own taxing and borrowing powers. The legal and administrative hurdles involved in establishing districts are relatively small, as they can usually be established by action of the legislature, or in some cases by cooperative action of local governments, without constitutional changes, popular referenda, or other time-consuming procedures.

It is sometimes suggested that the creation of a single purpose special district is a means of achieving metropolitan government through the "back door." It is very difficult to get voters to approve a plan for the establishment of a metropolitan government in an area, so this reasoning

---

[11] See discussion in Charles R. Adrian, *Governing Urban America* (New York: McGraw-Hill Book Company, 1961).

goes, but there is much less opposition to the creation of a special district to deal with a single problem. After its creation, however, it will be possible to add other functions to it one by one without great opposition; thus, in time a metropolitan government will have evolved where it could not have originally been established. The difficulty with this idea is that the facts just do not bear it out. Experience up to the present indicates no trend toward single-purpose districts gradually evolving into multipurpose governments. The best possibility for this exists in the Seattle area. When the Municipality of Metropolitan Seattle was created in 1958 to provide for sewage disposal and water pollution control, the state statute under which it was established provided that it could be expanded to include responsibilities for transportation, planning, water, parks, and garbage disposal, but up to the present time it has not expanded its activities beyond its original ones.

One criticism of special districts is that district officials are not forced to weigh the value of the service provided by the district against those provided by other governments. A city council, for example, must consider the need for additional policemen in relation to the need for more parks, better streets, or improved sewage disposal facilities. A single-purpose district does not have to make such comparisons, which means that if several districts are serving a given area there may be little coordination or consideration of the overall needs of the area among them. Critics also point out that creation of special districts complicates the governmental structure and may lead to duplication of effort and overlapping of functions. This situation can cause the district approach to be lacking where the criterion of responsiveness is concerned. Governing officials of districts are often appointed by general purpose governments in the area (one representative from each city and county for example), a system which insulates the district from direct citizen control. On the other hand, directly electing district officials lengthens what may well be an excessively long ballot to start with, and it is likely that only a small portion of the voters will be sufficiently interested to exercise their right to vote for district officers. The goal of public responsiveness seems to lose either way.

Most students of government are critical of the single-purpose district approach to metropolitan area problems. If the district could be expanded to take on the responsibility for a number of functions, those who are interested in rationality, responsiveness, coordination, and similar standards could give it more support, but there is little evidence that this will occur. In spite of this attitude, nevertheless, recent experience indicates that the rapid creation of special districts will continue, although they may continue to find their greatest usage outside metropolitan areas.

Contractual Arrangements

Los Angeles County, in southern California, has been the scene of the most extensive use of intergovernmental contractual arrangements to solve common problems. Almost every city in the county contracts for the provision of certain services. The county provides the services contracted for, and is then reimbursed by the city at an agreed upon rate. In 1961, the county made 42 different services available to municipalities and was providing a total of 1278 services to 73 cities.[12] While some cities contracted for only a few services, others contracted for over 30 of the total of 42 available, and the program has become sufficiently large that a special office has been established in the county government to handle contract administration. The county establishes cost schedules and offers the services "cafeteria style" to cities, allowing the municipalities to choose any or all of them that they want.

Beginning with the city of Lakewood in 1954, a number of newly incorporated municipalities have carried the contract system to its logical end; they purchase virtually all of their services from the county. "Lakewood Plan" cities have full legal status as municipalities, they have taxing and borrowing powers, and they elect city officials who adopt ordinances and set policies just as other cities. The main difference is that the staff will ordinarily be quite small, and its main job will be coordinating with the county to see that the services for which the city contracts are provided as called for. Policies, tax rates, service levels, and similar matters remain within the power of the city to determine. One city of 20,000, for example, may decide to contract for the services of one police car on a round-the-clock basis while another city of similar size may want the services of three cars.

The contract system has proved to be very popular because of its simplicity of initiation and operation. Services are provided within the framework of existing governments, and contracts can be negotiated and approved without popular referenda or additional state action. No stigma of being a supergovernment is attached to the role of the county in the system, and with policy decisions remaining in the hands of local officials, the system has met with a minimum of political opposition. The provision of services in this way lowers unit costs and prevents some duplication of staff and equipment. One can surmise that this system may also have the advantage of heading off the establishment of special districts and the

---

12 Martin, *Metropolis in Transition,* p. 13.

resulting problems of overlapping and lack of coordination. Martin's study suggests that a side effect has been the upgrading of county government.[13] Since the county must provide services under the watchful eye of each contracting municipality, it must be constantly alert and continually striving to improve the quality of its services.

The most significant criticism of the contract system is that it has given impetus to a host of new incorporations. Many small communities which were not large enough to accept all of the responsibilities of providing municipal services find that they can now incorporate, thereby assuring their continued "independence," and buy a package of services from the county. In most areas where contractual arrangements exist, there is no effort made by the county to use the contract as a lever to get local governments to undertake certain desirable programs, such as regional planning or area-wide cooperation on given projects. Thus it is possible for each municipality to become a tiny principality unto itself with no obligation to consider the problems of the larger area.

A second criticism is that local governments which rely heavily on the contract system become very dependent on the county. In theory they are free to use or reject any county services according to their own preferences. In practice, however, once a city commits itself to buy a particular service—police protection, for example—it is very difficult for that decision to be reversed because the capital expenditure which would have to be made would be prohibitive. The outlay that would be needed for police cars, crime detection equipment, and other necessary items make breaking off from the county a very difficult decision. Because municipalities find themselves in this dependent status, they are forced to be highly solicitous of county officials, according to the Martin study.[14] Martin suggests that city officials have sometimes even become political legmen for county supervisors in an attempt to win favor and assure good services for their cities.

This second point would seem to contradict the former criticism that contractual arrangements make it possible for small communities, through incorporation, to retain a degree of local independence. In reality there is no contradiction because countries have not used their position in such a way as to cause this to be true. The contract system has made it possible for many small municipalities to come into existence, thereby avoiding annexation by nearby larger cities, and there is little doubt but that they are heavily dependent on the county for services. On the other hand, this

---

[13] *Ibid.*, p. 23.
[14] *Ibid.*, pp. 22–24.

is a dependency only for services and does not necessarily impel them toward a more responsive attitude where area-wide problems are concerned.

The contract system is by no means limited to the Los Angeles area; it is in use in greater or lesser degree in virtually every urban area of the nation. In most cases the county serves as the contractor, but there are also areas where the central city provides services on a fee basis for neighboring suburbs. The use of such arrangements appears to be growing rapidly and probably will continue to do so.

Suggested Readings

Adrian, Charles R., "Metropology: Folklore and Field Research," *Public Administration Review*, Vol. XXI, No. 2 (Summer, 1961), pp. 148-53.

Alternative Approaches to Governmental Reorganization in Metropolitan Areas (Washington: Advisory Commission on Intergovernmental Relations, 1962). A good summary of the various approaches in use.

Bollens, John C., *Special District Government in the United States* (Berkeley: University of California Press, 1957).

Martin, Roscoe C., *Metropolis in Transition* (Washington: Housing and Home Finance Agency, 1963). Contains chapters on several of the alternative approaches to governmental reorganization in metropolitan areas.

Metropolitan Councils of Governments (Washington: Advisory Commission on Intergovernmental Relations, 1966).

Performance of Urban Functions: Local and Areawide (Washington: Advisory Commission on Intergovernmental Relations, 1963).

chapter 6

Governing the Metropolitan Area: Some Far-Reaching Approaches

The approaches to metropolitan reorganization discussed here differ from those in the previous chapter in that they make much more basic changes in the structures of existing governments, even to the extent of abolishing some and radically altering others. The result of this is that these proposals are likely to arouse much more public discussion and controversy and usually face more intense political opposition. We shall discuss four such approaches: consolidation of similar governmental units, city-county consolidation, city-county separation, and metropolitan federalism.

CONSOLIDATION OF SIMILAR GOVERNMENTAL UNITS

Seemingly one of the simplest ways to combat the proliferation of governments and the resulting confusing governmental structure would be for similar units to consolidate. The many cities of a metropolitan area, for example, might combine and become one, or if this were not feasible the dozens of very small municipalities which exist in many areas might be consolidated into four or five relatively large ones. The best example of consolidation of this type is what has occurred with regard to school districts since the 1940's.[1] In the 1930's there were over 120,000 school districts in the United States, but by 1965 there were less than 35,000. This was brought about through the consolidation of small districts into larger ones with more students and a broader financial base, but it was accomplished only with much controversy and debate. For many this was seen as a trend that meant the sacrificing of local autonomy and the end of the community school.

The impetus for this movement came sometimes from those in local districts interested in a higher quality educational program and an expansion of the curriculum to include a wider variety of courses, for such people recognized that these goals could be accomplished only in larger and wealthier districts. More often, however, consolidation was the result of a "carrot and stick" strategy used by states in the distribution of state aid. In Illinois, to illustrate, state law provides that state financial aid may not be made available to elementary school districts with an average daily attendance of less than fifteen students or to high school districts with an average daily attendance of less than sixty. In other states, such as Kansas, Florida, and Nevada, consolidation has been made compulsory by state action. In spite of local interest in consolidation in some areas, it is probably safe to say that the dramatic reduction in the number of districts would not have occurred without these various types of prodding by the states. Left entirely to the wishes of the electorate without such threats as loss of aid or accreditation, it is highly questionable whether the consolidation movement would have ever got off the ground. The fear of what was perceived as a large impersonal school system and the nostalgic memory of the little red school house would have been too much to overcome.

The advantages and disadvantages, the desires and the fears, which were present in the movement to consolidate school districts are also applicable to consolidation of cities. The sequence of events involved in an attempt to consolidate the cities of Champaign and Urbana, Illinois, illustrate the difficulties that stand in the way of this type of metropolitan reorganization.

The Champaign-Urbana Controversy

In the mid-1950's a movement was instigated to consolidate the cities of Champaign and Urbana, Illinois.[2] The two cities are contiguous not

---

[1] See Clyde F. Snider, *American State and Local Government* (New York: Appleton-Century-Crofts, 1965), pp. 440–41.

[2] For a more complete analysis, see Phillip Monypenny and Gilbert Y. Steiner, "Merger? The Illinois Consolidation Case," in Richard T. Frost (ed), *Cases in State and Local Government* (Englewood Cliffs, New Jersey: Prentice-Hall, Inc., 1961), pp. 267–79.

only to each other but also to the University of Illinois, the campus of which extends into both communities. Champaign, with a population of around 40,000 at the time, was about twice as large as Urbana. The area is not unlike many other university communities, including a degree of tension between town and gown. Politically the cities and the general central region of Illinois are conservative and generally vote Republican. Within the Democratic party there is a split between the organization minded party regulars and the more ideologically oriented members who come primarily from among university faculty and graduate students.

The impetus for consolidation originated with the Urbana Civic Committee. Although UCC had a few business and professional people among its membership, it was made up primarily of university faculty who were interested in community improvement. The organization supported long-range planning, improvement of city parks and similar projects, and on a previous occasion it had campaigned unsuccessfully for a merger of the school districts in the two cities. Some of the members were also interested in the council-manager form of government and the original merger plan called for consolidation under that form, but it was discovered that state statutes provided only for consolidation under the aldermanic or commission forms, so their final plan provided for the aldermanic form.

As soon as it became known the UCC was circulating petitions calling for a referendum on the consolidation issue, an Anti-Merger Committee was formed. The opposition leadership came mainly from among members of the Urbana Association of Commerce and representatives of various governmental units such as the city of Urbana, the township, school board, park board, police pension fund, and firemen's pension fund. The leaders of both parties were also among the opposition. The initial strategy of the opposition was to challenge the legality of the proposed consolidation on a series of technical points. This strategy succeeded in involving the issue in litigation and postponing the referendum for several months, long enough for the drive of the proponents to lose much of its momentum, but the state supreme court ultimately upheld the legality of the proposal clearing the way for the referendum.

At first both sides assumed, mistakenly it turned out, that Champaign would support the proposal since it was much the larger of the two and Urbana would in effect be merged into Champaign. Thus the major activity of both sides took place in Urbana. The pro forces directed their campaign toward general advantages to be gained from consolidation: improved services, more efficient administration, better planning, etc. The opposition emphasized the loss of identity with relation to city name, street names, and other matters of local pride and made a strong point of letting governmental officials know that their positions might be in jeopardy in a consolidated government. They also suggested that larger cities seem to have higher tax rates. The final results were so one-sided that it is unlikely that any amount of campaigning could have changed the results. The proposal was defeated by about three-to-one in each city.

In retrospect it appears that the broad base of the forces in the opposition and the advantages attached to the *status quo* were important factors in the outcome. The merger advocates were primarily university people, they lived mostly in the residential areas near the campus, and their organizational affiliations were related to university activities with very limited ties to the rest of the community. In contrast, the opposition forces had close ties with all aspects of business and professional life, civic and religious organizations, and the political parties. In addition they also had several prominent members of the university faculty in their organization, as the university community was by no means unanimous in its support of the proposal. The local papers took a hands off attitude until very late in the campaign, when one of the two local papers endorsed consolidation.

The Champaign-Urbana experience is indicative of the problems faced by proposals for municipal consolidation. In the absence of some immediate crisis, it is tremendously difficult to get citizens sufficiently interested to sell such a basic change in the form of local government. Advocates are forced to base their case on very general points, such as improved administration and better planning, which are usually valid but seldom exciting. Their limited base of support must be built on civic improvement associations, the League of Women Voters, university groups, and similar organizations. Opposition groups, on the other hand, can usually put together a coalition of many forces who feel directly threatened by consolidation and who will therefore become directly involved in the campaign to kill it. This would include office holders who fear that their positions will be abolished or merged, city employees who fear that "improved efficiency" really means fewer jobs, and the many citizens who have strong nostalgic attachments to the city and other institutions related to independent existence. It is noteworthy, for example, that Champaign and Urbana each had a First Presbyterian Church, and it became an issue of some import as to which would have to give up the title of "First."

Some Consolidation Successes

The consolidation movement has not been entirely fruitless. In 1958 Warwick and Newport News, Virginia, consolidated. In 1961 the town of Winchester and the city of Winsted in Connecticut were merged, and the two cities of Tampa and Port Tampa, Florida, became one. One of the larger recent consolidations was that of Sacramento and North Sacramento, California, in 1965 to form a city of over one-quarter million inhabitants.[3] Voters in that area had rejected consolidation in 1963 by a narrow margin of 102 votes but reversed themselves in a subsequent referendum and supported it by an even narrower margin, just 16 votes. It is worth noting that prior to the referendum, all employees of North Sacramento had been guaranteed employment by Sacramento in case the proposal passed. They were assured that they would not receive a cut in pay and that their employment would not be contingent on passing a civil service test or physical examination. Campbell, Milton, and Fulton Counties in Georgia were consolidated in 1931 and 1932, but consolidation of counties is even less frequent than of cities.

In spite of isolated successes, the future of consolidation does not appear optimistic. In recent years efforts have failed in most of the larger metropolitan areas where consolidation has been proposed, including Pittsburgh, Cleveland, and St. Louis. The forces which can be mobilized in opposition to such plans are impressive, and it is usually easier in politics to prevent change than to provoke it.

CITY-COUNTY CONSOLIDATION

With few exceptions cities are located within counties, and the two governments perform many similar functions. This may lead to conflict, but it has also led to the recommendation in many cases that city and county should be consolidated into a single government providing for the needs of all the people within the county. Advocates hope that this will eliminate conflict, overlapping and duplication, and lead to a government that is more efficient and, because it is simpler, more easily held accountable by the voters. Examples of such consolidations are not numerous. In the early 1800's a consolidation of the city of New Orleans and Orléans Parish (county) was effected, and in 1854 the boundaries of the city and county of Philadelphia were made coterminous, twenty-eight local governments in the county were made part of the city, and the city was given many county powers. In both of these cases, however, the consolidation was incomplete because certain county offices continued in existence. A constitutional amendment in 1951 cleared the way for more complete consolidation in Philadelphia. Since 1871 Boston has performed the county functions for Suffolk County although other independent municipalities continue to exist in the county. In Hawaii, the city and county of Honolulu were consolidated in 1907, and the entire island of Oahu is now governed by this one government.

---

[3] Christian L. Larsen, "Two Cities Merge in California, "*National Civic Review,* Vol. LV, No. 2 (February, 1966), pp. 106–08.

Perhaps the best known consolidation is that in the New York City area. Through a series of four consolidations in 1730, 1894, 1898, and 1912 the city and county governments were consolidated into New York City. This arrangement is unique in that areas kept their individual identity in the form of boroughs, and the boroughs also retained certain administrative powers as well as representation on the city council. The only other two city-county consolidations of major importance in the twentieth century are in the Baton Rouge and Nashville areas.

The Baton Rouge Consolidation

Prior to 1949 the Baton Rouge, Louisiana, area was governed by the city of Baton Rouge, East Baton Rouge Parish (county), several small municipalities in the parish, and a number of special districts most of which were organized and operated through the parish government.[4] Discussion of possible consolidation had begun in 1944 when the Baton Rouge Chamber of Commerce had appointed a committee to study the possibilities of reorganizing local government in the area. The committee's work resulted in the hiring of consultants in planning and governmental organization, who ultimately recommended a consolidated city-parish government.

Under the charter the parish was to be divided into three sections— urban, rural and industrial. The city of Baton Rouge and surrounding densely populated territory would constitute the urban district, and district residents would pay a higher tax rate than the rest of the parish in return for which they would receive the usual municipal services—street lighting, sewers, refuse collection, etc.—in addition to the services provided for the entire parish. Residents of the rural area would pay a lower tax rate and would receive only general parish services in return. The industrial area was taxed at the general parish rate, received parish services, and occupants were expected to provide their own municipal services.

Although several members of the commission had wanted to establish a government organized along the lines of the council-manager plan, public opposition developed to this, and the final plan called for a mayor-president to be directly elected for a four year term. The charter called for him to be the chief administrator of the parish, to prepare the annual budget, appoint major department heads, and preside over council meetings.

---

[4] The best study of Baton Rouge is William C. Harvard and Floyd L. Corty, *Rural-Urban Consolidation: The Merger of Governments in the Baton Rouge Area* (Baton Rouge: Louisiana State University Press, 1964).

The general governing authority was placed in two councils. The city council was to consist of seven members elected at-large from the city of Baton Rouge. The parish council would consist of these seven plus two others elected from the rural areas of the parish. The mayor-president was to preside over meetings of each. Because of legal difficulties and the danger of arousing intense opposition, certain offices such as sheriff, assessor, coroner, and clerk of the court were little changed by the charter.

The patterns of support and opposition were not surprising. Civic clubs, many business leaders, and major newspapers gave the plan support while opposition came from a few political leaders and those who feared a "takeover" of the parish by Baton Rouge. Geographically, the city gave the plan the strongest support, and opposition was most intense in the outlying parts of the parish. In the campaign the proponents talked about efficiency and progressive government, and the opponents emphasized the Baton Rouge takeover and the danger of higher taxes. Some of those in opposition also pointed to the three area division as a potential means which industry might use to avoid taxes. On August 12, 1947, the plan was adopted by a close vote. City voters supported the plan by about four-to-one, but stronger opposition in the rural areas made it a tight race.

In the years since its establishment the government appears to have worked well, although some problems have arisen. The rural members of the parish council have sometimes felt that the city council takes action affecting the entire parish without their having any voice in such issues and have suggested that the two councils be merged so that all nine members vote on all issues. The increasing urbanization of areas throughout the parish has led to establishment of several special districts to provide services, pointing up the need to revise the basis on which urban services are provided by the parish. In spite of certain difficulties such as these, the government is now firmly established and appears to have won "the tacit, and perhaps the enthusiastic, support of the great bulk of parish residents."[5]

The Nashville Consolidation

City-county consolidation came to Nashville and Davidson County, Tennessee, on the second try.[6] In 1958 a proposal to merge the two into

---

[5] *Ibid.,* p. 43.

[6] On the Nashville consolidation, see David A. Booth, *Metropolitics: The Nashville Consolidation* (East Lansing: Michigan State University, Institute for Community Development and Services, 1963), and the bibliography contained therein; Brett W. Hawkins, *Nashville Metro: the Politics of City-County Consolidation* (Nashville: Vanderbilt University Press, 1966).

the "Metropolitan Government of Nashville and Davidson County" had carried in Nashville, but approval required separate majorities both within and outside the city, and the county residents opposed it by a three-to-two margin. Between 1958 and 1962, when consolidation was approved, several events occurred which caused many citizens to become angry toward the city and thus look with interest toward alternative forms of governmental organization. The city had passed a ten dollar "green sticker'" fee which was required for all automobiles using the city streets regardless of whether the owners were city residents. The city also embarked on an aggressive annexation program to bring area into the city which it obviously would not be able to provide with full municipal services for some time. Both of these factors angered residents in the outlying areas, some of whom had already been annexed and some of whom feared future actions of the city, and made them sympathetic toward consolidation. The fact that the mayor, who had supported the merger in 1958, was now opposed to it only intensified the support of these people for the proposal.

The consolidated government approved June 28, 1962, divided the county into a general services district and an urban services district. The urban services district would receive all those services usually provided by city and county governments. The remainder of the county would comprise the general services district, and only county services would be provided here. Separate tax rates would apply in the two districts, with residents of the urban services district paying the higher rate in return for the additional services. Several smaller municipalities in the county were allowed to retain their identity in order to minimize opposition, but they have virtually no services to perform and their existence is mostly in name only.

The chief executive official of the new government is the metropolitan county mayor, elected for a term of four years and limited to three consecutive terms. He has the power to appoint department heads, prepare the executive budget, and generally exercise the authority of a strong mayor. The forty-one member council consists of a vice-mayor elected at-large, five additional members elected at-large, and thirty-five members elected from districts. In contrast to Baton Rouge where education was affected very little by consolidation, the Nashville plan placed this function in a nine member county board of education appointed by the mayor with the approval of the council. The board did retain some autonomy in that the charter provides for a popular referendum on the school budget if the council does not approve the budget recommended by the board.

The fact that the 1958 and 1962 plans were very similar indicates that ultimate success depended on a change in the political environment more than on differences in the proposals. There was actually more open opposition in 1962 than in 1958. The mayor and one of the two metropolitan dailies, both of whom had supported the 1958 plan, were in opposition in 1962. Nevertheless, the supporters had the advantages of better organization, good financing, support of civic groups like the League of Women Voters and the Junior Chamber of Commerce, and most important a change in public attitude from apathy or opposition to support. The Citizens Committee for Better Government was well organized at the precinct level and was of major importance to the Pro-Metro campaign of 1962. The 1962 proponents also had the advantage of being able to point to concrete issues (annexation, green sticker) rather than having to rely on the more general points on which reforms must often be sold.

Observers of both the Baton Rouge and Nashville governments indicate that they are operating well and gaining public support. The fact remains, however, that these plans represent dramatic changes from our traditional forms of local government and include the emotionally charged action of actually abolishing long existing municipalities. It should also be noted that for many larger metropolitan areas, successful utilization of this approach would involve the merging of several counties into one. On the other hand, if the problem of public opposition based on tradition can be overcome, experience in these two counties suggests that this can be a worthwhile approach in metropolitan areas where the population is concentrated in a single county.

CITY-COUNTY SEPARATION

In the nineteeth and early twentieth centuries separation of large cities from the county was advocated as a means of eliminating the duplication of government agencies and services. There were several reasons why this was attractive. City dwellers were convinced that they paid the bulk of county taxes but got few benefits in return since they also provided their own police protection, streets, and other urban services while the county sheriff, county roads department, etc. devoted their efforts mainly to the rural unincorporated parts of the county. The residents outside the city looked upon the city as a domineering force in county government which was too large for them to counterbalance. This mutual disaffection led to much sympathy for the separation concept. In 1851 Baltimore was separated from its county, San Francisco followed suit in 1856, and St. Louis in 1876. Denver was separated from the county by constitutional amendment in 1902, but legal problems postponed the implementation of the separation until about 1912.

Separation is pretty much a dead issue today. The only exception to this would be in Virginia where cities may separate from the county when they reach a population of 10,000. Upon separation the city becomes completely independent with the county giving up all jurisdiction including taxation. There are currently over thirty independent cities in Virginia.

In most major metropolitan areas any attempt to separate city and county today would intensify rather than alleviate most problems. With urban populations already spilling over city and county boundaries, separation would create even more fragmentation of government and set another barrier in the path of intergovernmental cooperation. Except for the unique situation in Virginia, city-county separation is not given serious consideration as a solution to metropolitan area problems today.

METROPOLITAN FEDERALISM

Undoubtedly the best known efforts to establish means for dealing with intergovernmental problems in metropolitan areas have been those concerned with metropolitan federalism. Metropolitan federalism, like national federalism, is an attempt to devise a system that includes both a general government covering the entire area concerned and providing services of an area-wide nature and some type of subunit of government which has a more narrow geographic base and provides essentially local services. By leaving local communities intact, it overcomes one of the major objections (from a political, not an administrative, point of view) to city-county consolidation. Plans based on this principle have been proposed in St. Louis, Boston, and Pittsburgh, among other cities, only to be rejected. Two areas where federation governments are in operation are Toronto, Canada, and Miami, Florida.

The Toronto Plan

The Municipality of Metropolitan Toronto is unique in that it was created by the provincial government, and approval by the local electorate was not required.[7] In the early 1950's the city of Toronto petitioned the Ontario provincial government to provide for a consolidation of the twelve suburbs with the central city. At the same time, the suburban community of Mimico asked the province to establish some type of administrative organization that could be responsible for certain urban services on an

---

[7] On Toronto, see Webb S. Fizer, *Mastery of the Metropolis* (Englewood Cliffs, New Jersey: Prentice-Hall, Inc., 1962), pp. 117–25; John G. Grumm, *Metropolitan Area Government: The Toronto Experience* (Lawrence: University of Kansas Publications, 1959).

area-wide basis. This led to extended hearings by the Municipal Board, an agency of the province, and eventually to a recommendation that the provincial legislature create a federal system of government for the Toronto metropolitan area.

Following the recommendation, the legislature created the Municipality of Metropolitan Toronto and gave it jurisdiction over the thirteen municipalities in the area. The twenty-five member governing board consists of twelve members from the city of Toronto, the council chairman of each of the twelve suburbs, and a chairman elected annually by these twenty-four. The chairman may be either an outsider or one of the twenty-four.

The new government was given jurisdiction over certain enumerated functions: water supply, sewage disposal, arterial highways, some health and welfare services, housing and redevelopment, regional parks, metropolitan planning, and the establishment of a uniform property assessment for taxing purposes. Because the new metropolitan municipality replaced the county, it inherited the county's authority over the courthouse and the jail. The government also reviews proposed bond issues of local governments and manages bond sales for the local governments. Education is the responsibility of a Metropolitan School Board, but the metropolitan government provides some financial support for the schools. The Toronto Transit Commission was continued in existence with its members now being appointed by the governing board of the new government. Although police protection was made a local responsibility by the enabling legislation, an amendment in 1956 gave the metropolitan municipality the power to provide for area-wide law enforcement.

The local governments are responsible for fire protection, local law enforcement, local streets, water distribution, local parks, public relief, most public health services, local planning and zoning, libraries and building regulation and inspection.

This new form of federated government has not been without problems. The system of representation on the governing council has been criticized as being unrepresentative of the actual population distribution, and it has been suggested that the boundaries of the entire government have now been outgrown and should be expanded to take in the additional growth that has occurred in the area in recent years. As in most federal systems the distribution of powers between local and central governments has been a continuing point of contention, with some functions including law enforcement and property assessment, having already been shifted from local to metropolitan jurisdiction.

One writer makes the interesting observation that the plan probably would never have been enacted if it had depended on a local referendum but that it has now won the approval of local citizens. Webb S. Fizer comments:[8]

> It is generally agreed that had a popular majority been required in each of the 13 municipalities the federation would not have been ratified. It is also generally agreed that if the people of the metropolitan area were asked today whether they approved of the federation it would be overwhelmingly supported.

No reference to 1966 Reorg. "Bill 81" — merging 13 into 6

Miami Metro

Any discussion of metropolitan reorganization in the United States almost always brings Miami to mind, for government there is the nearest that any major urban area in this country has come to metropolitan federalism.[9] Reorganization began there in 1956 when the voters of Florida adopted an amendment to the state constitution allowing Dade County to draft its own county charter. The amendment gave the county broad powers to reorganize county government and transfer functions from city to county. A charter was subsequently prepared and adopted by a very narrow margin (51 per cent) in May, 1957.

The new charter provided for a county-manager form of government with the manager to be appointed by, and responsible to, the county commission. The charter originally provided that the commission would consist of eleven members: five elected from districts, five elected at-large and one from the city of Miami. An amendment later changed the method of representation to provide for a commission of nine members all of whom would be elected at-large.

Although the twenty-six municipalities continued to exist and retained jurisdiction over certain matters of purely local concern, the charter gave the county responsibility for certain municipal functions, including fire and police protection, water supply, sewage disposal, traffic control, and administration of traffic courts. Much more important, however, was the fact that the charter provided that the county could expand its authority

---

[8] Fizer, *op. cit.,* p. 118.

[9] From a technical point of view Miami is not really an example of metropolitan federalism but rather a reorganization of the county government. This author, and many others, take the view that the reorganization has been so basic as to actually constitute a new form of government, i.e., metropolitan federalism. See Gustave Serino, *Miami's Metropolitan Experiment* (Gainesville: University of Florida Press, 1958); Edward Sofen, *The Miami Metropolitan Experiment* (Bloomington: Indiana University Press, 1963).

to include other functions, and it was unclear just what limits were to be placed on this expansion. Significantly, the state courts have interpreted the county's authority very broadly and allowed it to move into numerous additional functions. The county may also set minimum standards which municipalities must meet in the performance of local functions, and the county is authorized to take over the function from a municipality if it fails to meet those standards. Thus the new county-wide government emerges as much the stronger in the newly created federal relationship between county and municipality.

Although the new government can point to many accomplishments,[10] it has been beset with problems from its inception. Conflict between county managers and the commission has caused a rapid turnover in the manager's office. The new system has also been faced almost constantly with strong opposition that has included many municipal officials and the Dade County League of Municipalities. The opposition has attacked through two main channels, the courts and proposed charter amendments. Largely unsuccessful in the courts, the opponents have come close to overturning "metro" through referenda on charter amendments. In 1958 a so-called "local autonomy" amendment which would have had the effect of nullifying the most important parts of the charter was defeated by a wide margin (59 per cent of those voting opposed it), but in 1961 a series of amendments also designed to limit severely the powers of the new county government received 48 per cent of the vote. In 1963 an amendment was adopted which made the sheriff an elected official once again, a move which obviously weakened the county manager. Metropolitan government has now been in operation in the Miami area for over a decade, but survival has been a nip and tuck battle and the final outcome remains to be seen.

Concerning metropolitan federalism in general, it can be said that it has the advantage of providing for an area-wide government to assume responsibility for certain problems while at the same time allowing municipalities to retain their identity as well as responsibility for some local functions. One of its biggest drawbacks is the difficulty, common to any federal system, of satisfactorily distributing powers between the two levels of government. Because metropolitan area governments represent a new approach to local government, another problem is that their adoption often requires amendment of the state constitution and extensive revision of the state statutes. In neither Toronto nor Miami does county government exist separate and apart from the metropolitan government, but if this were to

---

[10] O. W. Campbell, "Progress Report on Metropolitan Miami," *Public Management,* Vol. XLI, No. 4 (April, 1959) pp. 85–89.

be the case in some area the problem of working out the relationship between these two might prove to be a difficult one.

METROPOLITAN REORGANIZATION:
AN APPRAISAL

If there is anything that observation of metropolitan areas has taught us it is that there is no single "best solution" to the problems of governing these areas. Metropolitan areas that extend across state lines have different problems than those located entirely in one county. Variables such as the racial composition of the population, the distribution of taxable resources, and the strength of political parties in an area will affect the issue. The extent to which a crisis situation exists will affect the willingness of citizens to alter their forms of government.

If we refer again to the criteria discussed in the previous chapter—organizational simplicity, responsiveness to the public, political acceptability, and comprehensiveness—we see that even these can be applied in only a very general way. It might be generally agreed that approaches like annexation, consolidation of similar units, and city-consolidation rate high on organizational simplicity, and it might also be agreed that whatever the merits of metropolitan federalism the tedious relationship between governments in any federal system could not be called simple. On the other hand, it is a matter of individual opinion how the Lakewood Plan would rate on organizational simplicity. Admittedly, it creates no new governments, but some would question the simplicity of the intricate maze of contractual arrangements which result.

Different people may have exactly opposite views about how to achieve responsiveness to the public will. A good case can be made that a city-county consolidation such as that in Nashville concentrates the decision-making process in one government and thereby allows the press, civic groups, and interested citizens to direct their attention to a single government and insure responsiveness. Others, viewing the same situation, would suggest that eliminating local governments and placing their powers in the county is a step in the wrong direction. The local government is the most responsive, this reasoning would say, and any consolidation downgrades their responsiveness. Those with this point of view would be more inclined to advocate a system of metropolitan federalism which retains some authority for local independent municipalities. This disagreement between those who believe responsiveness is accomplished through relatively large units of government in which governmental power and public attention are concentrated and those who see responsiveness as best protected through small independent municipal governments is illustrative of the difficulties involved in applying this standard.

It is possible to make some rather generally applicable statements about political acceptability. As a rule the more local officials or other interests feel their position to be threatened by a particular proposal for metropolitan reform, the more likely they are to oppose it. In Miami, as an illustration, local officials have been a major source of opposition to metropolitan government. If local officials were faced with a choice, however, between metropolitan federalism and city-county consolidation they would undoubtedly prefer the former because, while both alternatives may be undesirable from their point of view, a federal approach would at least leave them with some authority and status. Political parties, likewise, will react to reorganization plans on the basis of how they think their position in the area will be affected. The same usually would be true of racial groups, businessmen, or any other interest.

Comprehensiveness is a criterion that can be objectively applied in many cases. We can say, for example, that any attempt to deal with the problems of the Chicago metropolitan area through reorganization of the government of Cook County would not meet this standard. Even here, however, we are rapidly developing population masses where metropolitan areas become contiguous and overlap, and one might suggest that here only the federal government is really comprehensive.

It might be preferable if a set of criteria could be applied that would objectively measure the effectiveness of plans for governing metropolitan areas, but this is not to be. In the first place, there is no agreement on what criteria should be used, and even if there were, our discussion here shows that such criteria can serve only as broad guides rather than as specific standards. Moreover, in governing the metropolitan area as in other political issues, the ultimate outcome is likely to depend less on objective standards of measurement than on the complex interplay of political forces that is always present with issues that touch large numbers of people. For this reason we devote the next chapter to an analysis of the political implications of metropolitan reorganization.

Suggested Readings

Booth, David A., *Metropolitics: The Nashville Consolidation* (Lansing: MSU, Institute for Community Development and Services).

Grumm, John G., *Metropolitan Area Government: The Toronto Experience* (Lawrence: University of Kansas Publications, 1959).

Havard, William C., and Floyd C. Corty, *Rural-Urban Consolidation* (Baton Rouge: Louisiana State University Press, 1964). A study of the city county consolidation plan in Baton Rouge, Louisiana.

Sofen, Edward, *The Miami Metropolitan Experiment* (Bloomington: Indiana University Press, 1963).

Studenski, Paul, *The Government of Metropolitan Areas in the United States* (New York: National Municipal League, 1930). One of the earliest studies recognizing the problems of government in metropolitan areas.

chapter 7

The Politics of Metropolitan Reorganization

It is to be noted that the only well established system of metropolitan government in North America is in Toronto, where no referendum was required and the new government was established by the provincial legislature. In the Miami area, on the other hand, crippling amendments and threats of repeal have plagued the new government throughout its existence, and fear of voter reaction has constantly cast a shadow over Metro's activities. It is very significant to the entire study of metropolitan politics that the democratic tradition in American local government demands that the people have a direct voice in such matters as reorganization of local government structure in almost every state. If this were not the case, if structural changes were left in the hands of the regularly elected representatives or perhaps made the responsibility of a specially elected body, the history of metropolitan reform might read much differently. There is no assurance that such reforms would have had easier sledding had they been removed from direct popular control, but it would have created a set of circumstances where the question of political acceptability would have had a much different meaning. As it is, when we speak of making a reform politically acceptable we have to mean not only winning the consent of many public officials but also winning the approval of a public whose attitude is more one of mild skepticism or lack of interest than outright opposition. This fact points up the importance of understanding the political forces involved in such moves. In the paragraphs which follow the discussion pertains primarily to reaction to the far-reaching approaches, although there will be times when similar patterns will emerge in controversies over more moderate approaches.

PROPONENTS AND OPPONENTS

It is easy to overgeneralize about sources of support for and opposition to proposals for metropolitan reorganization. As with all political issues, the particular circumstances in a given area at a given time make each situation somewhat unique. One variable that will cause seemingly different public reactions in similar circumstances is what the public perceives as alternatives. One might discover support for establishment of a voluntary organization such as ABAG coming from sources that would be expected to oppose such action, but this would be understandable if it were generally believed that the alternative would be some more radical change, such as consolidation or federation. Support in this case would not be for a voluntary organization as such but merely for what certain people believed to be the more acceptable of two undesirable alternatives.

With this reservation in mind, we can still make some relatively broad generalizations about the most likely sources of support and opposition. Proposals of this nature appear almost sure to win support from certain university groups and women's groups. In most areas where some form of metropolitan reorganization has been discussed, college professors have played a key role in the background research and preparation of the proposal as well as in the campaign for approval. The metropolitan reformers have had few supporters more ardent and more loyal than the League of Women Voters, and they are often joined in the battle by other women's groups interested in community affairs. In Nashville, the Council of Jewish Women and the Federation of Business and Professional Women were loyal supporters of city-county consolidation. Service clubs, church groups, and chambers of commerce are potential sources of support.

Major business and industrial organizations whose interests cover all or most of the metropolitan area will usually be found among the supporters. This would include banks, large insurance firms, public utilities, real estate interests, major law firms, etc. This support may come because direct benefits are expected. Utilities and real estate firms, as an example, might expect to benefit if a single system of planning and zoning replaced the present system where each community performs these functions independently of its neighbors. The benefits expected may be more direct, as in the case of young attorneys who see participation in the campaign as a way to get their name before the public and build a reputation for civic interest and leadership. Many times support will come from major business firms not because of any direct interests but simply because support for the proposal seems in some general way to be support for "progress" or "reform." It just seems to be the right side to be on.

Support also comes from another type of business with an area-wide interest, the major metropolitan dailies. In almost every case, the press has played an important role not only in getting the issues before the public but also in campaigning for adoption through editorials, special series, and features. In St. Louis, both the *Post-Dispatch* and the *Globe-Democrat,* which ordinarily oppose each other in city, state and national politics, gave strong support to the proposed metropolitan district plan. The *Miami Herald* and the *Cleveland Press* were strong supporters in their areas. In Nashville, both papers, the *Tennessean* and the *Banner,* supported the proposed consolidation in 1958, although in 1962 the *Banner* opposed the change, partly because of its close association with the mayor who was leading the opposition fight.

A good summary of the sources of support has been provided by Professor Norton Long:[1]

> The revolutionaries who wish to overturn the status quo (in metropolitan areas) are most often university professors, League of Women Voters, Chambers of Commerce, civic leader businessmen especially those with a stake in downtown, those with a concern in the planning of major metropolitan highways and utilities, suburban residents, officials and real estate promoters needing sewer and water facilities, the media people seeking a cause and the intellectuals of local government who follow the thinking of *Fortune,* The National Municipal League and "the authorities."

On the other side of the issue, we will usually find key officials among the leaders of the opposition. It is to be expected that those who see the very existence of their positions threatened will react strongly. Suburban officeholders in both St. Louis and Miami were among the active leaders of the opponents of change, and in Nashville in 1962 the mayor of the central city spearheaded the campaign against consolidation. In Baton Rouge, Nashville, and some Virginia counties certain county offices were left untouched by consolidation not only because of the legal difficulties involved but also to minimize the role the incumbents would play in the opposition. There are frequent exceptions to this rule, in fact, almost every movement for metropolitan reform has had some political officials among its leadership, but in general one can expect to find a good representation of elected officeholders among the protectors of the *status quo.*

---

[1] Norton E. Long, *The Polity* (Chicago: Rand McNally & Co., 1962), p. 160.

The same motivations that bring elected officials into the camp of the opposition—fear for their positions—often affect the attitudes of city and county employees also. Governmental reorganizations can upset seniority systems and pension rights and may even threaten jobs themselves, so it is not surprising that they cause much consternation in the affected bureaucracies. In Nashville city policemen and firemen distributed anti-Metro-literature, and one writer says that policemen "occasionally harassed speakers at pro-Metro meetings."[2] The assurance given by the city of Sacramento that the employees of North Sacramento would be brought into the merit system without civil service tests or physical examinations in case of consolidation is illustrative of the efforts that must be made if this source of opposition is to be overcome.

In contrast to large business firms and news media which have area-wide interest, neighborhood businesses and newspapers tend to oppose major governmental change. They are oriented primarily toward the immediate vicinity or, in the case of the suburban areas, toward their own municipality, and metro proposals often appear to be just another step toward making government more complex, far-removed and inaccessible to the little guy. Local newspapers in particular depend on the existence of neighborhood or community identity and can be depended on to react vigorously against anything that seems to threaten that identity.

Racial minorities have usually been among those opposing metro plans. These groups are concentrated in the central city and in most areas their numbers in relation to the total central city population have been growing rapidly, giving them a long awaited strong voice at city hall. Any reorganization plan which enlarges the electoral base through the addition of suburban residents (mostly white middle-class residents) tends to dilute the strength of the minorities in local government and gives them good reason to look with skepticism at such plans. Also, minority groups are usually oriented more toward their own immediate communities than toward the metropolitan area as a whole in the same way that neighborhood businesses and newspapers are, and they tend to react in the same way. A study of Cleveland has shown that as the Negro population in the city has increased, the opposition to metro proposals in the central city has also increased.[3] In St. Louis the Negro wards were found to vote in opposition to reform, but it was also found that their voter turnout (12 per cent)

---

[2] David A. Booth, *Metropolitics: The Nashville Consolidation* (East Lansing: Michigan State University, Institute for Community Development and Services, 1963), p. 86.

[3] Richard A. Watson and John H. Romani, "Metropolitan Government for Metropolitan Cleveland: An Analysis of the Voting Record," *Midwest Journal of Political Science*, Vol. V, No. 4 (November 1961), pp. 365–98.

was far below even the turnout (19 per cent) in non-Negro wards with similar socio-economic characteristics.[4] While this pattern is not especially unusual, it does seem to indicate that the minority population was not aroused by any great feeling one way or the other on the issue.

As a general rule it appears that central cities are somewhat more sympathetic to metropolitan reform than are the surrounding areas. In Baton Rouge the voters supported city-county consolidation by almost four-to-one and adjacent areas gave the plan a comfortable majority, but more distant parts of the county voted against the plan. When the St. Louis metropolitan district plan was defeated in 1959, central city voters opposed it by about two-to-one, but suburban voters voted three-to-one against it. In the Nashville referendum in 1958 city voters supported city-county consolidation while county voters opposed it; in 1962 both city and county voters supported it but the margin in the city was considerably larger. This characteristic is difficult to explain. It is obvious that suburban communities often fear losing their identity and being gobbled up by the city whereas the reverse would not be true. It is also a fact that the large businesses which are most likely to support change are more often located in the city than in the suburbs. On the other hand, certain sources of strong opposition, such as the minority groups just mentioned, are concentrated in the central city while the middle classes which would seem to be most likely to respond to the appeals of the League of Women Voters and the university "experts" are more likely to be found in the suburbs. Firm conclusions on this point must await more research.

In the metropolitan areas where research has been done, findings show that there is a positive relationship between such characteristics as income and education and support for proposals for metropolitan reform. Those who are wealthier, have more income, and live in the more expensive neighborhoods are more likely to support metro proposals than those at the other end of the socio-economic ladder. This was found to be true in the St. Louis study,[5] and the results of research on the opposition of minority groups would tend to confirm this idea. This is only a general tendency, however, and can be changed by other intervening variables. In St. Louis, for example, certain low income areas in the city supported the district plan apparently because the political party organization in the area was actively supporting it.[6] Suburban communities with high income and

---

[4] Henry J. Schmandt, Paul G. Steinbicker, and George D. Wendell, *Metropolitan Reform in St. Louis: A Case Study* (New York: Holt, Rinehart and Winston, 1961), pp. 52–53.

[5] *Ibid.*, pp. 54–56.

[6] *Ibid.*

educational levels may also have a strong orientation to the local municipality and neighborhood in which case they might be motivated to oppose the metro idea. As with the variable of geography, the relationship of variables such as income and education to support or opposition to metro proposals can be stated only generally and is quite subject to being influenced by other intervening cross pressures.

THE ISSUES

There has been much consistency from area to area in the issues raised in campaigns directed at metropolitan reform regardless of the specific type of reform involved. The proponents of change usually have a somewhat more difficult time in selling their case not only because advocating change is harder than blocking it, but also because they are forced to rely on points that are general and often vague. They will talk about increased efficiency and more economy and point out the need for an area-wide approach to area-wide problems. A survey in the St. Louis area among citizens who said they believed more cooperation was necessary in the city-county area showed that, when asked why they favored more cooperation, their answers used such terms as "growth," "progress," "more order," "improve services," "equalize costs," and "more efficient."[7] The difficulties encountered by the merger advocates in Champaign-Urbana show the problems proponents meet in trying to tie down their issues to hard, specific points. In Nashville in 1962, when the pro forces could point to certain specific issues like the green sticker and city annexation policies and to the mayor who became the symbol of all that was wrong with the *status quo,* advocates had a much greater advantage.

The opponents can rely on several issues which have strong appeal to the voters. The charge that taxes will go up is usually heard, often true and in any case almost impossible to combat. In spite of promises that change will bring increased economy, the fear of more taxes makes this a strong selling point for the opponents. The issue of local identity is nebulous but strong. As shown in the Champaign-Urbana controversy, matters such as street names, community identification, or the location of city hall are important to many people. It would seem that in a highly mobile society where people move often and form few deep roots in particular areas, issues related to local attachments would decline in importance. This may indeed be happening, but it has not yet advanced to the point where this can be considered an insignificant matter. In some areas, in-

---

[7] Scott Greer, *Metropolitics: A Study of Political Culture* (New York: John Wiley and Sons, Inc., 1963), Chapter 5.

cluding Miami, Champaign-Urbana, Baton Rouge, and Nashville, reform opponents have questioned the legality of the proposed change and emphasized the legal complexities involved in establishment of a new form of government.

One of the most effective assets of the opposition is the ability to appeal to groups which may be specifically threatened. Depending on the specific reform involved, this may include city employees, elected officeholders, and others, and a suggestion that their positions may be in danger can mobilize a strong block of opposition. Given the low voter turnout at referenda of this type, a strong block of voters, such as city employees and their families, may make the difference in the outcome.

Two of the major advantages to the opposition forces are simply the *status quo* and apathy. There is a natural tendency to oppose change, especially when it involves substitution of that which is unknown for that which is known. In most cases where metropolitan federalism, city-county consolidation, or similar reforms are concerned, substitution of the unknown for the known is what is involved. The citizen hopes that taxes may go down, but he also fears that they may go up. He may not like city hall, but he understands it and is familiar with terms such as mayor, council, county, city, etc. When he is asked to do away with these and to approve proposals for consolidated government, metropolitan mayors, county councils, or other strange sounding innovations, there is a strong temptation on his part to say "no thanks."

As important as resistance to change is the apathy of the voter. We have discussed metropolitan reorganization in Miami, St. Louis, Nashville, and elsewhere as if this were an important and controversial issue in these areas. So far as the majority of the voters in these areas are concerned, this has not been the case at all, for most of them have been generally uninterested in the whole matter. In St. Louis after an active and controversial campaign only 21 per cent of the registered voters in the city and 40 per cent in the suburbs voted in the referendum. A sample survey taken immediately after the election showed that only 9 per cent of the city residents could identify even one prominent leader who had supported the reform proposal and in the suburbs the figure was 22 per cent.[8] Similar results have been found elsewhere. The highly controversial Miami Metro was adopted with only about one-fourth of the voters voting, and in Baton Rouge only about one-third of those eligible to vote on city-county consolidation did so.

One conclusion to be drawn from this is that the citizen reacts mainly to crisis situations. If he could be shown that his water supply or fire pro-

---

[8] *Ibid.,* pp. 99–101.

tection will collapse if drastic reforms are not made, he might well react with interest and action. Usually he cannot be shown this, and he is not inspired much by the usual promises of better planning or more efficiency.

THE POLITICAL PARTIES

One of the more ambiguous aspects of the politics of metropolitan reorganization has been the role of the political parties. This may be because in many metropolitan areas the role of the parties in local politics is itself ambiguous. In many cities today, and especially in the suburbs, elections are nonpartisan, and the role of the parties in these area ranges from covert to overt involvement to complete lack of interest and activity in local elections. This uncertain position of the parties makes it difficult for them to judge their stakes in metropolitan reform.

It seems safe, if not trite, to say that they will take that position which they perceive will best advance or protect their own position in the area. In rare cases the issues may be quite clear. If a city-county merger were proposed and if the Democrats were in the majority in the city while the Republicans outnumbered them in the county, it would be simple to evaluate the stakes of the game. If the Democrats were in the majority in the entire area, they would favor the plan and Republicans would oppose it, for it would enable the Democrats to push beyond the central city and control the entire area. If the Republicans held a majority in the entire area, party positions would be reversed.

In few, if any, cases are the issues so easily defined, and it is not uncommon for party leaders to be divided among themselves. In St. Louis Mayor Tucker opposed the district plan, but the party took no official position. A few Democratic ward leaders actually supported the plan and managed to carry the vote in their wards for it. Other party leaders quietly opposed the plan and succeeded in getting it overwhelmingly defeated in their wards. In Cleveland, the Democratic party officially endorsed the proposal, but Mayor Celebrezze opposed it.

There are times when a party may serve as a channel for intergovernmental cooperation. In the Syracuse area the fact that the Republican party is in the majority in both the city and the surrounding areas means that there is no threat to party power, and it has thus been both willing and able to serve as a facilitator of cooperation.[9]

There seems to be some tendency for those who identify with the Republican party to be more likely to favor metropolitan reform than

---

[9] Roscoe C. Martin *et al., Decisions in Syracuse* (Bloomington: Indiana University Press, 1961), pp. 326–28.

those who call themselves Democrats, but this may just be another way of saying that those with high socio-economic status are most likely to support area-wide reform. In some areas there may be a split between the central city party activists and their counterparts in the suburbs. This is especially true among Democrats, where the city party is likely to have many leaders oriented toward traditional organization politics while their Democratic brethren in suburbia are primarily of a middle class reform orientation. There was some evidence of such a city-suburb division among Democrats in St. Louis.[10]

The study of the St. Louis district election suggests that the role of political parties is crucial in metropolitan reform. "No metropolitan plan *can* pass over the active opposition of the political parties," they conclude, and "no such plan *is likely* to pass without active partisan support."[11] It is our opinion that there is not yet sufficient evidence to be sure of the validity of these hypotheses, but they offer an interesting point of view which, if found to be generally valid, will have a profound effect on the future of campaigns for metropolitan reorganization.

In most instances so far the parties have not taken official positions on such issues, although exceptions would be the Democratic party in Cleveland and a few ward organizations in St. Louis. Both parties usually have more to lose than gain from outright endorsements. Prominent party members are commonly involved, and party organizations are sometimes quietly mobilized for action, but the parties as such stop short of open involvement. In controversies where the issues, the stakes, and the outcome all are unclear, as is often the case with metropolitan reorganization, this seems like a logical position for the parties to take. In summary, the cases of metropolitan reform up to the present time have each presented the parties with such unique situations and the party responses have been so influenced by the local environment that it is difficult to present any general statement about the role of parties in controversies of this nature.

THE ATTACK FROM THE RIGHT

At least a word should be said here about the strange attacks by extreme right wing organizations on almost all attempts at metropolitan area reorganization or even cooperation. For over a decade rightist commentators and organizations have concerned themselves with a number of local issues. Their attacks have been directed at water flouridation, mental health programs, urban renewal, "social science experts," and the major

[10] Schmandt, p. 41.
[11] *Ibid.*, p. 59.

foundations which have supported research on issues opposed by the right.[12] The council-manager plan has been attacked as a device that provides for local dictators who take over responsibilities of elected officials and reduce the functions of the elected officials to that of rubber stamp.

Coming in for special attacks has been "1313," the label given to those organizations with headquarters at 1313 East 60th Street in Chicago.[13] These organizations are supposedly part of a world conspiracy which is associated with communism and which is dedicated to accomplishing the goal of world government. The association of some of these organizations with the International Union of Local Government Authorities, a European based organization which includes local government members from both sides of the Iron Curtain, is offered as evidence of the communist association.

The attack on metropolitan reform appears to have first gained momentum at the time metro became an issue in the Miami area. The fact that Public Administration Service, a "1313" organization, was hired to study the governmental problems of the Miami area and that the charter finally adopted established an adaptation of the council-manager plan added coal to their fire. Proposals for metropolitan reform, whether it be consolidation, federation, or more moderate proposals such as San Francisco's ABAG, have been referred to as "supergovernments," which by taking over the powers of local governments are supposed to be a step in the direction of an all-powerful federal government and ultimately a world government.[14]

There is no evidence that these attacks have had a major influence on the outcome of any proposal for metropolitan reform in a major area, although there are areas where they have had some temporary effects. In the Los Angeles area attacks of this nature have been at the center of several controversies over whether certain local governments should join a voluntary association known as SCAG (Southern California Association of Governments). Some right wing activity was in evidence in Nashville in both 1958 and 1962. The views of the rightists are widely circulated

---

[12] For a general discussion of the right wing attack, see H. G. Pope, "New Peas in an Old Shell Game," a special paper published by Public Administration Service in 1960.

[13] There have been numerous discussions of 1313. In particular see Jo Hindman, "Terrible '1313'," *American Mercury*, Vol. 88, No. 420 (January, 1959), pp. 5–15; Jo Hindman, *Terrible 1313 Revisited* (Caldwell, Idaho: The Caxton Printers, Ltd., 1963).

[14] See "Metropolitan Government," Dan Smoot Report, Vol. 11, No. 5 (February 1, 1965), pp. 33–39; Jo Hindman, "The 'Metro' Monster," *American Mercury*, Vol. 89, No. 426 (July 1959), pp. 50–62; E. G. Grace, *What is Metropolitan Government?* (Published by the author, 1958).

through books, newsletters, and radio and television shows which are well financed, and the possibility that this source of opposition might prove important in some future controversy over metropolitan reform should not be overlooked. Up to the present time, however, the leaders of those in opposition to proposals for reform have not chosen to accept the assumption or make use of the charges of the right wing in their opposition campaigns to any large degree.

MUST METROPOLIS BE REORGANIZED?

There was a time when those who study local government had little doubt about how people felt about metropolitan governments. Those who favored the idea were the enlightened, progressive, civic-minded citizens, and opposition came only from the uninformed and those with selfish interests to protect. Fortunately this type of dogmatism has disappeared from most writing about metropolitan problems, and there are many highly respected authorities who question whether it is really necessary to undertake broad scale reorganization of the governments in our metropolitan areas.[15]

Those who hold this point of view point out that there is a difference between the existence of problems in metropolitan areas and the existence of problems *because* of a lack of any type of metropolitan government. Thus Banfield and Grodzins say that there may be a lack of adequate parks and playgrounds in many metropolitan areas, but the creation of some form of metropolitan government is not going to solve this problem.[16] Banfield emphasizes elsewhere that the deep cleavages which exist in large urban areas cannot be made to disappear simply by encompassing all of them under a single governmental umbrella.[17] Divisions of party, race, income, ethnic background, and social class will remain and may even become more intense when brought within a single governmental structure. Duane Lockard has commented on this point as follows:[18]

> If there is an advantage to being able to take an overview of the whole metropolitan region, there is a concurrent disadvantage in

---

[15] See, for example, Vincent Ostrom, Charles Tiebout and Robert Warren, "The Organization of Metropolitan Areas: A Theoretical Inquiry," *American Political Science Review,* Vol. LV, No. 4 (Dec., 1961), pp. 831–42.

[16] Edward Banfield and Morton Grodzins, *Government and Housing in Metropolitan Areas,* (New York: McGraw-Hill Book Company, 1958), p. 32.

[17] Edward Banfield, "The Politics of Metropolitan Area Organization," *Midwest Journal of Political Science,* Vol. 1, No. 1 (May, 1957), pp. 77–91.

[18] Duane Lockard, *The Politics of State and Local Government* (New York: The MacMillan Company, 1963), pp. 534–35.

having to encompass a broad range of policy questions that pit antagonistic elements in all out conflict. If the logic of integration has appeal, there is also some persuasiveness about the counter-proposition that the smaller unit of government poses fewer divisive questions because it is likely to contain a more homogeneous collection of people. Right or wrong, the case against consolidation says in effect that, like India and Pakistan, it is better to remain separate if the price of unification is disunity.

Any alteration in governmental structure in metropolitan areas will involve some costs as well as benefits. Approaches calling for governmental reform on an area-wide basis may eliminate duplication, overlapping, parochialism, and other ills associated with the present system, but the costs of such revision may be the sacrifice of local control, community identification and individual choice among communities, and who is to say that the former values are inherently more important than the latter? As Charles Adrian puts it, the metropolitan reformers "sometimes exclaim in wonder and horror, 'Why there are seventy-five different fire departments in the metropolitan area!' But to the suburbanite, who wants a voice in policies that affect his place of residence, this may spell 'good' rather than 'bad.' "[19]

Essentially what those who support his view are saying is that there are ways to solve the problem of governing the metropolitan area other than the establishment of metropolitan federations, consolidations, etc. and the sacrifices of such things as identity, access and representation involved in broad governmental reorganization make the search for other alternatives desirable. Indeed they would point out that there are already many forms of intergovernmental cooperation in most areas and that these have been developed largely within the traditional framework of government. The moderate approaches discussed in Chapter 5 would be included here, as would the multitude of informal relationships between city managers, police chiefs, planners, and other functional specialists which are based on personal acquaintance and which lead to much cooperation in most metropolitan areas.

A new factor to be considered is the role of the federal government, which now requires evidence of area-wide cooperation before making aid available for certain functions, such as urban planning and transportation facilities. This trend toward tying federal aid to local cooperation will undoubtedly continue and will lead to even greater development of patterns of cooperation among governments in metropolitan areas, cooperation

---

[19] Charles R. Adrian, "Metropology: Folklore and Field Research," *Public Administration Review,* Vol. XXI, No. 2 (Summer, 1961), p. 150.

which still leaves independent local governments in existence and with control over many local matters.

It cannot be denied that there are many problems connected with the present governmental system in metropolitan areas. Intergovernmental cooperation, for example, cannot overcome the fact that the greatest service needs are in the central city and the greatest financial resources are in the suburbs. A city is not likely to enter into an agreement to pay for another city's problems. Nor can one deny that the present system probably makes some sacrifice of efficiency through its duplication and overlapping. On the other hand, metropolitan politics involves competition between competing values and competing goals, and the accomplishment of some will mean the sacrifice of others. We are not saying that plans for metropolitan consolidation or federation should be rejected, but it should be remembered that there are ways other than metropolitan governments for governing Metropolis.

SOME GENERAL STATEMENTS

On the basis of the cases of metropolitan reform on which there is information available, it is possible to make some tentative statements which seem to generally apply.

(1) Support for proposals for metropolitan reform comes most often from university groups, women's groups, large business and professional firms which have an interest either in downtown in parfessional firms which have an interest either in downtown in particular or the metropolitan area as a whole rather than in neighborhood areas only, and the metropolitan press.

(2) Opposition will center around local political officials, some party leaders, neighborhood businesses and newspapers, and minority groups.

(3) There is generally a positive relationship between socio-economic status and support for proposals for metropolitan reform.

(4) Metro supporters usually base their case on rather general issues such as more economy and efficiency, better planning, elimination of duplication and overlapping, and encouragement of an area-wide rather than a parochial view of local problems.

(5) Opponents will emphasize the possibility of increased taxes and the danger of the loss of community identity and access to government. They will point out to municipal employees and incumbent

officeholders that their positions may be threatened by the proposal.

(6) In every major metropolitan area one significant factor in metropolitan reform is a requirement that any proposed alteration in governmental structure be voted on by the citizens. Because of the difficulties involved in getting the voters to support structural change, this requirement works to the benefit of those supporting the *status quo*. The only major reform to have been established without difficulty was in Toronto, where a popular referendum was not required. The tradition of voter choice on issues of this nature is firmly established in the United States and is unlikely to be changed by any state.

(7) The most characteristic response of the public to proposals of this type is neither support nor opposition but apathy. The leadership on both sides involves a very small number of people, and the voter turnout in referenda is ordinarily very low. In the absence of some real crisis, voters do not get concerned about questions of metropolitan reform.

(8) The role of the political parties has been a varied one. If they were to take a strong stand either supporting or opposing a reform proposal it might well have an important effect on the outcome, but they have not usually chosen to do so. In most areas the parties have been officially neutral, with various party leaders involved, sometimes openly, sometimes behind the scenes, on both sides of the question.

(9) Proposals for metropolitan reform have been a target of various right wing groups, which have attacked them as being part of a communistic plot leading to the establishment of an all-powerful national government or world government. In the reform compaigns that have taken place so far, these particular attacks have not made much impact, although they have been an irritating and possibly a delaying factor in some areas, such as Los Angeles.

(10) There is a growing number of authorities who believe that the solution to metropolitan area problems need not come through reorganization of governmental structure. They point out that much cooperation can take place through informal arrangements or through moderate approaches which work within the existing structure of government, and they believe that the problems involved in far-reaching metropolitan reform are often sufficiently great that it is worthwhile to search for less drastic alternatives.

Suggested Readings

Booth, David A., *Metropolitics: The Nashville Consolidation* (Lansing: MSU, Institute for Community Development and Services, 1963).

Factors Affecting Voter Reactions to Governmental Reorganization in Metropolitan Areas (Washington: Advisory Commission on Intergovernmental Relations, 1962).

Greer, Scott, *Metropolitics: A Study of Political Culture* (New York: John Wiley and Sons, Inc., 1963). A discussion of the political aspects of metropolitan reorganization in three cities, Cleveland, St. Louis, and Miami.

Long, Norton, "Who Makes Decisions in Metropolitan Areas" and "Some Observations Towards a Natural History of Metropolitan Politics," both published in Charles Press (ed.), *The Polity* (Chicago: Rand McNally & Co., 1962).

Martin, Roscoe C., Frank J. Manger *et. al., Decisions in Syracuse* (Bloomington: Indiana University Press, 1961). A theoretical discussion of the political process built around a series of case studies taken from the Syracuse metropolitan area.

Schmandt, Henry J., Paul G. Steinbicker and George D. Wendell, *Metropolitan Reform in St. Louis: A Case Study* (New York: Holt, Rinehart and Winston, 1961).

Sengstock, Frank S., *et. al., Consolidation: Building a Bridge Between City and Suburb* (Worcester: Hefferman Press, 1964). A case study of the 1962 consolidation effort in the St. Louis area.

chapter 8

The Metropolitan Area in the Federal System

It has often been said that federalism is not a principle but a compromise. Federal systems are established when the citizens are divided, as they were when our constitution was written, over whether they want a strong central government or a loose association of strong states, and federalism becomes a convenient middle road to follow. When we speak of a federal system of government we mean a system of government in which power is divided between a cental government and some type of regional governments (usually called states or provinces). The United States, Canada, Mexico, and Australia would be examples.

Because we have historically thought of federal systems as being two-layer governments, the question of where those governments existing below the regional level—municipalities, counties, school districts, etc.—fit into the system remains a subject of controversy. There is no mention of local governments anywhere in the national constitution, so from the beginning the establishment of systems of local government has been a state responsibility. Until the turn of the twentieth century, and in most cases until after 1932, this system caused few difficulties, but as the nation became more industrialized and urbanized and as many urban problems came to be looked upon as national problems, the question of what part the national government should have in working with urban governments to solve their problems became more and more important. Sometimes, as in the case of public education, the states stepped in to provide large amounts of financial aid and technical assistance to local school systems. With many problems, however, the state government was not only unable or unwilling to come to the aid of local governments itself, but it resented the attempts of the national government to come to the assistance of these governments. This set of circumstances meant that the evolution of the federal system into one where local governments took their place as a third level came about only with considerable friction and controversy.

THE STATE-LOCAL RELATIONSHIP

In every state local governments are created by and exist at the pleasure of the state. The state can alter their structure or even abolish them. For a while after the adoption of the constitution some people supported a theory of the inherent right to local self government, which suggested that there are certain basic rights that states give to local governments by the act of creating them. There were only a few states that ever relied on this doctrine in their judicial rulings, and in the 1860's it was finally laid to rest by the famous decision of Judge J. F. Dillon. Dillon, in what has become known as Dillon's Rule, established this interpretation of local powers:[1]

> It is a general and undisputed proposition of law that a municipal corporation possesses and can exercise the following powers, and no others: First, those granted in express words; second, those necessary or fairly implied in or incident to the powers expressly granted; third, those essential to the accomplishment of the declared objects and purposes of the corporation,—not simply convenient, but indispensable. Any fair, reasonable, substantial doubt concerning the existence of power is resolved by the courts against the corporation, and the power is denied.

The states have universally adopted this principle, and the very restrictive interpretation of local powers implied here continues to prevail in most judicial decisions concerning local governments. This means, of course, that states hold a tight rein over the activities of their municipalities. It also means that state legislatures are often faced with the problem of considering much legislation each session which pertains to purely local issues.

Strict interpretation of local powers means that municipalities have only those powers which have been specifically authorized by the legislature or the state constitution. All of the citizens of a city may believe that a municipal sales tax is the best way to solve the city's financial crisis but unless the state legislature has authorized municipalities in the state to enact such a tax the city is not free to do so. In an age when new and previously unknown problems are constantly presenting themselves to urban govern-

---

[1] J. F. Dillon, *Commentaries on the Law of Municipal Corporation,* 5th ed. (Boston: Little, Brown & Company, 1911), Vol. I, pp. 448–50.

ments this means that the cities are often asking the legislatures for changes in the laws concerning local authority.

In order to provide the proper legislative framework for local government many states have adopted classification systems, usually based on population. For example, a state might divide municipalities into first class cities (those with over 100,000 population), second class cities (50,000 to 100,000), third class cities (25,000 to 50,000), and fourth class cities (under 25,000).[2] The legislature would then legislate for each class, prescribing which powers each class of cities is entitled to exercise. It is common for the legislature to enact legislation stating which forms of government each class may adopt. They may, for example, allow cities in a class to choose between the strong mayor-council, weak mayor-council, council-manager, or commission forms of government, or they may be more restrictive and allow them a choice among only two or three alternatives. In Indiana, as an illustration, municipalities are not authorized to adopt the council-manager plan.

In order to give local governments more flexibility and at the same time relieve the state legislature and other state officials of much detail work, some states have granted "home rule" to all or some local governments.[3] This reduces the close ties that the state has over municipalities, but states have been reluctant to go very far in this direction, the result being that even so-called "home rule cities" must still operate within certain state imposed limits in particular areas.

States have been particularly reluctant to grant local governments discretionary powers over matters involving budgeting, finance, and taxation, and state regulations concerning these issues usually apply to home rule and non-home rule municipalities alike. Not only may cities levy only those taxes authorized by the state, but limitations are usually placed on the levels of local taxation and indebtedness. States, for example, often limit municipal indebtedness to some stated percentage of assessed valuation, as in Illinois where the figure is 4 per cent.[4] Arizona law states that a city's budget may not increase more than 10 per cent over the preceding year's total without special authorization of the state tax commisison. In states which have classification systems for their local governments, differing taxing and bonding laws may apply in different classes.

---

[2] The figures used are for illustration only. States may use any population categories they desire.

[3] On home rule, see Chapter 4.

[4] See Leonard E. Goodall, *State Regulation of Local Indebtedness in the United States* (Tempe: Arizona State University, Bureau of Government Research, 1964).

In a somewhat more positive approach, states generally provide some financial aid to local governments. This may come through allocation of a portion of certain state taxes, such as the gas tax, for distribution to local governments. States may provide aid on some type of formula basis for certain functions, such as education, where the amount is commonly based on the average daily attendance. Some state governments provide assistance through offering to collect certain taxes for municipalities. California and Illinois, to illustrate, will collect municipal sales taxes along with the state sales tax for those municipalities which want them to do so. The questions of whether to levy the tax and in what amount are still local decisions, but if after levying the tax city officials want the state to collect it for them, it will do so. This takes advantage of the economies of large-scale tax collection and also minimizes the accounting efforts of businessmen who must pay the tax.

States also play a significant part in the process of making federal aid available to local government through passing enabling legislation. Because municipalities derive their powers from the state they may not participate in programs to receive financial aid from the national government without state authorization. Thus, the states make the basic decision as to whether their municipalities will be able to participate in a given federal program. With few exceptions, they have passed such legislation with little controversy.

States must also pass enabling legislation authorizing local governments to participate in programs of metropolitan cooperation. State action has preceded the establishment of cooperative arrangements in virtually every case, whether it involved structural alterations as in Miami, Nashville, and Baton Rouge, or more moderate reforms such as ABAG. Therefore, state governments may profoundly affect the direction of cooperation in metropolitan areas through deciding what alternatives will be made available, and it is not unlikely that in some states the major battle in the metropolitan cooperation issue will be fought at the state level when the legislature determines what choices are to be open to metropolitan areas.

State Departments of Local Government

The pattern of state-local relations in most states has developed along the lines of functional specialization, state welfare officials dealing with local welfare officials, state tax officials with local tax officials, etc. There has in most cases been no attempt at overall coordination of state-local relations. Recognition of this problem has led officials in some states to explore the possibility of establishing a state department of local government to assume responsibility for the direction and supervision of state activities concerning local government. George S. Blair has summarized the functions that such departments might perform:[5]

> First, they would assist the governor in coordinating information and action regarding local government problems in developing appropriate legislative programs and administrative policies. Second, they would serve as the central point in the state government for information, study, and evaluation of proposals relating to local governments and their affairs. Third, they would serve as a collection point and clearing house for studies of local governments conducted by private and other public agencies. Fourth, they would act as a coordinating agency for local governments seeking assistance from other local, state or federal agencies. Fifth, they would carry out legislative requirements relating to local standards of performance or service. And sixth, they would initiate and recommend to local government useful state services which do not currently exist.

Advocates of such departments point to the need for general coordination of the many state activities affecting local governments. They also suggest that a state department of local government could provide leadership and initiative in attacking urban problems and would serve to emphasize and dramatize the interest of the state in solving urban problems. Opponents say that state-local relations must of necessity be on a functional basis, specialist dealing with specialist, and any attempt to provide overall supervision would just add more bureaucracy and might even hamper good relations.

State departments currently exist in one form or another in several states, including Alaska, New Jersey, New York, and Pennsylvania. The oldest such office and probably the one with the broadest responsibilities is that found in New Jersey. In many states where there is no such official agency, the governor has appointed a specialist in urban affairs to his staff to advise him on matters concerning this subject. In addition, the legislatures in a number of states have appointed special legislative committees on urban problems.

Criticisms of State Governments

The states have often been criticized for being unwilling or unable (or both) to meet their responsibilities to their growing urban areas. Al-

---

[5] George S. Blair, *American Local Government* (New York: Harper and Row, Publishers, 1964), pp. 76–78.

though this criticism has taken many forms, it is well summarized by Roscoe C. Martin in his recent book, *The Cities and the Federal System.*[6] Martin divides the substance of his criticism into six categories: state constitutions, representation, administrative organization, resources, programs, and horizons. Most of our state constitutions were drafted in the nineteenth century or earlier and were designed to serve an agrarian society, says Martin. They are very restrictive and excessively long and detailed, often containing much material that would ordinarily be found in statutory rather than constitutional law. The result is that state constitutions are inflexible and tend to be something of a straitjacket within which states must operate.

Closely related to restrictive constitutions is the problem of legislative apportionment. Until recent Supreme Court cases such as Baker v. Carr[7] and Reynolds v. Simms,[8] most states operated under systems of representation in their state legislatures which were weighted in favor of rural areas. States allowed one, or sometimes both, houses of the legislature to be appointed on some basis other than population, e.g. political subdivisions or geographic area. Illustrative of the results is California where Los Angeles County with over 6 million population had one state senator while a rural district with about 14,000 people also had one. In Arizona, where each of 14 counties was entitled to two senators, the two largest counties with 75 per cent of the total population elected only four of twenty-eight members of the legislature.

For years federal courts held that state legislative apportionment was not within their jurisdiction, but in 1962 in Baker v. Carr the Supreme Court reversed this position and later ruled that both houses of state legislatures must be apportioned primarily on the basis of population. What the long run effect of this will be is uncertain. Legislatures should become more responsive to urban problems, but just how they will respond remains to be seen. It should be noted that it is not the central cities but the metropolitan suburbs that will be the big gainers through reapportionment, since the rapid population growth in recent years has caused these areas to be most under-represented.

The executive branch, according to Martin, has long shared with the legislative a structural inability to live up to its responsibilities. Influenced by the principles of Jacksonianism and reformism, many states have given their governors only a two-year term, surrounded him with a multitude

---

[6] Roscoe C. Martin, *The Cities and the Federal System* (New York: Atherton Press, 1965), Ch. 3.

[7] Baker v. Carr, 369 U.S. 186 (1962).

[8] Reynolds v. Simms, 84 S. Ct. 1362 (1964).

of independent boards and commissions, and elected him on a long ballot. The latter means that even his department heads in the executive branch—attorney general, state treasurer, secretary of state, etc.—are elected independently of him and he thus has no formal power over them. He is in a weak position, therefore, when it comes to providing unified leadership and coordination to the state government.

In the area of administrative organization, however, Martin sees a ray of hope. Administrative reform has been a subject of serious discussion ever since administrative reorganization commissions were appointed in Wisconsin (1911), Massachusetts (1912), and New Jersey (1912). Several states, of which Michigan and the newer states of Alaska and Hawaii are examples, have recently moved in the direction of correcting these problems, and interest in other states is high.

The concepts of resources, programs and horizons that Martin mentions are closely related. He suggests that states have virtually the same *resources* available as does the national government. But states have hamstrung themselves through constitutional restrictions, taxing and debt limitations, and other restrictive measures to such an extent that they have not used their resources to meet urban needs. Consequently, the states have not taken the initiative in developing new *programs* to meet urban challenges, and initiative for new programs such as mass transit and urban planning has come almost entirely from the national level. Also, state financial aid to local governments continues at a relatively low level and is concentrated in the traditional areas where states have long provided aid, mainly education, roads, and welfare, with little emphasis on the growing urban needs for support of other functions such as libraries, law enforcement, housing, and planning.

This situation arises from what Martin calls the limited horizons of the states. He characterizes their horizons as provincial and oriented toward the rural society of an earlier era. The typical attitude of state leaders, particularly those in the legislature, is skeptical of big government, the big city, the big state, and the national government. They yearn for a world that is no more. If this is true it is not surprising that the states have not responded adequately to the needs of an urban society.

In spite of this rather harsh criticism of the states, Martin does not write them off. He does see the cities emerging as a full partner in the federal system and continual expansion of direct federal-local relations. The function of the states is consequently currently in limbo. If they choose to direct their attention and their resources to urban needs, there will be a place for them as partners with national and local governments and there will be plenty of challenge for all three. If they choose to abdicate responsibility for newer urban problems and concentrate on their traditional functions, they may do so and still find much to do, but if they follow this road they may be sure that their own cities and towns will continue to look increasingly to Washington for help. Whatever road the state choses to follow, it is already established that the national government will be very much involved in determining the directions that urban policies take in the future, and it is to this subject that we now turn.

THE NATIONAL-LOCAL RELATIONSHIP

Most writers point to 1932 as the turning point in national-local relations. Prior to that time direct relations between the two were infrequent and unsystematic, while after that date national programs resulting from the crisis of depression and different political philosophy brought about rapid expansion of cooperative national-local projects. A number of recent writers have shown that national-local relations are nothing new and have existed from the beginning of the nation. Advocates of federal aid to education, for example, like to state that "It's older than the constitution," since the national government provided land for educational purposes in the Northwest Ordinance of 1787. National aid to local governments for canal projects and the financial aid for the movement of the railroads west are other examples.

For the most part, however, direct relationships between the two levels are a twentieth century, in particular a post-1932, phenomenon. Prior to 1932 several forms of assistance were made available by federal agencies to local governments. The F.B.I. has long worked closely with local police departments and law enforcement, and local police officials regularly attend F.B.I. police training schools. The United States Civil Service Commission provides advice to municipalities on establishing civil service systems and preparation of examinations. The data collection services of the Bureau of the Census have always been of service to municipalities, and in recent years the Bureau has expanded its services through a regular census of governmental units every five years and annual reports on city finances and debt, city taxation, city employment, and related subjects. In the 1920's the Department of Commerce prepared numerous reports that had application to local governments, probably the most significant of them being a model planning and zoning ordinance for municipalities.

The year 1932 is looked upon as a turning point because at that time the emphasis shifted to cash grants-in-aid as opposed to technical assistance and on some projects to direct national-local relations rather than to national-state-local relations. The Public Works Administration (PWA) came into being to provide grants and loans to muncipalities for public works projects in order to stimulate employment. Later in the 1930's programs for housing, public welfare, and slum clearance expanded direct national-local relations. Succeeding decades have seen continual expansion until today federal programs of assistance are available for municipal projects from air pollution control to zoning administration.

Federal grant-in-aid programs tend to have certain common characteristics regardless of the particular program. First, they usually involve cash grants, and these are provided on some type of matching basis. With many programs this is on a fifty-fifty basis, the local government providing a dollar for each dollar provided by the national government. In other programs the national government contribution may be two-thirds or in a few cases as high as ninety per cent of the total costs. The national government has sometimes paid a higher portion of costs on projects at first in order to encourage participation by local governments and then scaled down its contribution. For example, the community development and urban extension programs provided for in the Higher Education Act of 1965 were to receive seventy-five per cent support from the national government during the first two years after the bill was enacted and fifty per cent support thereafter. It was the hope of Congress that local governments would be encouraged to establish programs under the bill by the provision for seventy-five per cent national government support and would be sufficiently interested to continue them when national government support fell to fifty per cent.

Another characteristic of grant-in-aid programs is that they are voluntary. No local government is required to participate. It is true that the opportunity to get matching money to supplement local funds and the fear that if we do not spend the tax dollars that are going into a certain program some other community will often makes it difficult to reject such grants. The fact remains that the decision to participate is up to the local government.

A third characteristic of these programs, however, is that once a local government has made the decision to participate it must then meet the requirements and standards established by Congress and the agency administering the program. A significant trend so far as metropolitan areas are concerned is the requirement in many recent bills that evidence must be provided of area-wide planning and cooperation before federal aid will be available to communities in a metropolitan area. The programs for interstate highway construction, open space, and urban planning all require such evidence of cooperation. This cooperation need not be of any particular type. Regional planning associations and voluntary associations of governments may meet the requirements as well as consolidation and federation schemes.

The rationale for direct national assistance to local governments is simple. It is that the state and municipal governments have not adequately met the many problems facing urban areas and that in an urban society these must be considered national problems and cannot be ignored by the national government. It is also suggested by advocates that the national government is in the best position to provide the large financial resources necessary for such undertakings. The grant-in-aid device also gives local governments encouragement to tackle problems they might otherwise feel inadequate to attack, and when need is a factor in the distribution of grants, the system has the effect of reducing inequality of financial resources among cities. Critics of the system say that a strict interpretation of the federal constitution does not provide for direct relations of this nature by national and local governments, and they also point to the danger of excessive control of local policies by the national government.

An evaluation of the grant-in-aid program shows that it has enabled cities to deal with problems that would otherwise have seemed beyond their financial ability. Perhaps the best testimony to the success of the program is the almost universal support it has received from city officials. The question of excess federal control is a hard one. There are some things critics can point to, such as the charge that all federally supported public housing seems to have the same boring look, which suggests the danger of federal control leading to an excessive emphasis on conformity. On the other hand, while there can be no question that aid has brought certain controls, it appears that these controls have usually been desirable. The construction standards established for federally aided highways or sewers, the requirement that local officials handling aid monies must be part of a merit system, requirements for metropolitan area-wide planning are controls that can hardly be criticized as harmful to local governments. Moreover, increasing emphasis is being placed on allowing local initiative in the design of programs to receive grants-in-aid. This has been particularly true with the poverty program of the Johnson administration, where goals established by Congress were stated very broadly and local agencies were encouraged to design their own plans for fighting poverty within the limits of these general goals. The apparent success of the grant-in-aid system and the satisfaction of both national and local officials suggest that the system is here to stay as an integral part of the federal system.

Urban Representation in Washington

One indication of the close national-local association is the large number of organizations representing local governments whose headquarters are located in Washington. Leading the list would be the National

League of Cities (formerly the American Municipal Association), a federation of state municipal leagues and the main organizational representative of municipalities in Washington. It provides representation before Congress on issues of concern to cities, undertakes research, holds a regular annual conference and many special conferences, and publishes a periodical, *Nation's Cities*. With the National League of Cities having to represent all municipalities, the United States Conference of Mayors places special emphasis on representing the larger cities, with its membership being open to cities of 50,000 and over (in certain cases, to cities of 30,000 or over). The National Association of County Officers, once oriented primarily toward rural problems, is beginning to reflect the attitudes of urban counties and is now often found united with the above organizations in working for legislation of interest to urban areas. The International City Managers' Association has recently moved its headquarters to Washington and several large cities maintain their own representatives in the nation's capitol on a permanent basis. This by no means exhausts the list of urban organizations in Washington, but it is an indication of the concern cities have about national government activities.

In addition to organizational representatives, it is becoming common for mayors, city managers, and other urban officials to make frequent trips to Washington to appear at congressional hearings, search for federal aid, and confer on special problems. In most cities, even relatively small ones, it would make an interesting study to determine how many trips are made to Washington by city officials in any given year.

HUD

At least as early as 1912 it had been recommended that a Department of Municipalities be established in the President's cabinet, and the subject was of continuing interest to students of local government thereafter. At various times proposals were made for a Department of Civic Economy, Department of Urbiculture, Department of Community Development, Department of Urban Affairs and Department of Housing and Urban Affairs. Cynics suggested such an agency might be called the Department of Urban and Metropolitan Problems, and it could then be known by its initials, DUMP!

Regardless of the name, the issue had become a topic of serious discussion by the 1950's. Bills providing for establishment of such a department were introduced at every congressional session beginning with the 84th Congress, and support for such a department became part of the official policy of the American Municipal Association and many other urban oriented organizations. Although President Eisenhower was cool to the idea, the Democratic platform of 1960 and the Kennedy administration supported the proposal. The National Association of Manufacturers and a large segment of the business community opposed the plan, evidently fearing that a department of this nature would lead to large increases in national government expenditures on urban projects.

Supporters of the department argued that as the nation became urbanized a department devoted to city problems was as necessary as a Department of Agriculture had been for a rural nation. Also, it was evident that the national government was establishing many programs of aid to cities and that these were scattered among many different agencies, so establishment of an urban affairs department would provide a single agency to supervise and coordinate the many programs of this type. The need for an office to support research and serve as a center for information was also mentioned. Finally the political argument was made. The cities needed a voice in the national government, and it was obvious that a cabinet level office would have much more prestige and influence than a special commission, presidential assistant, or sub-cabinet level office devoted to urban matters.

A good case was also made by those opposing the department idea. In the first place it was pointed out that the comparison with the Department of Agriculture was not entirely valid because that department is organized, like other departments, on the basis of a single function, the economic activity of agriculture. A Department of Urban Affairs, on the other hand, would be organized strictly on the basis of geography. There was also a strong fear that establishment of the department might lead to increased centralization of governmental powers. It was recognized that a cabinet department might increase rather than decrease administrative conflict because other agencies could not be expected to give up the urban functions to a new department without opposition. It was suggested finally that there were other ways of providing for an urban voice in the national government, such as a special commission or council devoted to urban problems.

As the debate went on during the late 1950's and early 1960's foundations for the new department were already being laid, for the Housing and Home Finance Agency was steadily expanding its scope of activities to include many urban functions besides housing, and it became obvious that if a department were established the HHFA would be one of its most important units. This became an issue in the battle because Dr. Robert C. Weaver, head of HHFA, was a Negro and many southern congressmen were not happy at the idea of a potential Negro cabinet member.

The debate ended with the creation of the Department of Housing and Urban Development in 1965, and as many had expected Weaver became the first secretary. Transferred to the department were the duties of HHFA, including the Community Facilities Administration, Urban Renewal Administration, Public Housing Administration, and the Federal National Mortgage Association. The creation within the department of the offices of Assistant Secretary for Metropolitan Development and Assistant Secretary for Demonstrations and Intergovernmental Relations indicates that much attention would be given to metropolitan areas and the problems of the role of local governments in the federal system. Although many functions will be placed under HUD, it will by no means be the only agency dealing with urban problems. The Department of Commerce, Public Health Service, Health, Education and Welfare, and the proposed Department of Transportation if established, to name only a few, would continue to be actively engaged in certain functions in urban regions.

ACIR

Another agency which is rapidly gaining a position of responsibility in the national government is the Advisory Commission on Intergovernmental Relations created by Congress in 1959 to make studies and recommendations in the general area implied by the title. The commission's membership of twenty-six include: nine officials of the national government (including six from Congress), fourteen from state and local governments, and three public members. The commission has built a highly competent professional staff and has prepared a series of special studies and recommendations concerning metropolitan areas, the federal system, interstate relations, and related problems. Because of the respect which the commission has earned, its pronouncements have the ear of both the White House and Congress. Professor Deil S. Wright suggests that the general policy orientation reflected in commission statements and recommendations appears to be[9] (1) support of a system of cooperative federalism; (2) preference for decentralization in decision-making whenever possible; (3) a preference for general purpose rather than special

---

[9] Deil S. Wright, "The Advisory Commission on Intergovernmental Relations: Unique Features and Policy Orientation," *Public Administration Review,* Vol. XXV. No. 3 (Sept., 1965), pp. 193–202; also see Daniel J. Elazer, "The Continuing Study of the Partnership: The Publications of the Advisory Commission on Intergovernmental Relations," *Public Administration Review,* Vol. XXVI, No. 1 (Mar., 1966), pp. 56–68.

purpose governments; (4) a belief in the responsibility of the national government to encourage and foster programs of state-local action; (5) a special interest in the problems of urban and metropolitan areas.

THE FUTURE OF FEDERALISM

There is little doubt that the now popular term "marble cake federalism" is descriptive of our present federal system in which the three levels of government mesh together and function through intricate interrelationships rather than operating as three distinct governmental layers. The growth of our metropolitan areas, the increase in direct national-local relationships, the vast system of federal grants-in-aid, and the creation of HUD have all contributed to the evolution of this system.

In the future this working relationship will have its greatest effect on metropolitan areas. One effect will simply be the increasing availability of funds to apply to the problems of these areas. Another will be the role of HUD in providing research and experimentation to give urban governments new ideas and know-how. Still another will be the growth of intergovernmental cooperation fostered by federal programs which makes such cooperation a requirement for receiving financial aid.

A major difficulty that is currently appearing is the inadequacy of coordination among the many urban programs of the national government. The freeway program conflicts with the open space program, while the federally aided airport and the federally aided housing project are built next to one another, and each is a nuisance to the other. The creation of HUD should help with the problem of coordination but there is a big job to do.

Many of the unanswered questions about the future of the federal system concern the part to be played by the states. Should all funds from the national government be channeled through the state so that the state government can provide direction and coordination or does this merely add an unnecessary bureaucratic middle man to the grant-in-aid system? Should states create their own HUD-like departments of urban affairs? Regardless of the answers to these questions the state need not fret about becoming archaic. Traditional functions such as education and highway construction will continue to be primary responsibilities of the state. In addition reapportioned legislatures have the opportunity to take positive action to facilitate the operations of governments in metropolitan areas. Provision for state collection of local taxes can be a help to both local governments and those who pay the taxes. State laws simplifying annexation procedures and restricting new incorporations would help stop the proliferation of urban governments. State statutes or constitutional amendments making it possible for governments in metropolitan areas to cooperate through federation, regional councils, consolidations, or other plans would make it possible for metropolitan areas to work out systems for local cooperation. The recommendations of ACIR have consistently urged an important role for the states in approaching metropolitan area problems. In short, the extent of participation by the states in our dynamic federal system is limited only by their own imaginativeness and willingness to take action.

Suggested Readings

Bollens, John C., *The States and the Metropolitan Problem* (Chicago: Council of State Governments, 1956).

Connery, Robert H., and Richard H. Leach, *The Federal Government and Metropolitan Areas* (Cambridge: Harvard University Press, 1960).

Goldwin, Robert A., (ed.), *A Nation of States* (Chicago: Rand McNally and Company, 1963). A series of essays on the federal system.

Graves, W. Brook, *American Intergovernmental Relations* (New York: Charles Scribner's Sons, 1964). An encyclopedic study of the subject.

Maass, Arthur, (ed.), *Area and Power, A Theory of Local Government* (New York: Free Press, 1959).

Martin, Roscoe C., *The Cities and the Federal System* (New York: Atherton Press, 1965). The most complete study yet of the role of the cities in mid-twentieth century federalism.

chapter 9

Financing Metropolis

By any measure city government is big business. In 1965 city governments in the United States received revenues of over twenty billion dollars, double their budgets of just a decade earlier. City revenues and expenditures for years have been rising faster in percentage terms than those of the national government although they still trail school districts, which have the dubious honor of recording the most rapid rise in revenues and expenditures of all governmental units. In most parts of the country private and secondary education is administered and financed by independent school districts, so most of the rising cost in this area is not directly reflected in city budgets. Even without this cost, however, increasing population with its accompanying social and economic problems as well as the constant demand for more and better services has placed a strain on the financial resources of the cities.

CITY REVENUES

The Traditional Sources

Historically the property tax has been the primary revenue source for local governments, especially so since the depression of the early 30's when many states abandoned this tax as a source of state revenue and left it to the counties, municipalities, and school districts. As revenue needs have increased, the cities have supplemented this source with other revenues, including general and selective sales taxes, special fees and charges, and intergovernmental revenues.

The Property Tax. The property tax is theoretically a tax levied against all property. In reality it usually reaches mainly land and buildings, with tangible property (furniture, appliances, jewelry, etc.) and intangible personal property (stocks, bonds, mortgages, etc.) either going untaxed or being taxed in an unsystematic and "catch as catch can" way in many states. The administration of the tax involves three steps: assessment, establishment of the tax rate, and collection.

Assessment, i.e. placing a value on property for tax purposes, is the responsibility of a city or county assessor who is usually elected and often has little formal training in the job of property assessment. In addition to the problem of lack of training, the office of assessor is especially susceptible to pressure and attempts at corruption since the decisions made there affect the amount of taxes people pay. Consequently the office of assessor has had a stormy history and has come in for much criticism by students of government, economics, and taxation.

The tax rate is set by the legislative body of the taxing unit (the city council in the case of cities). To illustrate, if the assessed valuation of property in a city were one million dollars and the council determined that it needed to raise twenty thousand dollars from the property tax, the tax rate would be set at two dollars on each one hundred dollars of assessed valuation. The owner of property assessed at five thousand dollars would then have to pay a property tax of one hundred dollars. After the tax rate is established, collection is usually the responsibility of a city or county collector. Since a piece of property will often be taxed by several different governmental units—county, city, school district, etc.—it is the practice in many states for a single agency, often the county collector or county treasurer, to collect all the tax and then distribute it to the various governments. This way the taxpayer pays his total amount at one time instead of having to pay separate amounts to each individual government.

The property tax has long been the largest single source of revenue for local governments. As Table I indicates it produced three billion seven hundred sixty-seven million dollars in 1955 and six billion five hundred thirty-seven million dollars in 1965. Although the dollar amounts are increasing, the percentage of total city revenues coming from the tax is gradually decreasing. Ont reason for this is that cities have reached out for new taxes in an attempt to meet their needs. Another is that property tax revenues do not respond to growth of the economy as rapidly as other taxes, such as general and selective sales taxes and the income tax.

The property tax has been the target of much criticism by students of taxation. They have pointed out that assessed values often have little relation to real values; that assessors are usually elected and thus may be guided by political considerations in setting assessments; that property assessment is a complex task for which many assessors are not trained; and that the tax usually discriminates against those whose wealth is in the form of real rather than personal property. It is also true that today the property tax is not closely related to ability to pay, and, in many cases, it is probably actually regressive. Although these criticisms are certainly justified in many cases, the property tax appears destined to remain an important source of revenue for municipalities. There are several reasons for this. First, even though the percentage of local revenue coming from

Table I

CITY REVENUE SOURCES*
(Dollar amounts in millions)

	1965		1955	
Total Revenues	$20,318	100.00%	$10,227	100.00%
General Revenues	15,884	78.18%	7,824	76.50%
Intergov'tal Revenues	3,534	17.39%	1,438	14.06%
From State	2,745	13.51%	1,236	12.09%
From Federal	557	2.74%	NA	NA
From other Local	232	1.14%	NA	NA
Taxes	9,289	45.72%	5,100	49.87%
Property	6,537	32.17%	3,767	36.83%
General Sales	1,184	5.83%	433	4.23%
Selective Sales	611	3.01%	295	2.88%
Other	957	4.71%	606	5.93%
Charges & Misc.	3,061	15.07%	1,285	12.56%
Utility Revenue	3,760	18.51%	2,080	20.34%
Liquor Stores	92	.45%	57	.56%
Insurance Trust	582	2.86%	267	2.61%

* Figures may not add because of rounding
Source: U.S. Bureau of the Census, *City Government Finances in 1955*
U.S. Bureau of the Census, *City Government Finances in 1965*

this tax is declining, it continues to be a major source of revenue for local governments, and it is unlikely that a substitute source capable of providing equal amounts could be found. Second, it is one tax that can be levied and collected with relative efficiency at the local level. Finally, the force of inertia will probably help to retain the tax since it now exists, and, in the minds of many, "any old tax is a good tax and any new tax is a bad tax."

The Sales Tax. The sales tax is ordinarily a tax levied on retail sales and collected by the retailer. This has been a very important revenue producer for state governments since the 1930's, but municipalities in some states are also beginning to levy a retail sales tax. In states where muncipalities are authorized to levy a general sales tax, the state will commonly levy a tax of two or three cents on the dollar and the municipality will levy a tax of one-half or one per cent on top of that. In some states, like Illinois and California, the state will collect the municipal sales tax along with its own, making it simpler for the retail merchant to pay the tax as well as provide a service to the muncipalities. The state collecting agency then distributes the funds to the cities in which they were collected.

Sales taxes may be either general or selective. A general sales tax applies to nearly all retail sales. A selective sales tax applies to only certain items. A tax of so many cents per gallon on gas or per carton on cigarettes would be examples of the latter. Sales taxes are attractive because they are good revenue producers, and they arouse little resistance from the public since people do not seem to protest a tax of a few cents here and a few cents there. On the other hand, the total sales tax load has now reached five per cent in a few states, and there is surely some point at which there will be a public reaction. A few cents here and there is one thing; a nickle or a dime here and there is another. Sales taxes have become one of the main sources of city revenues, with general and selective sales taxes providing almost nine per cent of all city revenues in 1965.

A criticism often heard of the sales tax is that it is regressive. Because those in low income categories must spend most of their earnings on necessities such as food, clothing, and shelter, they are the ones who are hardest hit by a sales tax. A low sales tax that is part of an overall progressive tax system may not be too vulnerable to this charge, but the higher the sales tax rises the more valid the criticism becomes.

One criticism of the municipal sales tax, especially in metropolitan areas, is that it may tend to "drive business out of town." If one city has a sales tax and nearby cities do not, people may trade in the neighboring cities to avoid the tax. This will not happen on small purchases because the potential saving is too small, but it may occur on larger purchases such as automobiles or major appliances. In metropolitan areas where some municipalities have a sales tax and some do not, this can lead to marketing battles among merchants, where some will advertise, "Buy your new car in Village Meadows and avoid the sales tax." An approach to eliminating this problem is the enactment of a use tax, usually set at the same level as the sales tax and levied against items bought outside the city but brought into the city for use. A use tax is almost impossible for a city to enforce on purchases of appliances or smaller items, but it can be enforced on auto purchases because the purchaser ordinarily must give his address in applying for a car license. This assumes that the state auto license agency will cooperate with cities in enforcement.

Fees and Charges. Certain services provided by municipalities lend themselves well to financing on a fee basis. Water, sewers, municipal golf courses, toll bridges, parking lots, and city owned utilities commonly fall into this category. Fees are much like taxes if the citizen has no choice about paying them. This is often the case, as when he must pay a monthly amount for garbage collection or sewage disposal and does not have the option of not using the service. On the other hand, there are many instances where the amount paid depends on how much the individual chooses to use a given service. One's water bill will be affected by whether he chooses to water his lawn every day or once a week, and he also decides for himself whether he wants to use the municipal golf course.

Fees and charges have the advantage of placing the costs of services on the users and thus removing them from the shoulders of the general taxpayer. They also have the advantage of linking costs and benefits, something which cannot be done where services are financed out of general tax revenues. This makes it possible for officials to determine whether a particular service is carrying its own weight financially and adjust fees accordingly. Of course there may be times when officials want to set fees below cost in order to encourage use of a service. The costs of public subway or bus transportation, for example, may intentionally be kept low if officials believe that it costs less to subsidize a loss on public transportation than it would cost to build the streets and freeways necessary if those people decided to drive to work.

The use of fees also discourages waste on the part of the user. It would be possible to finance water costs out of general tax revenues or by levying a flat rate fee (in fact, some cities do it this way), but where this is the case there is no incentive to remember to turn off the water sprinkler or get the leaky faucet fixed. The use of a fee based on amount used encourages the consumer to use the service efficiently and to save where possible.

In summary, the use of fees is advantageous where they can be efficiently collected, where the benefits accrue solely or primarily to those who pay the fees, and where the service might be wasted if a charge were not made. This method of financing is generally popular with the taxpayer since it is based on the principal that those who use a service pay for it. In 1965 over fifteen per cent of city revenues came from general fees and charges, and another eighteen per cent came from fees charged by municipally owned utilities. In both cases most of this money is not available for general use but goes directly to finance the service producing the revenue.

Intergovernmental Revenues. An increasingly important factor in city financing is the money received from state and national governments. At the national level the grant-in-aid system discussed in the preceding chapter is the most important means for providing financial assistance to local governments. As mentioned previously, the fact that the national government seems to have access to more taxable resources, the necessity of equalizing resources and needs, and the desire to provide incentive to local governments motivated the national program of grants-in-aid. The figures in Table I do not indicate the full impact of national funds on local finances since such funds are sometimes channeled through the state, and many times national aid to states equals or surpasses the amount of state aid to local governments, thus influencing state ability to provide local aid.

An alternative to providing assistance through grants-in-aid is the use of shared revenues, a technique employed by many states. Many states return a certain percentage of the income tax, sales tax, gas tax, or other taxes to local governments. This varies from the grant-in-aid system in that shared revenues are usually returned to their point of origin without reference to matching funds or other requirements; in addition, they are not tied to specific projects and thus may be spent as desired. An exception to this is shared gas tax revenues which are often earmarked for use on streets and highways.

Shared taxes are economical to administer since the entire process is handled by the state. They give municipalities the advantage of access to a tax source that they might not have otherwise, and there is the added benefit for city officials of receiving revenues without the usual accompanying political burden of having to levy taxes. Shared taxes are levied by the state, and the formula determining the amount to be returned to municipalities is set by the state. This can occasionally be hazardous for municipalities because it means that in times of economic crisis, just when they need funds the most, the state may choose to cut the cities out and retain the entire amount for state functions. Especially significant is the fact that the shared revenue approach is usually used with taxes that are highly responsive to economic expansion and are therefore good revenue producers.

Closely related to shared revenues is the principle of state collection of local taxes mentioned above. The main difference is that with the latter the decision about levying the tax remains with the municipality and the state acts merely as the collecting agency.

The Newer Sources

The greatest amount of city revenue comes from the sources discussed above, but two other sources should be given some attention. One is the municipal income tax, already in use in many cities. The other is the Heller plan, not yet a reality but under discussion in Congress.

Municipal Income Tax. Beginning with Philadelphia in 1940 and Toledo in 1946, about five hundred cities have enacted municipal income taxes up to the present time.[1] The tax is often called an earnings tax because it is usually a tax on corporate and personal earnings rather than

---

[1] The best source of information on the municipal income tax is Robert A. Sigafoos, *The Municipal Income Tax: Its History and Problems* (Chicago: Public Administration Service, 1955).

on income. Unearned income in the form of rents, interest, dividends, and capital gains is usually excluded.

Several characteristics are common to municipal income taxes: (1) as mentioned, they are levied against earnings rather than total income; (2) there are ordinarily no exemptions, exclusions, or deductions such as are found in state and national income taxes; (3) it is usually a flat rate tax of one-half or one per cent; (4) it is levied on all earnings within the city limits regardless of where the recipient lives and also on the income of residents earned outside the city.

These facts make it obvious that the tax is meant to be simply a revenue producer and not an instrument for such social policies as income redistribution. Because of this these taxes have usually faced the opposition of organized labor and other groups with a similar point of view, making it difficult to secure passage in those cities where adoption is dependent on a general referendum. On the other hand, the main selling point of the tax is that the suburban dwellers will help pay it. Because it is levied on income earned in the city without regard to the residence of the earner, a large portion of it will be paid by those who live in the suburbs and drive into the city to work.

Some suburban communities have retaliated by levying earnings taxes of their own. This creates the possibility of an individual being taxed twice, by the city in which he works and by the city in which he lives. To avoid this danger over half of the cities levying the tax have reciprocity agreements with other nearby cities that also levy it. The city of Toledo, for example, has an agreement with neighboring cities whereby the tax is paid only once, and the amount is then shared equally by the city of residence and the city of employment.

Because cities may levy an income tax only when authorized by the state, nearly all the cities are located in a few states, mainly Pennsylvania and Ohio. Besides Philadelphia and Toledo, other larger cities with a tax of this nature are Detroit, Louisville, St. Louis, and Kansas City. The tax has only two primary advantages: it is a good revenue producer and it enables the central city to tax the suburbanite. These two facts make the tax sufficiently attractive that we may expect to see it spread gradually to other cities. One thing which might change the picture would be enactment by the national government of the Heller plan, which could alter the form in which cities would receive revenue from taxes on income. Let us turn now to a discussion of this plan.

The Heller Plan. The Heller plan is essentially an attempt to apply the shared revenues principle at the national level. Professor Walter W. Heller, professor of economics at the University of Minnesota and former chairman of the President's Council of Economic Advisors under Kennedy and

Johnson, has proposed that some portion of the national income tax revenue, perhaps one per cent, be returned to the states for use as they see fit.[2] Details have not been worked out, but there seems to be some general agreement among those discussing the idea on these points: (1) each year the national government would place in a special trust fund a certain percentage of income tax revenues for distribution to the states; (2) the funds would be returned to the states with no or few limitations. Some have suggested limits which would prevent use of the funds for highway construction and certain other functions that already receive large amounts of federal aid. Other suggested limitations are that a stated minimum amount must be spent on education or that a certain minimum amount must be redistributed by states to the municipalities and school districts; (3) most of the funds would be distributed on some basis such as population or point of origin, but some portion, perhaps twenty or twenty-five per cent, would be distributed on a formula based on need.

This proposal has evoked mixed reactions. Advocates like the fact that this plan would make available to state and local governments funds from what most people agree to be the most progressive and fairest tax in the federal tax system. By attaching few requirements the plan would strengthen the decision-making process at the state and local level and widen the flexibility and latitude of these governments. At the same time critics question whether this is good or bad. They believe that the past record of state governments and state legislatures has not shown that they are capable of spending wisely this large new source of funds. They prefer to channel any new revenues into the traditional system of grants for specific programs in which standards and regulations can be imposed.

In discussing city revenues it should be pointed out that enactment of the Heller plan would not necessarily make new funds available for cities. This would depend entirely on the form in which the plan is adopted. If a requirement were written in that a certain amount must be redistributed by the states to municipalities this would assure them of help. Otherwise the extent of help received would depend on the attitudes of the legislature in each state. Various forms of the plan have been introduced in Congress, but no action has yet been taken.

A variation of the Heller plan has been recommended by Mayor Schmied of Louisville. He suggests that cities be allowed to levy a small gross income tax of one or two per cent to be paid directly to the city. The tax would then be deductible from the amount of federal income tax

---

[2] For a general discussion of the concepts embodied in the Heller Plan see Harvey E. Brazer, "Our Hard Pressed State and Local Governments," *Challenge,* Vol. XIV, Nov. 3 (Jan.-Feb. 1966) pp. 7–9, 41; *Congressional Record,* Appendix, August 25, 1965, pp. PA4780–81.

which the individual owes. This would leave administration of the tax at the local level and would allow each city to decide whether it wanted the tax.[3] It is safe to say that nearly all cities would want it, but there would probably be a few that would not.

CITY EXPENDITURES

The figures for city expenditures in 1955 and 1965 are shown in Table II. Although the table shows cities spending somewhat over twelve per

Table II

CITY EXPENDITURES

(Dollar amounts in millions)

	1965		1955	
Total Expenditures	$20,680	100.00%	$8,363	100.00%
General Expenditures	16,012	77.43%	6,524	78.01%
Education	2,489	12.04%	1,103	13.19%
Highways	1,807	8.74%	720	8.60%
Public Welfare	927	4.48%	470	5.62%
Hospitals Health	1,115	5.39%	546	6.53%
Police Protection	1,739	8.41%	681	8.14%
Fire Protection	1,146	5.54%	495	5.92%
Sewerage & Sanitation	1,774	8.58%	731	8.74%
Parks & Recreation	775	3.75%	323	3.86%
Housing & Urban Ren.	686	3.32%	205	2.45%
Airports	182	.88%	60	.72%
Water Tran. & Term.	73	.35%	40	.48%
Parking	94	.45%	42	.50%
Libraries	267	1.29%	102	1.22%
Gen. Govt.	1,088	5.26%	392	4.69%
Interest	603	2.92%	209	2.50%
Other	1,247	6.03%	404	4.83%
Utilities	3,966	19.18%	1,541	18.43%
Water	1,820	8.80%	689	8.24%
Electric	1,291	6.24%	366	4.38%
Transit	662	3.20%	444	5.31%
Gas	193	.93%	43	.51%
Liquor Store Exp's	78	.38%	11	.13%
Insurance Trust	624	3.02%	288	3.44%

Source: U.S. Bureau of the Census, *City Government Finances in 1955*
U.S. Bureau of the Census, *City Government Finances in 1965*

[3] Speech before the Southern Conference of the Council of State Governments, Houston, Texas, July 21, 1966.

cent of their expenditures for education, this is misleading. In the first place most cities spend little or nothing on education because the function is the responsibility of an independent school district whose budget is separate from that of the city. Second, the few cities that do operate school systems spend far more than twelve per cent of their budgets on education. In 1965 New York City used twenty-six per cent of its total expenditures to operate its schools, and in Washington, D. C., the figure was about twenty-two per cent.

The most interesting point revealed by the data in Table II is how little the proportionate amounts have changed in the ten year period. With the exception of the "other" category, the share of the total allotted to each function was within one percentage point of the share alloted to that function a decade earlier. This may indicate the extent to which inflexibility is built into city budgets through state restrictions, earmarked revenues and the like. It may also reflect the fact that department heads come to think in terms of their "rightful share of the pie," and it thus becomes very hard to make meaningful changes in the budget. In any case, it is obvious that all of the talk about new emphasis in local government, such as the shift in interest from physical and engineering problems to human problems, is not reflected in the expenditures of city dollars up to 1965.

CITY INDEBTEDNESS

Cities have found it virtually impossible in recent years to operate on a pay-as-you-go basis. Huge expenditures, especially for capital outlays, have caused the cities to have to borrow large amounts. In 1965 the total indebtedness of city governments was thirty-one billion eight hundred sixty-two million dollars, more than double the 1955 total of thirteen billion one hundred eighty million dollars. Most municipal indebtedness is in the form of either general obligation bonds or revenue bonds.

The most common means of borrowing funds for general municipal purposes—municipal buildings, fire fighting equipment, parks, etc.—is the issuance of general obligation bonds. Such bonds are ordinarily retired from property tax funds. These bonds are referred to as "general obligation" or "full faith and credit," bonds because they are guaranteed by the full taxing power of the government unit issuing them.

Revenue bonds are bonds which are issued to finance a revenue producing facility, such as a public utility, airport, turnpike, or toll bridge. Revenue bonds are usually secured solely by the revenues of the facility for which they were issued, and if these revenues are not sufficient to cover repayment of the bonds, the related governmental unit is not obligated to provide tax funds for repayment. Because these bonds are not tax secured, they represent somewhat greater risk for the investor than general obligation bonds, and therefore they often must bear a higher interest rate than would general obligation securities.

Debt Limits

Every state places either statutory or constitutional limits on the powers of local governments to incur debt.[4] This reflects a historic interest on the part of states in the financial well being of their local governments and also is probably illustrative of the conservative posture which Martin says is typical of state governments. There are five common types of limits used by the states, the most common of which is a limit on the maximum amount of debt which a municipality may incur. The amount of debt that local governments are allowed to incur is usually stated as a percentage of assessed valuation. About thirty states have constitutional provisions of this nature, with the limits ranging from 1.5 per cent to 25 per cent of assessed valuation. The most generally used figure is 5 per cent, with eleven states fixing the limit at this amount. Limits based on assessed valuation usually apply only to general obligation bonds since revenue bonds are not related to property values or property taxes.

A second type of limit used by states is a maximum time limit on the maturity of the bonds. Examples would be limits of twenty years (Illinois), twenty-five years (Oklahoma), thirty-four years (West Virginia), and forty years (Kentucky). A third type is a limit on the interest rate that bonds of local government may bear. Such a limit allows the impersonal forces of the bond market to limit the amount of debt that local governments may incur. If a local government may pay only four per cent on its bonds, there is a limit to the amount of bonds the government is able to sell at that rate or lower. Municipalities are generally allowed to pay somewhat higher interest rates on revenue bonds than on general obligation bonds because of the greater risk involved.

Over half the states employ a fourth type of limit, a restriction on the purposes for which indebtedness may be incurred. State constitutions often say that municipal debt must be for "public purposes" and specifically prohibit the incurring of debt for the purpose of subscribing to stock of, or otherwise aiding, private corporations. This type of limit dates back to the times when cities often borrowed in order to attempt to lure the railroad through town.

---

[4] See Leonard E. Goodall, *State Regulation of Local Indebtedness in the United States* (Tempe: Arizona State University, Bureau of Government Research, 1964).

Finally, many states require that local bond issues be approved by the voters in a referendum. Referendum elections are most often required to authorize local governments to exceed the established debt limits, but a few states require voter approval on all local bond issues.

Administrative Regulation

The techniques for state regulation of local debt have often been criticized for being inflexible and tied to unrealistic measurement standards such as assessed valuation of property. A number of states have attempted to overcome this problem by moving in the direction of state administrative supervision of municipal indebtedness. The best example of this approach is North Carolina. In that state the Local Government Commission, a nine-man state board, must approve all proposed local bond issues and also supervise the sale of all local securities. Administrative supervision is much more flexible than the more traditional types of limits and makes it possible to give considerations to specific problems, current monetary conditions, and other factors that are subject to change. Massachusetts, Indiana, New Jersey, and Michigan are other states that use various types of administrative supervision to regulate municipal indebtedness.

THE BUDGET PROCESS

Although the budget process varies from city to city, it generally proceeds through four steps: preparation, review, adoption, and administration. Budget preparation is usually the responsibility of the chief administrative officer of the city, either the city manager or the mayor. It is his responsibility to make estimates of revenues, get requests from the various department heads, decide where to recommend reductions if necessary, and present a recommended budget to the city council. In some cases the council will have provided some general policy direction by saying that this year they want to place special emphasis on police protection or recreation or whatever. At other times no such direction is given, and the executive must simply try to guess what kind of budget the council will accept.

There is a degree of difference between the role of a city manager and that of a strong mayor in budget formulation. A strong mayor is expected to provide policy leadership, and the budget is one of the tools by which he does this. He prepares the budget so as to give priority to his policy preferences and then attempts to use his persuasive powers to secure adoption by the council. A city manager on the other hand, as an appointee of the council, must be more cautious. He must attempt to discern the views of his council and to prepare the budget with those views in mind. He must be careful about the extent to which he attempts to reflect his own policy preferences in the budget. This does not mean that the manager must pretend to be completely neutral or that he cannot make policy recommendations, but he must be careful to perform this function in a more subtle manner and he must have a good working knowledge of his council in order to understand just how far they expect him to go in this direction.

After the budget is prepared, it is presented to the council for review and adoption. The council will hold hearings at which the city manager or budget director and sometimes department heads will answer questions about the budget. The exact procedure will vary from city to city. In some cities councilmen will be actively involved in preparing the budget by sitting in on conferences between the budget officials and department heads as each departmental budget is prepared. In such cases the councilmen are very familiar with the budget by the time it is presented to them. In other cities budget preparation will have been done entirely by the chief executive and his budget staff, and the councilmen will see the budget for the first time after preparation is completed. In the latter case, the hearings are much more important, because this is the first time the council has had an opportunity to review and discuss the budget.

In many cities it is required that a public hearing on the budget be held at which time any citizen may express his opinions. The amazing thing is the minute amount of public participation in the budget process. Very few citizens ever take an active part in the hearings, and as a rule "public" participation at the hearings consists of comments by representatives of the Chamber of Commerce, taxpayer organizations, and major taxpayers such as utilities or banks. After hearings are held and the council has reviewed the budget, it will usually make some changes in the various amounts provided for in the budget. The changes though are likely to be very minor.

In recent years we have heard much about incremental budgeting and zero based budgeting. Incremental budgeting means that the amount approved in the preceding year's budget is accepted as a given, and the budget process revolves around the amount of increase. If the police department had a seven hundred thousand dollar budget last year and they want seven hundred sixty-five thousand dollars this year, discussions will focus on the need for and use of the additional sixty-five thousand dollars with little time or attention given to the seven hundred thousand dollars. Without doubt this is how the budget process operates in most cities. There are actually some cases where the only figures the councilmen want to see are the amount of change from last year for each department.

Zero based budgeting, in contrast, means that each department head must assume that he starts from zero in preparing his budget request and justify the entire amount. Zero based budgeting, like performance budgeting and program budgeting, is being experimented with in some jurisdictions, but the vast majority of city budgets are still prepared on an incremental basis and probably will continue to be. Zero based budgeting is more difficult and time consuming than the incremental method and also more likely to evoke conflict since approval of entire budgets requires that councils make basic choices between programs and departments in allotting funds. The incremental system, by providing just about everyone with "a little more than last year" minimizes conflict and makes the decisions of the council much easier.

After hearings and review the council will ordinarily make a few changes and then officially adopt the budget. After adoption the last step in the budget process is budget administration, sometimes called budget execution. This involves seeing that the funds are spent properly and for the items for which they were budgeted. Budget administration is commonly the responsibility of a budget director, finance director, or city treasurer. Departments are often given their appropriate funds in monthly or quarterly allotments so as to assure that they do not spend their entire appropriation early in the fiscal year. The allotments may be equal or they may vary according to need. A parks and recreation department may want most of its funds allotted during the summer months while the public works department will need the bulk of its snow removal appropriations during the winter.

While we have discussed the budget process as if it were a number of discrete steps, it should be noted that it is actually a continual process. It is likely that the current year's budget is in the allocation and administration stage while next year's budget is being prepared and last year's is being audited.

THE CITY-SUBURB CONFLICT

Officials of central cities have long believed that they are subsidizing their suburban neighbors. According to this theory, the suburbanite who works in the central city drives to work on the city's streets, expects police and fire protection to be provided by the city while he is there, and brings his children to the city zoo or city park on the weekend, but he lives and pays taxes in the suburb. Also since the low income sections of the metropolitan area are usually concentrated in the central city, it is suggested that the suburban dweller is not carrying his fair share of the welfare costs of the metropolitan area. The municipal earnings tax has been adopted by many cities in an attempt to tax the suburbanite, and it is often sold to the city population on precisely this point. It has also been suggested that consolidation of the various governments into a single jurisdiction would spread the tax load over a wider area and relieve the burden of the central city taxpayer.

Recent research suggests that the problem of subsidization is not a major one.[5] A study in California and another in the Minneapolis-St. Paul area showed that while some subsidization does occur the amount is very small and tends to diminish even further as the suburbs mature and develop their own tax generating economy which contributes to the central city as well as to the suburbs.

Studies have also shown that the subsidization pattern occurs only if education costs are excluded from consideration. Suburban taxpayers commonly pay higher school taxes and still receive a smaller per-pupil expenditure for education than city dwellers. This is explained by the fact that the suburbs are inhabited primarily by young families with children of school age, while the central city has more family units without school age children and also is the location of most heavy industry, large warehouses, and commercial establishments which contribute greatly to the tax base but do not directly add children to the school system. If the various governmental units in a metropolitan area, including school districts, were to be consolidated into a single jurisdiction, the city residents might find themselves subsidizing the suburban schools in the area rather than drawing in suburban tax dollars to help pay city bills. The debate over who is subsidizing whom in metropolitan areas will undoubtedly continue, but our present knowledge indicates that this is not nearly as significant a matter as many have believed it to be. Depending on the particular metropolitan area, it is likely that the financial benefits and costs involved in consolidation would just about balance out, with neither city nor suburbs being a big gainer.

---

[5] See James M. Banovetz, "Metropolitan Subsidies—An Appraisal," *Public Administration Review,* Vol. XXV, No. 4 (December, 1965), pp. 297–301.

Suggested Readings

Alderfer, H. F., and R. L. Funk, *Municipal Non-Property Taxes* (Chicago: Municipal Finance Officers Association, 1956).

Financing Metropolitan Government (Princeton: Tax Institute, Inc., 1955).

Measures of State and Local Fiscal Capacity and Tax Effort (Washington: Advisory Commission on Intergovernmental Relations, 1962).

Mosher, Frederick C. and Orville F. Polant, *The Costs of American Governments: Facts, Trends, Myths* (New York: Dodd, Mead & Company, 1964).

Sacks, Seymour, and William F. Hellmuth, Jr., *Financing Government in a Metropolitan Area: The Cleveland Experience* (New York: Free Press of Glencoe, 1961).

Sigafoos, R. A., *The Municipal Income Tax* (Chicago: Public Administration Service, 1955).

chapter 10

Planning in the
Metropolitan Area

Very few cities are fortunate enough to have had a comprehensive plan guiding their growth patterns from the
earliest periods of their existence. In 1791 Pierre L'En-
fant began the preparation of a general plan for Washington, D. C., the results of which are still evident in the
beauty of much of our capital city. About a century ago
Brigham Young prepared a plan for the growth of Salt
Lake City. Philadelphia, thanks to the foresight and work
of William Penn, is another city that had the benefit of
good planning in its initial years. In recent years the South
American country of Brazil has planned and built a new
capital city, Brazilia, from the ground up.

These cities, however, are exceptions to the rule. Most cities which
have made the decision to attempt to guide their growth and development
in accord with some basic planning decisions have had to impose the plan
on an existing situation. During much of the nineteenth century many
people looked upon city planning as an unwarranted invasion on private
property rights. It was believed that the owner of a piece of property
should be able to do as he pleased with it without restrictions. The resulting chaotic patterns of development in most cities caused many to realize
that city planning could be an instrument for the protection, more than
for the restriction, of property rights. Good planning and zoning laws
could assure the owner of a home that no one was going to build a factory
or tavern on the lot next to him. Good planning could give some indication of where future schools, streets and fire stations would be needed.
By the turn of the century recognition of the need for planning in cities
and towns was becoming more widespread. In 1908 Hartford, Connecticut, became the first city to have a planning and zoning commission.
Belief in city planning spread rapidly to other cities, and today over

ninety-five per cent of the cities of over ten thousand population in the United States have made provision for some department to be responsible for city planning.

THE PLANNING FUNCTION

City planning is not an easy concept to define. If one were to walk into most municipal buildings in the country, even those in cities where planning is well established, and ask to see the city plan, he would probably get a puzzled look. This is because the elements of city planning are likely to be found in many different places. Part of the plan might be in a zoning ordinance or in a map showing the various zoning districts of the community. Part of it may be in the five-year capital budget prepared by the city manager. Still other parts may be in a table of future populations or in a map prepared by school officials showing locations for schools that will be needed in the future. Many cities are now trying to bring all parts of the plan together in a single publication or series of publications, and when this is done a city has something specific to show the person who wants to see a city plan. The important point to be made here is that city planning consists of many elements. Whereas it was once considered to be little more than zoning, i.e. establishing a land-use pattern for the city, it is now recognized as a much broader concept. Planning involves the setting of goals by city officials and others to establish what they want the city to become. It includes gathering statistical data on city population, industrial development, employment, income, and similar matters, and making projections about what these indicators will show five, ten, or twenty years hence. It means using these data to estimate future needs for schools, sewers, fire stations, streets, and all other public facilities, as well as to direct private land use through zoning. It means making budget projections to determine the revenue and expenditure trends in the city. Since it is almost inevitable that a city will find that it cannot do everything it would like to do, it also means determining which problems appear most crucial and setting priorities for projects that are most needed.

City Planning Organization

The most common organization for the directing of the community planning function is a board of citizens known as a planning board, planning and zoning commission, or similar name. The boards commonly consist of from five to nine members who represent a cross section of the city's population. In earlier years, planning and zoning boards were often dominated by people in the real estate business, but most cities now make an effort to provide for representation of varied interests. The members often serve relatively long terms which are staggered so that there are always some experienced members on the board. In some cities the planning director, public works director, or budget officer are ex officio members of the commission. Students of city planning do not entirely agree on the role that the planning and zoning commission should play in local government. There are three alternative roles that are suggested: (1) planning should be the function of an independent planning and zoning commission; (2) planning should be a staff function of the chief executive (mayor or city manager), and planning personnel should be responsible to him; (3) planning should be a function of the city council, and the responsibility of planning personnel should be to the council.[1]

The Independent Planning and Zoning Commission. The first theory of planning to gain wide acceptance was that of the independent commission. Around the turn of the century, at the time when planning first became a subject of general interest to those involved in local government, city officials enjoyed a very poor reputation. This was the day of the big city political machine, and people considered city councilmen to be, at best, political hacks and, at worst, dishonest and corrupt. Because city governments had this reputation, those interested in city planning attempted to isolate planning from the rest of city government. They urged that planning be the responsibility of a planning and zoning board and that this board be as independent of the city council as possible. Although the board members were usually appointed by either the mayor or council, they enjoyed a considerable amount of independence in that their terms were usually longer than those of the mayor and council and they could not be removed from office until the end of their term.

According to this theory the board was to consist of prominent citizens of the community, and advocates of this approach suggested that removing the board as much as possible from city politics would make it easier to find able citizens who would be willing to serve. Planning and zoning decisions were to be made by the board under this approach. The board was to adopt a general plan, establish zoning regulations to implement the plan, and make the decisions concerning when exceptions to the plan and the zoning regulations could be granted. The city planning director and other personnel concerned with planning were to be appointed by the board. The city council had little, if anything, to do with planning in

[1] The material presented here on city planning organization originally appeared in substantially this same form in *Gearing Arizona's Communities to Orderly Growth* (Phoenix: Arizona Academy, 1965). Appreciation is expressed to the Arizona Academy for permission to use the material here.

cities operating under this system. In those cities where the council was given the power to override the board's decisions, it was common to require that the council could take such action only when considerably more than half the councilmen—it was common to require the affirmative votes of two-thirds or three-fourths of the councilmen—agreed to the move.

It is obvious that one of the basic reasons for the support of this plan was the distrust of city councils. Another reason was suggested by those who took a somewhat more charitable view of the ability and honesty of city officials. According to this group, even when the councilman wants to do a good job the nature of his position prevents him from taking the long-range view necessary in community planning. Professor T. J. Kent has described the positions of those holding this view:[2]

> First, since councilmen are elected for relatively short terms, and since immediate political pressures are always present and dominant in their minds, they cannot be expected to have any long-range objectives or policies of their own that will serve as a logical basis for the decisions they must make every week on so-called short-range matters. Second, since the situation just described is assumed to be true and unavoidable, some way must be found to force these publications to permit a group of wiser men, whose tenure the council is not supposed to control, to make a general plan for the city and to limit the freedom of the council to legislate on all matters affecting the physical development of the community.

Those of this view believed that the independent board accomplished their desired goals. Still another justification for the independent board was simply the time element. The city council must concern itself with so many pressing current matters, according to this view, that it does not have the time to consider the problems of long-range planning, a function better handled by an independent board concerned exclusively with that subject.

This concept of planning was the most widely accepted one down to about the time of World War II. Since then it has gradually declined in popularity.

Planning as a Staff Function. A second concept of planning is that those concerned with planning should serve as staff assistants to the chief executive (mayor or city manager). In this system, the planning director is usually appointed by the chief executive, and the planning and zoning board serves only as an advisory group. Of the three alternatives discussed here, this one envisions the least important role for the board. The im-

---

[2] T. J. Kent, Jr., *The Urban General Plan* (San Francisco: Chandler Publishing Co., 1964), p. 58.

portant responsibility here lies with the planning director who serves as an advisor directly to the chief exectuive. This approach grew out of the emphasis in public administration on centralized management, executive unity, and clear lines of authority and responsibility. This concept reflects a fear that placing power in an independent board will result in unnecessary dispersion of power and possible internal policy conflicts which could impair the effective operation of the city government. In this system the channel of communication between the board and the city council is through the office of the mayor or manager. The board and the planning director make recommendations to the chief executive, and he in turn presents his recommendations to the council. If he disagrees with the recommendation of the board or the planning director, he is under no obligation to pass thoughts on to the council.

Very few cities today operate under this approach in its pure form, although many cities use it with some modifications. It is not uncommon to find cities in which planning is the responsibility of one of the regular departments of the local government. The planning director is appointed by and responsible to the chief executive, and the board serves the department in an advisory capacity. It is not currently common, however, for the board to be isolated from the council. In many cities recommendations of the planning and zoning board go directly from the board to the council for its action.

Planning as a Function of the Council. The third approach to community planning sees the city council as having the primary responsibility for planning. In this system the board and the planning director (and his staff) serve as advisors both to the council and to the chief executive. The reasoning behind this approach is that the council is the policy making body of the community, and since day-to-day policy making should be closely related to long-range planning, the council should have the final say on important planning decisions. The planning director and his staff are responsible for providing surveys, data, and whatever other information the council and board feel they need. The board should concern itself with planning problems and make recommendations to the council. The council, according to this approach, should be the body that establishes the final planning policies for the city and, after having established them, should attempt to insure that its other decisions are in accord with the long-range plans of the city.

In practice, most cities do not fit neatly into any one of these three categories. The first concept has been dated and is to be found in a continually diminishing number of cities. Many cities which have reorganized their administrative structure in accordance with modern principles of management—in particular, those cities which have adopted the council-manager form of government—have experimented with the second approach, but few have adopted it in its most extreme form. Most cities appear to use some combination of the principles included in the second and third approaches, with the exact practice varying from city to city.

The Model City Charter, prepared by the National Municipal League, recommends basically the second approach. It provides for a planning director to be appointed by the city manager (the charter calls for a council-manager form of government) and for a city planning board to be appointed by the council. The council would serve in a strictly advisory capacity and its members would not be allowed to hold any other official position with the city. In other words there would be no city officials, such as the public works director or finance director, serving as ex officio members of the commission.[3]

Regional Planning

As with other governmental functions in the metropolitan area, city planning is a function that cannot be considered on a purely local basis without regard to neighboring municipalities. When numerous municipalities have common boundaries, as is often the case in metropolitan areas, planning decisions must give consideration to the situation in nearby communities. Otherwise industrial plants in one city will be located beside residential areas in the adjoining city, or a street that has four lanes in one city will have only two in the next. Cooperation between city and county on planning matters is also important because area that is in the county today may be annexed and become part of a city tomorrow.

In an attempt to cope with this situation regional planning commissions have been established in many metropolitan areas. The organization of the Twin Cities Metropolitan Planning Commission, created in 1957 to serve the Minneapolis-St. Paul area, is typical of many such commissions. Its membership consists of: (1) two members from each of the two central cities, one the mayor or his representative and the other appointed by the council; (2) one member from each of the seven counties; (3) seven representatives of the suburban municipalities; (4) one representative of the public schools; (5) one member for each of the two special-purpose public corporations in the area; (6) two representatives

---

[3] *Model City Charter,* 6th ed. (New York: National Municipal League, 1964), Article VI.

of the towns; (7) seven members appointed by the governor, with at least three of them coming from the central cities and not more than four belonging to the same political party.[4]

The four areas of responsibility assigned to the Metropolitan Planning Commission are also typical: research, metropolitan planning, assistance to local governments in the area, and coordination of local activities. The commissions ordinarily gather data and publish reports of trends concerning population, economic activities, transportation, utilities, and similar matters.

Perhaps the most frustrating activity of the commissions is regional planning. While nearly all such commissions have the responsibility for preparing a comprehensive plan for the area, they are seldom given sufficient legal power to implement it. The normal procedure is for the commission to publicize its plan as widely as possible and urge individual local governments to coordinate their own plans with the regional plan. The arm-twisting power of the commissions, however, is not great. They can sometimes bring a bit of bad publicity to a community that consistently ignores the regional plan, but there is little more they can do. Their authority rests mainly in their prestige in the area and in their ability to mobilize public opinion. Their ability to coordinate local government activities is likewise limited to their persuasive powers.

The increasing interest of the national government in metropolitan areas is likely to enhance the authority of regional planning commissions. Most recent legislation at the national level has required evidence of local planning in accordance with some comprehensive plan for the entire metropolitan area in order to qualify for grants-in-aid. The regional planning commissions are the logical bodies to provide leadership in the preparation of plans that will help local governments meet this requirement. Thus even if states or metropolitan areas do not give the commissions legal authority to enforce their plans, the national government may give them *de facto* power to do so by placing such requirements on local governments.

This development raises other questions. If the commissions move from a simple fact-gathering role to one in which they can directly affect local planning decisions through their influence over the purse strings, their organization and functions become crucial to the political process. They may have to be reorganized on a strict one man-one vote apportionment

---

[4] For a discussion of the Twin Cities Metropolitan Planning Commission, see Roscoe C. Martin, *Metropolis in Transition,* (Washington: Housing and Home Finance Agency, 1963), Chapter V.

system. The authority of local planning departments in relation to regional planning commissions will need clarification. If both a regional planning commission and some other organization for area-wide coordination, such as a regional council, exist in the same area, the relationship of the two will have to be worked out.

The National Government and Urban Planning

The national government's interest in orderly planning in urban areas is not new. As early as the 1920's Secretary of Commerce Herbert Hoover spearheaded an effort in his department to aid the planning efforts of municipalities. The result was a series of reports on urban planning, including a model zoning ordinance. More recently the interest of the national government has increased, and a number of national programs have given impetus to local planning. A brief look at three programs— the "701" program, the open space program, and the Highway Act of 1962—will provide an indication of the nature of the national government's interest in planning.

The "701" Program. The urban planning assistance program, known as the "701" program, was established by section 701 of the Housing Act of 1954. The program is administered by HUD. The purposes outlined in the act are to:

1. Assist state and local governments in solving problems resulting from the increasing concentration of population in metropolitan and other urban areas, including smaller communities.

2. Facilitate comprehensive planning for urban development, including coordinated transportation systems, on a continuing basis.

3. Encourage state and local governments to establish and improve planning staffs.

The "701" program is specifically designed to aid urban planning in both small and large communities. Cities, counties, and other units of local government with a population of less than fifty thousand may apply for planning assistance through the state agency designated by the governor to administer the program. For metropolitan areas and urban regions with a central city or urban concentration of fifty thousand or more, federal grants may be made either through the state agency or directly to the official metropolitan or regional planning agency authorized to perform planning functions for the area. The program places special emphasis on area-wide or regional planning in metropolitan areas.

Grants are also available under the "701" program for state and interstate planning and for planning in disaster areas and areas experiencing the impact of federal installations. The national government normally pays two-thirds of the cost of the projects supported by planning assistance grants with the remaining one-third being paid by the state or local government.

Open Space Program. The Housing Act of 1961 authorized the national government to make grants-in-aid to help local governments in acquiring and developing land to be used as permanent open space. Land could be acquired under the program for parks and recreation purposes, conservation of land and natural resources, and preservation of historic and scenic areas. Parks, playgrounds, malls, and parkways are examples of projects that would come within this category.

Grants may amount to up to fifty per cent of the costs of acquiring and clearing the land. A community or region must have a comprehensive planning program in effect in order to qualify for participation in the program.

Highway Act of 1962. The Highway Act of 1962 goes beyond just encouraging local governments to engage in planning. It provided that all urban areas of more than fifty thousand population must have had a comprehensive transportation plan completed by July 1, 1965. Failure to have made a plan by that date was to result in the loss of federal funds for both the Interstate system and the primary and secondary system of highways. Three key points in the law are that the plan must be (1) comprehensive; (2) continuing; (3) cooperative.

To be comprehensive the plan must encompass the entire "urbanized area" as defined by the United States Census Bureau. It must also be comprehensive in terms of subject matter and must include information on such matters as present and future land use, population growth patterns, travel patterns, transportation facilities, and zoning codes.

There must be evidence that the planning process in the area is a continuing one. The local officials must be able to show that means exist for keeping their information and statistical data current and for adapting their plan to changing conditions.

Finally, the plan must be cooperative. The preparation of it must be accomplished jointly by the state government and the various local governments in the area involved. According to the law, the nature of the cooperation must be such as to insure that "the planning decisions are reflective of and responsive to both the programs of the state highway department and the needs and desires of the local communities."

There is little doubt but that this act has had a direct impact on urban planning. In many metropolitan areas regional planning programs were established as a direct response to the requirements imposed by this act.

State Governments and Planning

Several states have established state-wide planning agencies to undertake planning on a state-wide basis and to encourage and coordinate the planning activities of local governments. The case for a state agency is well stated in the following paragraph by Luther Gulick:[5]

> The time has come to strengthen greatly the powers and the staffs of state planning agencies, or to establish planning agencies in those states which now lack such departments. I happen to think that this is needed for the rural areas of the states and for guiding the general state-wide economic development. But I am urging the need for action here because it seems to me that strengthened state planning has now become a vital necessity as an aid to the evolution of the metropolitan areas. The time has come when we should consider limited and general state-wide land use controls in all areas which have no plans of their own. We should probably give any jurisdiction the right of appeal to the state if it thinks it is being injured by nonconforming developments next door. Terrific damage is being done by ill-planned developments and stupendous costs are being generated for the future. Proper state restrictions imposed where the localities fail to act adequately can save our children many a headache and will greatly increase the security enjoyed by the private developers who will in the end do most of the building of the new metropolitan areas.

It seems inevitable that states will display an increasing interest in urban planning in the future. In some instances this may take the form of an agency with strong powers to impose planning regulations. It is likely, however, that the more common case will be a state planning office that serves as a source of aid and information and attempts to upgrade and coordinate the planning programs of the various local governments.

THE ZONING FUNCTION

The terms "planning" and "zoning" are often confused and sometimes are used interchangeably. A thorough knowledge of the planning process requires an understanding of the difference between them. Planning is the

---

[5] Luther Gulick, "The Role of the State in the Solution of Metropolitan Area Problems," in Stephen B. Sweeney (ed.) *Metropolitan Analysis* (Philadelphia: University of Pennsylvania Press, 1958), pp. 174–75.

broader, more inclusive concept and encompasses all those activities discussed above. Zoning is one of several tools used to implement planning. It refers to the establishment of land use restrictions on privately owned land. A city normally establishes several zoning classes, including single family dwellings, multiple family dwellings, restricted commercial, general commercial, light industry, and heavy industry. Many times these general classes will be broken down into additional categories. The zoning system, which is one of the most important parts of any city plan, is now usually enacted by the city council. In the earlier days of the completely independent planning and zoning commission this was the commission's function, and the council had little or no voice in the process. The planning department and planning and zoning commission now commonly serve as advisors to the council in the preparation of zoning regulations.

As times change the zoning ordinance will have to be reviewed and amended, and this too is usually a council function. If an individual wishes to get the zoning changed on property that he owns he must get the council to amend the ordinance. In many cities the procedure is for the individual to present his case to the planning and zoning commission. The commission then holds hearings on the requested change and makes a recommendation to the council. The planning department may also investigate the case and make a recommendation. The council gives consideration to the recommendations but is free to make the decision as it sees fit. In a few cities a zoning administrator is authorized to make minor changes in the zoning law.

Zoning Restrictions

The particular types of restrictions included in a zoning ordinance are varied. They include the establishment of zoning classes such as those described above. Within each category restrictions such as the following will be established:

1. The height, number of stories, size of building, and other structures.
2. The maximum percentage of a piece of land which may be occupied by buildings or other structures.
3. The size of yards, lots, and other spaces.
4. The set-back distance required between streets and buildings or other structures on the property.

Some cities have attempted to establish restrictions on the minimum value of homes in an area in an effort to prevent the construction of inexpensive homes in high income residential areas. This practice is commonly known as "snob zoning." As a rule state courts have held zoning ordinances invalid with specifically set minimum dollar values on construction in given areas. On the other hand, cities have been able to accomplish about the same thing indirectly through establishing minimum lot size or minimum square footage restrictions.

Non-Conforming Uses

One of the major zoning problems which cities must deal with and one in which the rights of the individual property owner often come into conflict with the interests of the community as a whole, is non-conforming usage. A non-conforming use is the use of a piece of property which is contrary to the zoning ordinance but which existed prior to the ordinance. A city can prevent the establishment of commercial enterprises in a residential area through enactment of a zoning ordinance, but it faces a dilemma over what to do with those enterprises that existed there prior to enactment of the ordinance. If it does nothing with them the whole purpose of the zoning ordinance is defeated except in very new cities where planning and zoning restrictions precede actual development. On the other hand, it would be very unfair (and often illegal) to force the owners of such businesses to close them immediately after enactment of the ordinance.

While such business establishments may not be closed to eliminate non-conforming uses, there are certain laws which can legally discourage their continuance. To accomplish this end zoning ordinances have been used in the following ways:

1. To prohibit resuming a non-conforming use after it has been abandoned for a specified period of time;
2. To restrict the replacement of a non-conforming use destroyed through an "act of God" such as fire or flood;
3. To limit or prevent expansion of a non-conforming use;
4. To limit the amount of its repair and maintenance;
5. To force the retirement of conforming use of buildings over an amortization period;
6. To force the immediate or less than one year abandonment of non-conforming use of land not involving structures.

The extent to which powers such as these may be exercised varies from state to state and depends upon the degree of authority granted by the state to its municipalities. Certainly the last two of these are the most effective means of eliminating non-conforming usage on a broad scope.

State authorization for municipalities to eliminate non-conforming uses over time through amortization would seem to be a fair approach to balancing the community's need for good planning against the individual's right to make the best use of his property.

DOWNTOWN: A SPECIAL PROBLEM

Virtually every large city in the United States and many smaller ones are faced with a serious crisis in their downtown areas. Business is declining, the type of clientele is changing, and the appearance of the area itself seems to be deteriorating. The reasons for this are varied and complex, but many of them are related to other phenomena of urbanization which we have already discussed. The most obvious factor is that the largest group of potential customers, the middle class families, no longer live near the central business district. They have moved to the suburbs, and downtown is now far away.

Equally significant is the fact that the suburban shopping center has made it unnecessary for the suburban dweller to go to the city's central business district to shop. For a long time after the shopping center trend began, spokesmen for the central business district could argue that the shopping center was a poor substitute for going downtown. The shopping center offered only a limited variety of goods to choose from, it was said, and if one really wanted to have the widest possible choice of merchandise or if he desired to shop for speciality items, he still needed to go to the downtown area. If this were once true it is continually becoming less so. Regional shopping centers are growing in size, and the department stores in the shopping centers (usually owned by the same firms that own those in the downtown area) often rival in size to those located in the center of the city.

The decline of mass transit and the rise of the automobile has contributed to the dilemma of downtown. When most urban dwellers traveled by mass transit, the normal traffic patterns of the transit system brought huge numbers of potential shoppers to the central city area. The automobile changed all of that. Not only is it now easier to go to the shopping center, but the congested streets and lack of parking facilities make it difficult to shop in the downtown area even if one wished to do so.

There is little doubt that the changing population composition of the city has also contributed to this problem. In most cities residential areas nearest the central business district are now inhabited by low income families, in particular by minority groups such as Negroes and Puerto Ricans. This affects the downtown area in two ways. First, the suburbanite does not care to drive through the shabby neighborhoods that separate him from the city core. Second, downtown merchants adjust the type of merchandise they carry to serve the new market. The men's clothing section of the department store has fewer business suits and more work clothes for sale, the women's department stocks more suits and dresses in the low price categories, and these changes make the store even less attractive to the suburban shopper.

There is a general agreement that cities have a responsibility to do what they can to prevent the decay of the downtown area, but the question of what action will best accomplish this is yet unanswered. Some cities have attempted to approach this problem by creating civic centers in the downtown area. Complexes of government buildings—national, state, county and local—are designed to serve as a focus of activity in the center of the city. The San Francisco Civic Center, which includes the municipal buildings and the city's opera house with federal and state office buildings nearby, would be one example. The civic center complex in downtown Los Angeles would be another.

Civic Centers give a modern look to the city (if one likes the modern styles of glass and concrete in which government buildings are now so often constructed), and they provide employment for a large number of people, necessitating their coming into the city each working day. In addition where the centers include entertainment facilities they often attract many people into the city during the evening hours. The construction of a complex of government buildings may also give impetus to the erection of buildings to house related businesses and professions such as offices for attorneys and other professional people, title companies, banks, insurance companies, restaurants, etc. On the other hand civic centers take large amounts of expensive land off the tax books and some urban planners and architects say that their design is seldom such as to contribute to the liveliness and wide variety of activities that make downtown areas interesting and functional.

Most urban planners seem to believe that a mix of public and private efforts will be necessary if the problems of downtown are ever to be overcome. One assumption that is basic to any effort to rejuvenate downtown is acceptance of the fact that this area will never again be *the place* to shop. It may well be one of several very desirable areas for shopping, but the regional shopping center is here to stay and nothing that happens in the central district is likely to change that fact. While the central area cannot expect to regain a monopoly on retail merchandising, there are other functions in which it might reasonably expect to hold a position of dominance and leadership. There is a good possibility, for example, that downtown will continue to be the financial center of the community. It is a logical location for the larger banks, insurance firms, brokerage houses, and similar establishments which do not depend on walk-in customers for most of their business. As in the case of the civic center, the presence of these large employers will generate a certain amount of retail business as well as business for restaurants, service firms, office equipment stores, and other related businesses.

The center of the city also has the opportunity to serve as the cultural and entertainment center of the area. Most metropolitan areas can support several shopping centers but only one symphony orchestra or opera house, and the center of the city is a good location for such activities. The larger movie houses and theaters are also usually downtown.

Finally, the downtown area is the logical center for a metropolitan area's tourist and convention business. Visitors on vacation or attending a convention want to be where evening activities are available, and the entertainment centers and restaurants of a downtown area make that the ideal location for large hotels and convention facilities. If one were to survey the people strolling through Times Square in New York, the Loop in Chicago, or Market Street in San Francisco on most any evening, he would probably find that many if not most are from out of town. He would also find that people are there because they enjoy the concentration of activities in one place and the opportunity to see so much in such a small area. The unique functions of areas like these are hardly threatened by the suburban shopping center. In short, there is no reason why the city core must die. If the area adjusts to the fact that it may have to give up its traditional position of leadership as a retail trade center and concentrate more on its other potentialities, it can continue to be a vital and lively part of the metropolitan area.

NEW TRENDS IN PLANNING

Urban planning has really come into its own only since World War II. Although planning was recognized as a legitimate function of cities soon after the turn of the century, it usually was based on few data other than "hunch" and its scope was considered to include zoning and little else. One trend of recent years has been the recognition that urban planning must involve far more than just land use planning. Transportation, recreation, housing, and all other functions of city governments have come to be recognized as being of interest to those planning the long-range development of urban areas.

We might also identify as a trend the increasing recognition that planning is a vital part of the political process of a city. The early efforts to establish independent planning commissions and to isolate them from council influence was based on the assumption that it was both possible and desirable to keep planning "out of politics." Many planners today would question this. Because planning deals with the most important questions facing cities, it must be involved in the politics, i.e. policy making of the city.

This understanding of the close relationship between planning and policy has led to dramatic structural changes in city government planning organizations. The major responsibility for planning has now shifted from planning commissions to the chief executive and the city council. The planning director is now commonly appointed by the mayor or city manager rather than by the commission, and final decisions on planning matters are usually the responsibility of the council. The commission has become primarily an advisory body, and in many cities its role is very minor. Other citizen advisory groups, urban renewal organizations, and private organizations interested in encouraging orderly city development now share with the commission the function of advisor to the council on planning matters.

Another very important trend, perhaps the most important in the long run, is a new interest in the area-wide approach to planning. Most metropolitan areas are moving, however slowly, in this direction. The major difficulty in the past has been that regional planning agencies had little authority to enforce any kind of general planning, but recent federal laws tying acceptance of regional planning to eligibility for grants-in-aid make it likely that this will change. The impetus which has been given to regional planning in metropolitan areas may be the most significant result of the whole series of laws and new urban programs that have come out of Washington in the 1960's.

Suggested Readings

Jacobs, Jane, *The Death and Life of Great American Cities* (New York: Vintage Books, 1961). The comments of one who dissents from much of the dominant thinking among planners.

Kent, T. J., Jr. *The Urban General Plan* (San Francisco: Chandler Publishing Company, 1964). A good discussion by a professional planner of what comprehensive urban planning should include.

Long, Norton, "Planning and Politics in Urban Development," *The Journal of the American Institute of Planners,* Vol. 25, No. 4 (November, 1959), pp. 167-69. Long emphasizes the point that planning cannot be divorced from the political process.

Makielski, S. J., Jr., *The Politics of Zoning* (New York: Columbia University Press, 1966).

Meyerson, Martin, and Edward C. Banfield, *Politics, Planning and the Public Interest* (New York: The Free Press of Glencoe, 1955). A study of the process by which sites for housing projects in Chicago were selected.

chapter **11**

Housing in the
Metropolitan Area

The need for thousands of new dwelling units each year, the preference for single family dwellings, the desire to live in the suburbs, the fear of racial integration—all of these are factors that point to the immense challenge society faces in attempting to meet the housing needs of a growing population. Meeting these needs has made housing construction a large industry and a major force in the economy and has made the question of adequate housing a major concern of urban governments.

As might be expected the major housing construction activity in recent years has taken place in the metropolitan areas. The 1960 housing census showed 62.4 per cent of all housing units (a single room, apartment, house, or other structure that served as an individual housing unit) to be located in metropolitan areas, up from 58.8 per cent in 1950. As is to be expected the percentage of all housing units in central cities declined slightly (from 34.8 per cent to 33.6 per cent) while the figure for metropolitan suburbs increased (from 24.0 per cent to 28.7 per cent).[1]

The statistics also indicate that we are becoming a nation of homeowners. We indicated in an earlier chapter that the desire to own one's own home is a well established part of the value system of most Americans, and it appears that the dream is becoming a reality. In 1960, 62 per cent of the total number of housing units were occupied by owners. This represented a marked gain over the 1950 figure of 55 per cent and the 1940 figure of 44 per cent. Somewhat less encouraging is the progress made by minority groups in upgrading their housing conditions. Home ownership among the nonwhite population, for example, stands at a level

---

[1] U.S. Bureau of the Census, *Census of Housing: 1960,* Vol. 1, Part 1, pp. XIX-XXXI.

179

of 38.4 per cent compared with the above figure of 62.4 per cent for the population as a whole. The efforts of the urban middle class Negro to break out of the central city and move into suburban residential areas have also had only limited success. Nonwhites accounted for 15.4 per cent of the total population of central cities in metropolitan areas in 1960, but they made up only 4.1 per cent of that portion of metropolitan area populations living outside of the central city.[2] The social problems created by this *de facto* segregation have contributed much to the racial tensions that now exist in many urban areas.

Not to be overlooked in any analysis of housing statistics is the economic impact of housing and housing construction. In 1965 the total value of new construction in the nation for all purposes was over 71 billion dollars. Over three million workers are employed by the construction industry.[3] Such figures indicate that housing is related not only to the social problems of urban living, but also to such economic factors as employment, production, and the financial health of the nation. Because of the magnitude of such problems, governments at all levels feel a vital interest in issues related to providing adequate housing for the nation's population.

GOVERNMENT HOUSING

Public Housing

The national government first became actively involved in attempting to meet the nation's housing needs in the 1930's. Since that time activities of the national government have moved in two general directions. One has been support for government owned public housing, as established in the Housing Act of 1937, and the other would be assistance to privately financed and constructed projects through the federal urban renewal program. In addition the government has provided support and assistance through such programs as mortgage loans insured through the Federal Housing Administration and the Veterans Administration.

The United States Housing Act of 1937 provided the first long-range program of the national government directed toward meeting the nation's low cost housing and slum clearance needs. Prior to that time some state and city governments had initiated limited programs of public housing on their own, and the national government, through the public works administration, had even been involved to some extent. In 1934, the Public

---

[2] *Ibid.*

[3] *Statistical Abstract of the United States: 1966,* p. 735.

Works Administration had begun a program of direct construction and operation of low rent public housing projects, but the administrative problems and legal questions involved in direct ownership coupled with political opposition to the program made it desirable to look for a new alternative.[4]

The program that developed was the Housing Act of 1937, which provided for federal loans and subsidies to semi-autonomous local agencies, known as housing authorities, to construct and operate public housing projects. Loans were to be made to the local housing authorities to construct rental units, and the units were then to be rented to low income families. Because the families usually could not afford to pay a level of rent sufficient to cover the maintenance, debt service, and other costs, the act provided for a subsidy payment by the national government to help finance the projects. It was also required that the local government contribute by providing municipal services either free or for only a token payment.

The administrative device of the independent housing authority was used for at least two reasons. One was the need to stay free of debt limits imposed by most states on their local governments. Most municipalities were in financial straits in the late 1930's and were indebted up to their legal limits, so they would have been unable to receive the loans provided for under the act. Housing authorities, which usually had close working relationships with their municipalities, were nevertheless considered to be separate units of government, and they could accept the loans without reference to the municipality's debt level. The other reason was the desire to protect the projects from local politics as much as possible. The housing authorities were ordinarily governed by a board of prominent local citizens who served without pay and were not subject to removal by the mayor or council. It was believed that this arrangement gave some assurance that local political officials would not be able to use their influence to get construction contracts or other favors connected with the projects for themselves or their friends.

The act provided that for each new dwelling unit built one unit of existing substandard housing must be demolished. This had the effect of accomplishing two aims. First, it assured that the act would have some impact on slum clearance. Second, it made it certain that the act would not provide competition for the private housing market since the total number of units available would not be increased. Those involved in the private housing industry were very wary of public housing programs and

---

[4] Martin Meyerson, Barbara Terett, and William L. C. Wheaton, *Housing, People and Cities* (New York: McGraw-Hill Book Company, 1962), pp. 227–28.

brought no little amount of pressure on Congress and federal administrators to keep such programs from interfering with their sphere of activity.

Throughout the 1930's opposition to public housing was an important political force to consider. Those closely associated with the private housing market—contractors, developers, bankers, realtors, and others— fought hard to keep such programs off the law books or to minimize their scope. These interests directed their activities toward all three levels of government. Not only did they fight their battle with Congress, but they sought to keep state legislatures from passing enabling legislation making it possible for local governments to undertake such activities or to participate in the federal programs. At the local level they encouraged municipalities to pass ordinances or charter amendments requiring a popular referendum before a public housing program could be undertaken. This had the effect of making the procedure more cumbersome and also provided another chance to defeat public housing programs through working for a negative vote in the referendum. As time passed those who had opposed or feared public housing found it was not a direct threat to the private housing industry or the capitalist economic system. While most in this category did not become ardent champions of public housing, they found that they could live with it. Efforts continued (and still do today) to limit the size of the government's involvement in public housing, but most have come to accept the theory that the government has a legitimate role in providing adequate housing for its citizens.

The subdued intensity of the opposition that occurred with time does not necessarily indicate that the programs were entirely successful. In many ways they were not. Those who believed that crime, drunkenness, divorce, and other problems would disappear as a result of slum clearance and public housing were to be disillusioned. Crime and juvenile delinquency continued even among families in public housing, for it was too much to expect lifelong behavior patterns to change overnight. There were still broken homes, drunkenness, and illegitimacy. A lack of motivation and understanding about how to care for property caused some of the new housing units to be quickly turned into slums by those who inhabited them.

There was also criticism directed toward the maximum income limits established in order to determine who qualified for public housing. The exact figure varied from area to area, but the principle that some maximum had to be established in order to assure that those most in need were provided with the housing accommodations remained. This brought charges that the limits discouraged tenants from trying to better themselves for fear of losing their apartment. It was also suggested that the limit led to "snooping" by inspectors attempting to discover some evidence that individuals had lied about their income in order to qualify for housing. One of the most vexing problems concerns racial segregation in public housing projects. Because there is such a large representation of minority groups, especially Negroes, in low income areas, public housing projects often become in fact Negro housing projects. This was contrary to the policy of the national government which is to encourage integrated residential patterns. It also has created serious difficulties in choosing sites for projects. Residents of many areas have fought hard to prevent the location of a public housing project in the neighborhood for fear it would mean a large influx of minority group residents.

Other difficulties have involved the strong preference of Americans for single family homes. Public housing too often has appeared to have the characteristics of dormitory or institutional living, and even the poor are sufficiently imbued with our value system to reject such a living pattern if at all possible.

Critics and supporters now agree that public housing has been no panacea for the difficulties of life in the urban slum, but most also believe that it was an important first step in the direction of attacking a crucial social malady. With some modification in the Housing Act of 1949 and subsequent legislation the public housing program continues in operation today although it has not been a very dynamic program in recent years. In 1965 there were 737,920 low cost dwelling units in use which had been built through the public housing programs of the national government.[5]

Urban Renewal

The second major direction which national housing policy has taken is directed toward working through the private sector of the economy. The Housing Act of 1949 provided for the federal urban renewal program. Under this program local governments may buy and clear land in slum areas and then resell the land to private developers or in some cases to public housing authorities. Since the cost of purchase and clearance will usually amount to more than what the land will be sold for, the city will often incur a loss on the sale. The act provides that in such cases the national government will provide aid equal to two-thirds of the amount of the loss (certain cities qualify for a higher national contribution). The local government then contributes the remaining amount. To qualify to participate in the program a city must have a comprehensive land use plan and adequate zoning and land use controls. The urban renewal program has been highly successful in helping many cities improve the appearance and economy of slum areas or older neighborhoods. New Haven, Pittsburgh,

[5] *Statistical Abstract of the United States: 1966,* p. 755.

and Philadelphia are often pointed to as cities where urban renewal programs have met with much success.

Urban renewal has been a target of much criticism from right wing political groups who charge that it is a scheme to take away personal property rights and another step to socialism. While such charges can hardly be taken seriously, we should not overlook the fact that there are some legitimate criticisms to be made of the program. Perhaps the most pertinent criticism concerns the problem of relocation. When urban renewal land is sold to the private developer, he has considerable freedom in the kind of project he constructs, and because the land is normally expensive land (the return from, and therefore the costs of, land in slum areas tends to be very high) he will have to use it in such a way as to insure return on his investment. This means that often he will construct a high rent apartment complex for those in the upper income categories. Very seldom will he construct facilities that will be available to those who were displaced when the land was cleared.

The result is that, while the neighborhood now looks much more modern and aesthetically pleasing, those who formerly lived there must now find living facilities elsewhere. While the act requires local governments to plan for relocation and provides assistance to those affected, the fact is that most relocation efforts have been somewhat less than successful. Those who lived on the land previously are still in low income categories and thus must still seek housing at a relatively low cost. Critics suggest that this merely results in "moving the slums around," for too often the moving of people from the cleared land to other neighborhoods will increase the population density and add to the deterioration of these areas.

Relocation, of course, is a problem faced by any kind of slum clearance program, public or private. One of the basic characteristics of slum areas, indeed a part of the definition of such areas, is a high density of population. Even when projects (low rent public housing, for example) are designed specifically to house the same people who were living in the area prior to its clearance and redevelopment, it usually cannot house *all* of them because it will provide for a lower population density. Even in those cases, therefore, a relocation problem will arise. People who live in potential clearance areas quickly become aware of this dilemma, a fact which accounts for the intense opposition to slum clearance programs which often develops among the people the programs are supposed to help.

Another criticism directed toward renewal attacks the political manipulation that has been associated with the program. Charges are made that favoritism has been shown in sales of land, contracts for clearance, choice of site location or other matters. Whenever governmental agencies get intimately involved in programs involving large amounts of land—whether it is for slum clearance, freeways or other projects—the opportunities for such illegitimate activities inevitably exist and some malfeasance undoubtedly occurs. It is the author's view, however, that considering the size of the urban renewal program on a national basis the problems of corruption and political favoritism associated with it have been relatively small. Other criticisms, the relocation problem in particular, are much more pertinent.

Another approach to slum clearance that is separate from, but related to, urban renewal is the concept of neighborhood conservation and rehabilitation. Considerable criticism has been directed at the "bull dozer" philosophy of urban renewal, i.e. the idea of completely clearing a given area and starting redevelopment literally from the ground up. The Housing Act of 1954 authorized programs of conservation and rehabilitation in neighborhoods which are deteriorating and possibly in danger of becoming slums but which do not warrant complete destruction and clearance. Subsequent legislation has made available low interest federal loans to individuals to encourage fixing up homes and fighting encroaching blight. The enforcement of local housing and building codes is a part of this concept, and grants and loans are available to individuals who need assistance to bring their dwellings up to a level where they meet local code standards. This approach avoids many of the relocation and political favoritism criticisms of more far-reaching clearance and redevelopment approaches and has much potential for neighborhoods that are not yet "too far gone" to save.

Other Programs

The public housing and urban renewal programs are only two of the housing programs of the national government. While both are closely associated with slum clearance, other programs are directed at entirely different goals. One of the best known and most significant activities of the federal government has been making available a source of credit to finance home purchases by middle income families.

The program of credit expansion began in the early 1930's. The Home Loan Bank Act of 1932 and the Homeowners Loan Act of 1933 strengthened the savings and loan associations through providing for federal loans, deposit insurance, and a system for federal purchase of mortgages in danger of foreclosure.

The National Housing Act of 1934 extended to commercial and savings banks federal assistance similar to that provided savings and loan associations earlier. The act established a system of mortgage insurance under the Federal Housing Administration. Under its provisions an individual applies for a loan through regular lending institutions such as commercial banks. The FHA checks the borrower's credit and reviews the plans for the house, which must meet certain specifications. If FHA approves the application, it will then insure the loan which is made. FHA does not make the loan; it simply insures the loan which is made by the local lending firm. For the service the borrower pays a small insurance premium which goes into a national insurance fund.

A related program that has had far-reaching effects on the nation and the housing industry is the mortgage insurance program of the Veterans Administration. Begun in 1944 to assist servicemen returning from World War II, the program provided that the Veterans Administration would insure loans on home purchases by servicemen who qualified under the act for amounts covering the entire value of the loan. It also required no payment of insurance premiums by those receiving VA loans. The FHA and VA programs have played a very large role in the financing of housing construction since World War II. In the decade of the 1950's approximately 40 per cent of all mortgages insured were insured by one of these two agencies.

A new feature was added to federal housing programs by the Housing and Urban Development Act of 1965: rent-supplement payments. The act covers certain categories of low income families (for example, elderly, physically handicapped, those displaced by governmental housing programs, occupants of substandard housing) and provides for rent-supplement payments equal to the difference between twenty-five per cent of the recipient's income and the rent required for adequate dwelling units. After the rent-supplement program was adopted in principle, Congress was slow in providing funds to finance it, and sufficient time has not yet passed to allow for an evaluation of the program.

THE PRIVATE SECTOR AND NEW HOUSING CONCEPTS

The great need for new housing has given private industry incentive to experiment with new concepts in hopes of turning them into solid business profits. With the strong interest in conservation and rehabilitation much emphasis is being placed on developing techniques for repairing older dwellings in slum areas. One program to which the Federal Housing Administration is giving encouragement and support is an experiment with almost overnight rehabilitation of tenements on New York's Lower East Side. The plan is to take buildings which were built years ago with strong foundations and firm exterior walls and rehabilitate the interior portions by working through the roof. The inner sections would be torn out and removed through the roof and complete rooms which were pre-assembled would then be lowered through the roof and put in place by large cranes. The project would be completed with the attachment of heating and plumbing facilities and other minor installations. It is planned that the entire process can be completed in as little as forty-eight hours, thereby minimizing the difficulties of relocation. Residents can be relocated temporarily, and they will then be able to return to their homes within a few days.

A tenement renovation program being undertaken entirely by private industry is United States Gypsum's project in Harlem. The company has purchased several tenement houses there and is completely rehabilitating them. The project may ultimately involve an entire block in the East Harlem area. It is the firm's plan eventually to sell the dwellings at a profit. More important, however, is the hope that the experimentation undertaken in connection with the rehabilitation will lead to the development and marketing of several new building products that can be used in similar projects elsewhere.

The American Plywood Association has an experimental renovation program underway in Cleveland, Armstrong Cork Company is working on a project in North Philadelphia, and other companies are giving consideration to projects elsewhere. The expectation of making large profits from the projects themselves appears not to be a prime consideration in the programs undertaken so far (although this is not considered an impossibility). The main motivation has been research and experimentation in the hope of finding new techniques of slum renovation which will create markets for new products. A sincere desire on the part of the companies to do something about the deteriorating problems of the cities also should not be overlooked as a motivating factor. In some instances, for example, the projects have involved areas close to company plants or neighborhoods in which many company employees live.[6]

HOUSING PROGRAMS: THE GENERAL APPROACH

A few words of comment are added here to emphasize an important point: even with heavy government involvement in housing programs for over three decades, the primary emphasis of the programs has been oriented toward working within the free enterprise system of the American economy. When housing legislation was first being proposed in the 1930's it was widely attacked as "socialistic," and there was even doubt among many as to whether the constitution allowed the national government to

---

[6] A discussion of these programs is found in the *Wall Street Journal,* Nov. 14, 1966, p. 28.

be involved in housing matters. Even up to the present time there are strong interests opposed to any proposal to expand federal housing programs. In most cases the programs themselves reflect the desire to meet the objections of the opposition and the general preference of most citizens to work within a free enterprise framework. The earliest public housing legislation, for example, carefully provided that an existing substandard dwelling must be destroyed for each new dwelling unit built, as we noted earlier. The urban renewal program and programs for neighborhood conservation and rehabilitation operate primarily through the private sector of the economy. The national government's efforts to provide a source of credit for those buying homes have largely involved insuring loans made by private lending agencies instead of direct government loans in competition with private credit. There are certainly valid criticisms to be made of the varied housing programs of national, state and local governments, but the criticism that the programs are "socialistic" or anti-free enterprise is not borne out by the facts.

HOUSING AND MINORITIES

Of all the unaccomplished goals which the nation faces in relation to housing, none is more perplexing than the need to provide adequate housing for minorities. In virtually every metropolitan area the largest concentration of minority groups, particularly Negroes, is to be found in the slum areas and deteriorating neighborhoods of the central city. Even those Negroes who have become sufficiently financially successful to be able to purchase better housing have found barriers—legal and social—placed in the way of their moving into the more desirable, and predominately white, neighborhoods. Metropolitan suburbs, in particular, have often been especially concerned about preventing minority groups from moving in. Negroes have not been the only group to face housing restrictions. Roman Catholics, Jews, Chinese, and Puerto Ricans among others have also felt the sting of housing discrimination, but there is little doubt that the Negro has been the most obvious target of discrimination in recent years.

As hard as it may be to believe, it is a fact that those who sought to prevent integrated housing had the force of law on their side until rather recently. Two legal tools were used to accomplish these results, racial zoning and restrictive covenants. Racial zoning ordinances, like other zoning ordinances, sought to restrict land usage in given areas, but in this case restriction was on the basis of race. Louisville, Kentucky, had an ordinance prior to 1917 which forbade members of one race to live in areas where a majority of the houses were occupied by members of another race. Another approach, taken by New Orleans, provided that members of one race could move into an area zoned for another race only if a majority of the residents of that zone approved. Racial zoning was ruled unconstitutional by the United States Supreme Court in a 1917 case involving the Louisville law.[7] Efforts were still made to rely on the zoning laws to prevent integration even after the decision. Strict zoning ordinances requiring a very large minimum lot or house size were passed only to have the zoning authorities make frequent exceptions to the rule in dealing with Caucasians but enforce it rightly in cases involving Negroes.

The other legal tool used to enforce residential segregation was the restrictive covenant. Such covenants were agreements among property owners in an area, often written into the deed or title to the property, which provided that the property would not be sold or in any way conveyed to an individual not of the Caucasian race. In addition to Negroes, Jews were often the victims of restrictive covenants. This device remained in use until 1948 when the Supreme Court ruled that restrictive covenants could not be enforced by the courts.[8] This approach to the problem is most interesting. The court did not say that the covenants themselves were unconstitutional, but rather that it was a violation of the constitution for state or national courts to use their authority to enforce them.

From its inception in the 1930's until an abrupt change of policy in 1949, the policies of the Federal Housing Administration gave strong encouragement to segregated housing patterns. In establishing standards for developers who hoped to have their homes qualify for FHA insured loans, the Federal Housing Administration officially encouraged racial homogeneity. Its publications warned against the instability that can come from introducing diverse racial groups into a neighborhood, and it even recommended a model racial restrictive covenant for properties insured by FHA. After the restrictive covenant decision of 1948, FHA policies began to change, and its publications after 1949 contained no references which appear to encourage segregated housing. It also announced that it would not insure property that had a racial covenant recorded after February 15, 1950. Even after this change of policy much FHA insured development occurred which was for all practical purposes segregated even in the absence of restrictive covenants or other legal authority. Federal Housing Administration policy did not encourage segregation, but it tolerated it. It was not until President Kennedy signed the Executive Order on Equal Opportunity in Housing on November 20, 1962, that it became federal policy to bar all discrimination in federally owned, aided, or insured housing projects and officially to encourage integrated housing patterns.

---

[7] Buchanan v. Warley, 245 U.S. 60 (1917).
[8] Shelley v. Kraemer, 334 U.S. 24 (1948).

The last decade has seen much action by cities and states to encourage equal housing opportunities regardless of race. In 1957 New York City enacted the first law barring religious and racial discrimination in private housing. The particular significance here was that the law applied to all housing regardless of whether it had received any type of governmental assistance. The law applied to all sales and rentals of housing units except an apartment in an owner occupied duplex or a room in a private home. It also applied to real estate, lending institutions, and real estate advertising. Pittsburgh passed a similar law in 1958, and four states passed statewide anti-discrimination laws that applied to private housing in 1959. By 1966 sixteen states had enacted such laws.

Congress in 1966 spent much time debating Title IV of the Civil Rights Act which would have established a national prohibition against discrimination by real estate brokers, agents or salesmen, but it did not apply to private owners occupying dwellings that contained no more than three dwelling units. This provision was ultimately defeated, and the new Congress in 1967 seemed to be even less enthusiastic about such a provision than was its predecessor. It thus appears that the main responsibility for barring discrimination in private housing lies with state and local governments at this time.

One reason for the reluctance on the part of many to support integrated housing is the belief that the introduction of Negroes or other minorities into a neighborhood lowers property values in the area. Right or wrong, there is little doubt that this belief is held by large numbers of people. On the other hand, there is also little doubt that this belief is based more on myth or fear than on fact. Virtually all available research indicates that this is so. A study of seven cities by the Commission on Race and Housing found that the entry of nonwhites into a previously all-white neighborhood either had no effect on property values or caused them to go up. One reason the property values may go up is that since financially able nonwhites have less access to good private housing they will often bid up the price on that which is available to them.

The major exception to this pattern is found when the white residents of an area panic and decide to sell at any price. In such cases the decline in property values becomes a self-fulfilling prophecy as the fear of lower property values directly contributes to bringing them about. In many communities determined action on the part of residents and leaders has kept panic selling at a minimum and the result has been stable integrated communities.[9] Integrated housing has also been encouraged by several large

---

[9] See Lyle Schaller's two part series on "The Racial Crisis Comes to the Suburbs," in the November and December, 1964 issues of *Mayor and Manager*.

organizations which have constructed housing and apartment developments which are open to all without regard to race. Eichler Homes, one of the largest developers on the west coast, has been selling homes on open occupancy basis since 1954. Concord Park, near Philadelphia, is a well planned integrated suburban community. Racially integrated developments have proved to be profitable investments for many large organizations including the Metropolitan Life Insurance Company, United Auto Workers, and the International Ladies Garment Workers.

Some attempts have been made to accomplish racial balance in housing through a quota system. This is based on the theory that the main fear of a majority population is a complete domination or take over of an area by a minority group. The majority would not panic, so the reasoning goes, if it were assured that the proportion of the minority population would stabilize at some figure, perhaps twenty-five or thirty per cent of the total. This concept has been tried with considerable success in many areas. It has obvious drawbacks, on the other hand, and attempts to establish quotas through legal action would probably run into difficulties. Still there are numerous measures short of coercion that can be used to try to maintain a racial balance in accord with some general quotas. Advertising directed at particular groups, work with human relations organizations, cooperation among current residents in finding prospective new residents, and numerous other positive measures can help in attempting to maintain a racially balanced living pattern in an area.

HOUSING AND METROPOLITAN AREA GOVERNMENTS

A question is often raised about whether the fragmentation of government in metropolitan areas hinders orderly development and adequate provision of services. In the most comprehensive study of the question as it relates to housing, Banfield and Grodzins found that fragmentation itself could not be looked upon as a serious impediment to meeting adequately urban housing needs. They concluded that "when the distinction is made between 'problems which exist in metropolitan areas' and 'problems which exist by virtue of the inadequacies of governmental structure in the metropolitan areas,' the latter are few."[10] This does not mean that there are no difficulties which cannot be improved by area-wide cooperation among governments in the metropolitan area. Housing needs can be better met, for example, if there is cooperation among local governments in planning,

---

[10] Edward C. Banfield and Morton M. Grodzins, *Government and Housing in Metropolitan Areas* (New York: McGraw-Hill Book Company, 1958), p. 156.

subdivision regulation, code enforcement, and provision of essential services such as water and sewers. Banfield and Grodzins suggest that the central city in particular should take the lead in encouraging cooperation on such matters. With the rapid development of regional councils since their study was completed, it would appear that this provides another vehicle for the expansion of such coordination. The basic conclusion of the study that some form of metropolitan consolidation or federation would not in itself alleviate housing problems still appears valid. Urban slums, racial discrimination, and the many other problems of housing appear to be related to more basic social and economic issues than just governmental structure.

Suggested Readings

Anderson, Martin, *The Federal Bulldozer: A Critical Analysis of Urban Renewal* (Cambridge: Massachusetts Institute of Technology Press, 1964). It is exactly what the name says.

Banfield, Edward C., and Morton Grodzins, *Government and Housing in Metropolitan Areas* (New York: McGraw-Hill Book Company, 1958).

Davies, J. Clarence, III, *Neighborhood Groups and Urban Renewal* (New York: Columbia University Press, 1966).

Fizer, Webb S., *Mastery of the Metropolis* (Englewood Cliffs, New Jersey: Prentice-Hall, Inc., 1962).

Kaplan, Harold, *Urban Renewal Politics: Slum Clearance in Newark* (New York: Columbia University Press, 1963).

Laurenti, Luigi, *Property Values and Race* (Berkeley: University of California Press, 1960).

Meyerson, Martin, and Edward C. Banfield, *Politics, Planning and the Public Interest* (Glencoe: The Free Press, 1955). A study of the process by which sites for housing projects in Chicago were selected.

Rossi, Peter H., and Robert A. Dentler, *The Politics of Urban Renewal* (Glencoe: The Free Press, 1961).

Eldredge, Taming Metropolis

Hadden, et al. Metropolis in Crisis

chapter 12

The Urban Transportation Problem

There are pessimists who suggest that one of our major cities may someday find all traffic within its borders coming to a complete halt as the city bogs down in a giant traffic jam. While we can hope that this picture is an overly gloomy one, there is little question that transportation is becoming one of our most acute urban problems. Whereas there was a time when public transit systems (we use the term "public" to mean systems that carry large numbers of people and not to denote ownership; public transit systems may be either publicly or privately owned) of various types moved most urban transit, the trend in more recent years has been for transportation by private automobiles. The result has been a decline in the quality of mass transportation systems and an overcrowding of our urban streets and freeways. Over eighty per cent of all families in the United States now own at least one car and many own more than one. In Dallas, Texas, eighty-five per cent of the families own at least one auto, and thirty-one per cent own two or more. In San Jose, California, the figures are ninety-two per cent, and thirty-seven per cent.[1] The automobile is definitely the primary means of transportation in urban America today.

---

[1] Wilfred Owen, *The Metropolitan Transportation Problem,* (Washington: The Brookings Institution, 1966), pp. 27–28.

THE TRANSPORTATION DILEMMA

The Family Car

The reasons for the shift to the automobile are rather easily discerned. The improved economic position of the American worker has brought automobile ownership within the reach of the great mass of citizens, and most people consider the family car to be a necessity rather than a luxury. The wide dispersion of residential areas in most cities has also contributed to auto ownership. Mass transit systems depend upon high densities of population, and as living areas become scattered, mass transit systems find such areas increasingly difficult to serve. The result is more reliance on the private automobile. The relationship of the rise of automobile ownership to residential dispersion is actually a "chicken and egg" relationship. It is difficult to say which is cause and which is effect. Prior to the invention of the auto cities tended to grow outward along the main routes of trolley and railroad systems as these were the only means of getting from home to work. The coming of the car made it possible to develop residential areas in a much more diverse pattern. This residential dispersion in turn made auto ownership more and more of a necessity.

The increasing amount of leisure time has joined residential patterns in recent years as a factor in making the family dependent on the automobile. Even when living areas and working areas have sufficiently dense populations to make mass transit workable, the greater amount of leisure time now enjoyed by many families means that much population movement occurs along routes other than the traditional home-to-work routes. In most urban areas the desire to get to the country, the lake, or the state park can be met only by the auto.

We should not overlook the fact that the trend toward dependence on the automobile for our transportation needs has been encouraged by specific governmental policies. The national government has provided large sums of money to states for freeway construction for over a decade but only recently has it moved in the direction of providing assistance to urban mass transit systems. State and local governments have followed suit in placing first emphasis on automobile transportation. Many cities have allowed their transit systems to fall to miserably poor service levels, and while discussion has occurred in many urban areas about the possibility of limiting or even completely banning private automobiles in certain central business district areas, few cities have actually taken action to implement these ideas. State and local governments were very reluctant to initiate subsidies for privately owned transportation systems in financial difficulty, and many governments actually imposed artificially high tax loads on local transit companies. It is obvious that government officials at all levels feel that their constituents want them to give the private auto priority over mass transit systems in meeting our urban transportation problems. In this estimate of public opinion they are probably correct.

That the public should prefer the car to public carriers under current conditions is not surprising. Surveys have shown that commuters have numerous complaints about public transportation systems. They complain about the high costs, crowded conditions, long waits, and poor accommodations associated with public transportation. Their car, in contrast, is comfortable and available when they want it to take them where they want to go. In spite of the feeling of the automobile commuter that he creeps along on the freeway at a snail's pace, the fact is that he would likely travel even more slowly on public transit. A study made by *Fortune Magazine* in the late 1950's showed that in twenty-five of our largest cities the automobile averaged about twenty miles per hour during the peak rush hours while those traveling by public transit (mainly bus) moved at only about thirteen miles per hour.[2] Only in New York, Newark, and San Francisco did commuters traveling by public transit have a marked advantage over those traveling by private auto.

While the car appears to have advantages over mass transit for most commuters today, the growing number of automobiles on our streets and highways is creating tremendous problems. One of the major difficulties is that providing for an adequate system of transportation by automobile takes very great amounts of space. Los Angeles, famous (or infamous) for its vast freeway system, is now devoting two-thirds of all land area in its downtown section to serving the car. About one-third is being used for parking lots and garages and another third for roads and freeways.[3] It is estimated that by 1980 the Los Angeles freeway system will occupy land area equal to the entire area of the city of Miami.[4]

The financial outlay necessary to construct freeway systems is great. It has been estimated that the forty-one thousand miles of freeway in the interstate system will cost approximately 3.7 million dollars per mile. In densely populated areas with high land values, the costs are much higher. The five miles of the Cross Bronx Expressway cost over twenty-two million dollars per mile.[5] The eight mile Eisenhower Expressway (for-

[2] Editors of Fortune, *The Exploding Metropolis* (Garden City, New York: Doubleday & Company, Inc., 1958), pp. 39–41.

[3] Mitchell Gordon, *Sick Cities* (Baltimore: Penguin Books, 1965), p. 32.

[4] *Ibid.*

[5] Owen, *op. cit.*, pp. 44–45.

merly Congress Expressway) in Chicago cost fifty million dollars, and it took fifty-five million dollars to construct the Hollywood Freeway.[6] One of the frustrating aspects of providing for the automobile is that it seems impossible to catch up. Needs constantly out run new facilities. As soon as a new freeway is opened it is overcrowded, and freeway traffic gets more congested and moves more slowly each year.

Various plans have been devised by cities attempting to alleviate congestion. Decentralization of industrial and commercial facilities to outlying areas may be encouraged, although this may run counter to the policy of some cities to rejuvenate the central city and lure people back to it. In some areas decentralization has led to the erection of entire new communities; Reston, Virginia, outside of Washington, D. C., is an example of a new pre-planned community which will have its own industrial and commercial as well as residential facilities. While it will be sufficiently near Washington to take advantage of all that city has to offer, it is hoped that Reston will be a well-balanced community that provides for most of the employment and recreational needs of its residents. Other similar pre-planned communities are Columbia, Maryland, south of Baltimore, Litchfield Park, near Phoenix, and the Irvine Ranch in Southern California.

Some cities have tried to reduce traffic problems through encouraging large employers to stagger working hours. If working hours can be arranged so that some people work from 7 a.m. to 4 p.m. and others come at various intervals until as late as 9 a.m. to 6 p.m., this spreads out the problem of the peak hour traffic load. As the work week and work day shorten the possibilities of staggering hours will become even greater. There are, however, certain problems with this idea. Business executives in different firms need to be at work at the same time so that they can meet or communicate by phone, and this limits the possibility of too radical a variation in working hours. Coordination among employers in arranging for staggered shifts is also difficult. This is why the most extensive use of staggered working hours has been in Washington, D. C., where a very high proportion of the work force is employed by a single employer, the federal government, thereby reducing the problems of coordination.

Mass Transportation

The City of Los Angeles once possessed one of the finest mass transit systems in the nation. In the 1920's its electric railway system provided services over eleven hundred miles of track and one hundred fifty different routes. It extended twenty-eight miles north into the San Fernando Valley and forty-four miles south to Balboa, and as late as 1945 it carried over

---

[6] *Ibid.*

one hundred three million passengers. After World War II it began losing money as business declined, and conditions grew steadily worse until the last route was finally discontinued and the system went out of business completely in 1961.[7] In city after city the story of various kinds of transportation systems—commuter railroads, subways, elevated trains—parallels the story of Los Angeles. The widespread ownership of the automobile, the low population density in the newer metropolitan suburbs, and the coming of age of the freeway have all added their bit to the problems of urban mass transit.

Statistics tell the story well. In 1922 commuter railroads carried nearly four hundred thirty million passengers. After falling to a low of two hundred twenty-seven million in 1938, they recovered during the war and reached a peak of three hundred forty-five million in 1947, but they have been declining ever since. In the mid-1960's they were carrying less than two hundred million passengers annually.[8] If we look at the problem in terms of finances, we find that in 1929 about fifteen cents of every consumer dollar spent on transportation was spent for some kind of public transportation, but today the consumer is spending only four cents of his transportation dollar on public transit.

A large portion of the financial difficulties of public transit systems can be attributed to what is called the peak load problem. Public carriers get the largest portion of their business in two short doses, one at the morning rush hour and one at the evening rush hour. At these hours subways, commuter railroads, and the like will be tightly packed with passengers traveling between home and work, but the rest of the day the carriers will be almost empty. The peak load problem is amusingly illustrated by the Tokyo rapid transit system which hires "pushers," men whose job it is to push passengers aboard during the rush hours in order to get as many as possible packed into the commuter trains!

The uneven distribution of passengers throughout the day means that transit systems must invest huge amounts in equipment and hire large numbers of employees to provide for a passenger capacity that is utilized only a few hours a day. The rest of the time much of the system is idle, representing a large investment that is producing little or no revenue. The reduction of the work week from six days to five hurt transit systems because it reduced the total number of commuter trips a week. It will be of importance to public transit to see what form future shortening of the work week takes. If the work day is shortened but spread over five days per week, there should be little effect, but if the four day week becomes common this will put another crimp in the financial status of public transit.

---

[7] Gordon, *op. cit.*, p. 23.

[8] Owen, *op. cit.*, p. 235.

Some efforts have been made to even out peak load periods. Staggered working hours help public transit carriers as well as helping to alleviate traffic congestion. The carriers themselves sometimes offer special reduced "shoppers fares" for those who ride during the off hours, such as from 10 a.m. to 4 p.m. In general such efforts have met with only limited success, and most transit systems are still plagued with peak loads, huge investments and serious financial difficulties.

In spite of the generally dreary outlook for mass transit, recent developments in a few cities are most interesting and encouraging and give us hope for possible rejuvenation of transit systems. The city of Cleveland after World War II was in the unique position of being able to secure right-of-way land at relatively low cost because it had earlier been set aside for that purpose, and it constructed a new 13.5 mile subway route running east and west through its downtown section. The new route has been widely praised, but it has also been criticized by some who believe too much money was spent on a single route.

One of the most widely acclaimed new systems is the Yonge Street Subway in Toronto, Canada. The 4.5 mile subway serves the heart of the city and replaced the city's busiest street car line when it was opened in 1954. It has been credited with giving a boost to downtown business, contributing to a sharp rise in property values along its routes and helping alleviate the traffic problem. While Yonge Street is still the scene of daily traffic congestion, it is estimated that the subway keeps approximately ten thousand autos daily out of the central core of the city. Transit officials have been sufficiently pleased that they are now constructing a ten mile addition for the system.

A unique combination of transportation facilities is the Eisenhower Expressway in Chicago, where two commuter transit tracks have been constructed down the center of the eight-lane freeway. The transit lines are already carrying more passengers than the freeway and Chicago officials consider the experiment a success. At least one authority, however, has suggested that a more flexible transportation system could have been provided by substituting for the transit lines special lanes reserved for use only by buses. Wilfred Owen says that since buses are necessary as feeders for rail transit systems anyway, it might be more feasible to provide for a comprehensive bus transportation system in the first place.[9]

Bay Area Rapid Transit System

Beyond any doubt the most important new development in urban mass transit is the construction of the Bay Area Rapid Transit system (BART)

---

[9] *Ibid.*, p. 135.

in the San Francisco area. This will be the first completely new mass transit operation built in any of our major cities since Philadelphia began its system in 1907.

A suggestion for some form of mass transit for the area was first seriously discussed in the 1940's, but it did not make real headway until 1957, when a special commission presented a report on the Bay Area's transportation needs to the state legislature. Unlike many commissions which issue their reports and disband, this one worked actively to implement its recommendations. Led by many of the most respected leaders of the community, such as Alan K. Browne, Vice President of the Bank of America and commission chairman at the time it issued its report, supporters of mass transit got the legislature to create a multi-county transit district.

Some of the original counties dropped out of the plan. San Mateo county, to the south of San Francisco, withdrew because officials objected to the property tax assessments that were to be levied to help pay the costs of the system. Marin county, north of San Francisco across the Golden Gate Bridge, withdrew when engineers decided it would not be feasible to expand the bridge in order to accommodate rail traffic. As finally constituted, BART includes three counties, San Francisco, Alameda, and Contra Costa.

The system, when completed about 1971, will consist of seventy-five miles of track, including a subway beneath the bay. The modern light weight trains, which will be computer controlled, will move at speeds up to eighty miles per hour and average fifty miles per hour with stops. During rush hours trains will run at ninety second intervals. In an attempt to convert the automobile commuter the transit cars will be made as comfortable as possible. They will be air-conditioned and noise free, and they will have carpeting, wood panelling, and tinted glass windows.

The one billion dollars of costs involved will come from a number of sources, including transit revenues, property taxes, and toll bridge receipts. Eventually the property tax assessments for BART may cost the average homeowner in the area thirty dollars or more annually. Proposed transit fares may range from twenty-five cents for the eight minute ride from San Francisco to Oakland to a dollar thirty-five for the forty-five minute trip from Daley City to Concord.

One of the more noteworthy accomplishments of transit leaders was winning state appoval for using one hundred thirty-three million dollars in tolls from the Bay Bridge to build the Trans-Bay Subway tube. Although bridge tolls are usually used only to provide more highway and bridge facilities, it was agreed that construction of the subway tube would substantially reduce the need for additional bridges and was therefore a legitimate use of toll revenues.

As impressive as BART appears to be it is not without its problems. There have been disagreements among key officials of the system. Construction has lagged behind schedule and costs have increased more than expected. The key test, though, will come after the completion of the system when it is determined whether first class public transit facilities can lure the commuter away from his car. This question is as yet unanswered.

The Proper Balance

When we speak today of urban transportation systems the emphasis is on the word "system." No single mode of transit can meet urban transportation needs. The needs must be met through a balanced system of transportation that includes various forms of transit. The exact formula will vary from area to area, but one source suggests this general plan:[10]

1. For small cities: highways and cars
2. For medium size cities: highways and cars plus bus transit
3. For large cities: highways and cars plus buses, and maybe in some cases rail rapid transit.

In smaller cities the automobile is going to be the primary, usually the only means of transportation. Because of a lack of population numbers and density, smaller cities cannot begin to support mass transit operations. Even in larger cities it appears that the consumer preference will dictate a rather important place for the automobile in the total transportation system.

As cities grow larger there will come some point, even in cities where the private car is the primary means of transportation, at which the automobile alone cannot meet the total needs of the area. Buses are commonly the first form of public transportation to be added to the system. The bus, because it is not restricted to certain routes like subways or commuter trains, has much of the flexibility of the private car. At the same time it is able to offer many of the advantages of mass transit. The bus, of course, is susceptible to many of the same problems faced by the car. Buses, like cars, can get caught in traffic jams in congested business areas or on freeways. They can also be a cause of traffic problems because of their constant starting and stopping.

Some transportation planners have suggested providing special lanes for buses in order to remove them from the general traffic pattern and

---

[10] See Ardee Ames, "The Search for Balanced Transportation," *Nation's Cities,* Vol. 3, No. 1 (January, 1965) pp. 20–23.

allow them to move rapidly during peak hours. An example would be San Francisco, where street cars have exclusive lanes on Market Street. Providing such lanes gives bus transit a boost because it increases average speed, and it usually also amounts to a subsidy since the bus line (regardless of whether it is publicly or privately owend) seldom has to reimburse the city for exclusive use of the lanes.

The question of rail mass transit systems evokes considerable debate. There seems to be general agreement that cities which already have rail transit operations should keep them. The capital investment in rights-of-way and equipment represent a huge sunk cost, and as a result continuing the operation of existing systems is usually more economical than providing alternative means of moving equal numbers of people. The question of constructing new systems is more difficult. Walter McCarter, of the Institute of Rapid Transit, says "As a starting point, I think it fair to say that the twenty-three cities we have with more than one million inhabitants will have to have rapid transit sooner or later."[11] In contrast the position of the American Automobile Association is that "the current number of American cities in which fixed-rail transit makes economic and transportation sense is between six and ten. A few more might possibly be added to this category in the next several decades."[12] Obviously one's point of view is often influenced by the position from which the viewing is done!

It is accepted that rail rapid transit can move large numbers of people faster and usually cheaper than other methods, but it is feasible only where large numbers of people provide high population density. The public reaction to deteriorating transit lines in recent years also indicates that commuters will go to considerable trouble and expense to exchange the poor services of a mass transit system for the flexibility and comfort of the private automobile. The future of rail transit systems is presently unclear. We will know more about it after BART is in operation in the San Francisco area and we can see how the people of that area react to it.

The future of the more esoteric types of transportation involves even greater uncertainty. The monorail, for example, has received much publicity, but most cities that have seriously considered monorail systems have rejected them as impractical. In a few urban areas helicopters and similar rotary wing aircraft are now being used for special purposes, primarily for transportation between airports and downtown locations. It is possible that air transportation will gain greater usage for short trips within urban regions in the future.

---

[11] *Ibid.*, p. 21.
[12] *Ibid.*

It is the author's opinion that bus lines as a supplement to the private auto represent the most realistic approach to mass transit for most urban areas. The automobile cannot do the job alone in most areas, and if it could, most of us would not want it to, considering the consequences for urban planning and design that would result. Rail rapid transit, on the other hand, will probably be confined to only the largest metropolitan areas. Thus, for most areas a transportation system combining the private auto and an efficient bus operation will offer the best opportunity for moving large numbers of people with maximum flexibility, economy and convenience. It should be added that this solution will be satisfactory only when the air pollution problems of autos and buses are solved.

It should be pointed out that urban governments can if they desire invoke special policies to minimize the use of the auto. Some cities have experimented with prohibiting private autos in congested areas during certain hours. New York City officials have considered raising the rates on toll bridges during rush hours to discourage commuting by car. A municipality might obtain a monopoly over parking space in the city core and set parking fees sufficiently high to discourage all day parking by commuters. While such policies are theoretically possible, they are also highly unpopular and politically dangerous for elected officials. In addition experience up to the present time does not indicate that artificial efforts to separate the commuter and the car hold great potential for alleviating the traffic problem. Rome experimented with prohibiting autos in certain areas, but the result was such heavy traffic congestion in other areas that the plan was abandoned. In the long run urban officials must remember that their decisions must reflect to some extent the wishes of those whom they serve.

Transportation Finance

As with most public services, some of the major controversies over transportation concern the matter of finance. Is the automobile paying the way for street and highway construction and maintenance? Should the taxpayer be expected to support the auto or mass transit commuter? Is one mode of transportation cheaper than others? These are the types of questions that must be considered in developing policies for financing urban transit.

It is often difficult for the individual urban commuter to make accurate cost comparisons between alternate means of transportation. Many authorities can show statistically that use of the private automobile is far more expensive than using some form of public transit. Such figures take into account items like depreciation, insurance, highway taxes, and similar expenses when figuring the cost of automobile transportation, and comparison does show a lower cost for public transit. The average commuter, though, may not be convinced of this because he is more likely to compare only out-of-pocket costs rather than actual costs. He compares the cost of gas with the bus fare and then considers the convenience and comfort of his own car. Particularly when it is remembered that additional riders can be added to the automobile (as in a car pool) at no additional cost, public transit comes off second best in a direct comparison.

One reason the automobile commuter is not aware of his total costs is because, except in cases such as toll bridges and toll roads, much of the transportation system for the private car is financed indirectly through taxes and license charges. Even then taxes levied directly against auto users (gas and license primarily) seldom pay the full cost of providing for the transportation system. Likewise public transit systems today often fall short of being self-supporting and must rely on support from other sources for help.

Students of urban transportation disagree about whether we should expect a total urban transportation system to be self-supporting. The case can be made for subsidizing a transportation system from non-transportation related tax sources. Good freeways or an efficient bus system or subway will enhance property values, and it is therefore not unreasonable to support these means of transportation from the property tax. In a metropolitan area, a good transportation system to move people to the downtown area may be a necessity to minimize the loss of retail business to suburban communities. In such cases support of the system in the central city through sales tax revenues may be justified. Perhaps the simplest justification for tax support is that transportation, like police or fire protection, is vital in an urban area and therefore deserving of support by society as a whole.

Another point of view is that represented by Wilfred Owen, who believes that whatever type of transportation system an urban region ultimately adopts should be self-supporting.[13] Among his reasons for taking this position is that in a period when the demand for all kinds of public services is increasing rapidly the competition for the tax dollar will be so great that we cannot expect transportation systems to be adequately financed if they must depend on tax support. A self-supporting system is a possibility, according to Owen, if we make certain changes in our administrative and pricing practices. In many states, for example, gas tax

---

[13] Owen, *op. cit.,* Chapter V.

revenues are distributed in such a fashion as to favor highway construction in rural rather than urban areas. Distribution formulas work so as to cause urban areas to pay far more in gas tax revenues than are spent in the urban areas. Revision of the formulas in many states would help to make urban roads and highways more nearly self-supporting.

Pricing schedules based more closely on economic principles would also help in this regard. As an illustration, transportation prices—for bridge tolls, bus fares, subway fares, etc.—should be higher when demand is high, i.e. during peak rush hours, than when it is low. Many areas, however, do just the opposite. Through special prices for buying several fares or tokens at once, prices taken advantage of primarily by regular commuters, we actually lower the price of transportation during those hours when the law of supply and demand indicate that, if anything, it should be raised. We make a similar mistake, according to Owen, when we charge only a few cents to park on the street by a parking meter but charge much more to park in an off-street parking lot. Street parking spaces are usually the most expensive, especially when it is considered that they occupy space that might otherwise be an additional traffic lane. Revision in pricing policies, says Owen, would do much to increase the financial self-sufficiency of urban transit.

As interesting as Owen's proposal is, it faces serious problems. The idea of charging more for fares or tolls during the rush hours will face the accusation that this penalizes the working man and benefits those who are free to travel whenever they please. The political obstacles in the way of a completely self-supporting system are great. In fact various types of subsidies are already used. Several states provide direct subsidies to commuter railroads, and some states and cities provide assistance through relief from certain taxes, especially property taxes. The fact that publicly owned transit systems are ordinarily exempt from national and state income taxes and most local taxes improves their financial status and might be considered a subsidy.

While complete acceptance of Owen's suggestion that transportation systems be entirely self-supporting is unlikely, he makes a point which is often overlooked. That is that urban transportation systems must be viewed in their entirety, and this concept should be applied in the area of finance. There is no reason why toll bridge revenues or gas taxes must be used only on automobile transportation facilities if other forms of transportation are of greater need to the system as a whole. This concept strikes hard against many deeply held beliefs of those who want to emphasize only the auto and it will run up against large political obstacles, but it is basic to a comprehensive view of urban transportation problems.

ORGANIZING FOR URBAN TRANSIT

The Urban Transit Agency

An important issue in urban transit is what type of administrative unit is best suited for providing this service. Is it the private corporation, the city, the state, the public transit authority, or some other organization. The trend today is decidedly in the direction of some form of public ownership, due in large part to the financial conditions of the transit industry. In the decade ending in 1963, one hundred ninety-four transit companies went out of business, some being taken over by governmental agencies and some leaving cities without public transit.[14] The financial status of transit companies has deteriorated steadily in recent years, and many systems have accumulated large deficits, thereby adding impetus to the trend toward public ownership.

Ownership by the government raises the question of what form or organization is best suited to manage transit operations. The fragmentation of government in metropolitan areas confronts transportation with the same problems it presents for other functions. No single governmental unit is sufficiently comprehensive to cover the entire area in which mass transit is needed. The central city has the greatest need for public transportation, but it is also important in most cases that some transit lines extend beyond the limits of the city out into the suburbs. A metropolitan government (where in existence) or a county government (where it encompasses the entire urban area) might be utilized to provide comprehensive mass transit. The most common means, however, has been through establishment of a special district or authority. These have the advantages of wider jurisdiction than any single city, relative independence from other governmental units, and considerable flexibility on financial matters. On the other hand, the matter of coordination with other governments can become a real problem, as it often has in the case of the Port of New York Authority.[15] Since they are usually responsible for only a portion of the total urban transportation system, their existence works against the need to look into urban transportation from a comprehensive point of view. In spite of coordination problems this approach is widely used. The New York Transit Authority and the Chicago Transit

---

[14] *Ibid.,* p. 93.

[15] See Edward T. Chase, "How to Rescue New York from its Port Authority," *Harper's Magazine,* Vol. 220, No. 1321 (June, 1960), pp. 67–74.

Authority as well as the Bay Area Transit District would be examples of the district and authority forms of organization. In the absence of some unexpected sudden trend toward metropolitan governments, transportation districts and authorities appear likely to remain common organizational units for administering public transportation operations.

THE NATIONAL GOVERNMENT'S ROLE

The Department of Transportation

In 1966 the federal government gave new emphasis to urban transportation needs through establishment of the Department of Transportation as the twelfth department in the President's cabinet. The purpose of creating the new department was to bring together in one unit the many varied federal agencies concerned with transportation. A total of thirty-one agencies and bureaus were transferred to the department. Included were the Federal Aviation Administration, the Bureau of Public Roads, the Coast Guard, the St. Lawrence Seaway Development Corporation, the Alaska Railroad, the Great Lake Pilotage Administration, and the Under Secretary of Commerce for Transportation. President Johnson and many congressional supporters of the bill had hoped to move the Maritime Administration into the department, but political opposition to this was sufficiently strong to block any such action, leaving Maritime with an independent status.

The Secretary of Transportation has the responsibility for developing new transportation goals and objectives and for suggesting policy guidelines to the many national, state, and local transportation agencies. It is probable that expanded federal aid to urban transportation will become available and will enable the department to help shape future transportation policies. The creation of a new cabinet department inevitably creates problems of coordination and conflict. While many agencies are pulled together into one department, it is impossible to include all offices with an interest in transportation. The Department of Commerce and the Department of Housing and Urban Development, for example, will continue to be concerned with certain aspects of urban transportation, and a potential for conflict will certainly exist. Whether the new department will achieve the goal of coordination in clarifying national transportation goals remains to be seen. It should certainly have the effect of emphasizing the interest and support of the national government for urban transportation programs.

Highway Beauty and Safety

Closely related to transportation are two other areas in which the national government has taken an interest: highway beauty and safety. The Highway Beautification Act of 1965 was concerned with three main problems, control of outdoor advertising, control of junkyards, and landscape improvement. Regulations pertaining to size, lighting and spacing of commercial signs are dealt with in the act. Junkyards along the Interstate System of highways which are within one thousand feet of the highway right-of-way must be screened or relocated, and financial assistance is provided by the act for these purposes. The act also provides that three per cent of the federal aid highway funds apportioned to a state may be used for restoration and preservation of scenic beauty adjacent to Interstate Highways, and this amount need not be matched by the state.

In September, 1966, the President signed into law the National Traffic and Motor Vehicle Safety Act and the Highway Safety Act. The former places emphasis on national government action to reduce traffic accidents, deaths and injuries, while the latter provides aid to state and local governments to assist with traffic safety programs. The National Traffic and Motor Vehicle Safety Act includes safety standards to be applied to construction of motor vehicles and interstate commerce. The Highway Safety Act provides grants-in-aid on a dollar for dollar matching basis to encourage state and local governments to undertake research and development projects and experimental demonstration programs which are designed to promote highway traffic safety. The interest in highway beauty and safety represents new activities for the national government and hopefully are indicative of a desire and intention on the part of the national government to take a truly comprehensive view of the nation's transportation problems.

Suggested Readings

Ames, Ardee, "The Search for Balanced Transportation," *Nation's Cities,* Vol. 3, No. 1 (January, 1965), pp. 20-23.

Litch, Lyle C., *et. al., Urban Transportation and Public Policy* (San Francisco: Chandler Publishing Co., 1964).

Owen, Wilfred, *The Metropolitan Transportation Problem,* Revised Edition Washington: Brookings Institution, 1966). The best general discussion of the subject for the layman.

Simpson, H. S., "Mass Transit Can Be Saved," *Public Management,* Vol. 35, No. 4 (April, 1953), pp. 77-81.

Smerk, George M., *Urban Transportation: The Federal Role* (Bloomington: Indiana University Press, 1965).

Smith, Joel, *Some Social Aspects of Mass Transit* (East Lansing: Michigan State University, Institute for Community Development, 1959).

chapter 13

The Traditional Urban Services

In an era when much of the talk about urban areas concerns race relations, freeways, and metropolitan planning, it is sometimes easy to overlook the fact that the traditional services which urban governments have long provided are still a very important part of the responsibilities of these governments. As we near the close of this book, we now turn our attention to four of these services—education, health, welfare, and law enforcement. It would be impossible to discuss all issues related to these subjects in the limited space available here, so we shall limit ourselves to the political and governmental aspects of these services and to those aspects which have been most often the subject of public discussion and public policy debate.

EDUCATION

There is no service that evokes more discussion, has more long-range effects or takes more of the tax dollar than education. As we discussed in Chapter 2, education is an issue that will often arouse the intense concern of an otherwise passive citizenry. A commitment to high quality schools is part of the sacred ritual of virtually every political official and public figure.

There is a strong tradition of local responsibility for education in the United States. Both the state and national governments share in this responsibility, but education is still primarily a local function. The usual organizational structure for the provision of elementary and secondary education is the local school district. The school district is very much like any other single-purpose special district. It is ordinarily completely independent of other units of government and possesses its own taxing and borrowing powers. In some places the public school system is a part of the city (New York City, for example), township, or county government, but the independent district is the more common organizational form. The governing body of the district is a school board made up of lay citizens. The board is responsible for appointing the superintendent, establishing general policies for the district, and (usually) levying the school tax. Board members are commonly elected to their positions in nonpartisan elections, although where the system is part of the city government (as in Chicago and New York) they may be appointed by the mayor or council.

There is no area of public service in which the goal of "staying out of politics" is more firmly established than in public education. This is indicated by the independent district forms of organization, the use of non-partisan elections and the tendency to leave most decisions of consequence to the "professionals," i.e. the superintendent and his staff and faculty. As we have indicated earlier one must be aware of the idea of keeping a function out of politics. It may be possible to insulate the schools from partisan politics. However, if we remember that we define politics as conflict over public policy, it is obvious that a function that spends as much tax revenue and arouses as much citizen interest as public education is inevitably involved in political decisions. There is nothing intrinsically wrong in the myth of keeping the schools out of politics so long as the myth itself is not used to affect the outcome of political decisions—for example, by denying a citizen a seat on the board simply because he is active in a political party.

Students of public administration have often questioned the wisdom of creating an independent unit of government to provide education for the same reasons that they question the creation of special districts to provide other public services. They suggest that any time a government is created to provide a single service it is very difficult to weigh the value of that particular service against others. A city council must compare the need for fire protection against the need for more parks or better streets in allocating scarce tax dollars. A school board, or the board of any other single-purpose special district, is seldom forced to make such comparisons. Critics also charge that coordination of related functions, such as school site location and street planning, is more difficult when they are performed by different governments. In spite of criticisms of this type, the independent status of public schools is not only well established but also strongly supported by most citizens. Any proposal to merge school districts with city or county government would undoubtedly bring about intense public opposition in most places.

One point made by school officials, nearly all of whom support the independent district concept, is that education has so much influence on the formulation of public opinion and general societal attitudes that it must be kept independent to prevent any possible misuse of the system for propaganda or indoctrination.[1] This important consideration, it is said, overrides many arguments against the independent districts. Most would agree that this point is a very valid one, and for many it more than offsets the administrative difficulties attributed to the independent district system.

The independence of the schools has been maintained in most areas where some form of area-wide coordination of governments has been developed. In Nashville the position of the schools was one of the more controversial issues raised during the city-county consolidation discussion. Schools were finally made a part of the consolidated government, but the school board was given the right to appeal its case to the people in a referendum if the council cuts its budget. In Miami the school districts are continued as independent governmental units. Most regional councils that have been created up to the present time have not included school district representatives among their members in spite of the obvious importance of many area-wide problems to school officials.

One question that often becomes an important political issue with schools is school consolidation. As the nation has evolved from a rural to an urban society, the total number of school districts has decreased through district consolidation. This has occurred mainly in rural areas where small districts and one room school houses have been consolidated into larger units. The heated controversy and sharp debate that accompanied consolidation in many ways was ample evidence of the concern of the citizen for his schools. The fear of loss of local control and the inconvenience of bussing rural students to the nearest community were perhaps early manifestations of debates over education that still occur with only slight changes to fit the times.

While consolidation in the past has been a rural issue, it is now often a contributing factor to the fragmentation of government in urban areas. Most metropolitan areas are divided into even more school districts than municipalities, and district and muncipal borders are often not coterminous. Even in the large central cities, where consolidation has usually advanced sufficiently so that a single secondary system exists, there are still several cases where independent elementary districts exist side-by-side in the same city. The unified school districts that encompass an entire metropolitan area, suburb as well as central city and elementary as well as secondary schools, are few and far between. In fact, it is safe to say that the desire to escape the city school system and become part of a separate system has been a prime motivating factor in the movement of families

---

[1] The same reasoning is often used to support an independent status for public libraries.

to the suburbs and the desire to maintain the independent status of the suburban community. There is no reason to believe that any general trend toward school consolidation on a metropolitan area-wide basis will occur in the near future.

School Finances

A tradition of local responsibility for education has meant that the financial burden of providing schools falls mainly on the local district. As the following figures indicate, over fifty-six per cent of the revenues of elementary and secondary schools are raised locally:

Source of Public Elementary and Secondary School Revenues
(In Billions)

	1950		1960		1965	
Total	$5.437	(100.0%)	$14.747	(100.0%)	$22.484	(100.0%)
Local	3.116	(57.3)	8.327	(56.5)	12.800	(56.9)
State	2.116	(39.8)	5.768	(39.1)	8.708	(38.7)
National	.156	(2.9)	.652	(4.4)	.976	(4.3)

Source: Office of Education, *Digest of Educational Statistics, 1965.*

It can be seen that the proportion of total revenues provided by each level of government has remained fairly stable since 1950. Long-range trends show that the most significant change has been the increasing responsibility being taken on by the state. In 1920 the state governments provided only 16.5 per cent of elementary and secondary school revenues, and in 1940 this figure had increased to 30.3 per cent. The figures above show that the state's portion has been about 39 per cent since 1950. The main problem with local district financing is that the property tax is the only tax most districts are allowed to levy, and the short comings of this tax discussed in Chapter 9 apply with equal validity to the school district. The result has been increased reliance on the state for financial assistance.

Until quite recently financial assistance provided by the national government has been small and limited to particular fields. Aid has long been available, for example, for training in agriculture and home economics, and more recently there has been assistance for school lunch programs. The Russian launching of their Sputnik in 1958 was in many ways a great boost for American education because it shocked the nation into realizing that more emphasis and more expenditure would be necessary for educational purposes. Federal aid was soon made available to help finance education in mathematics, sciences, and foreign languages, and loans and scholarships were established to assist those continuing on to college. Even after Sputnik, however, federal assistance was limited to a relatively few subjects.

The first major broadening of the national government's program of assistance came with the passage of the Elementary and Secondary Education Act of 1965. This act authorized funds for school libraries and equipment, textbooks, and other instructional materials. Money was also provided for educational television, guidance and counseling, and remedial reading programs, and special funds were earmarked for schools serving low income families. In addition the Higher Education Act of 1965 established a program of federal scholarships and created a National Teachers Corps to serve officials in poverty areas. These two acts seem to have broken the tradition of providing aid only in a few fields of study, and the national government has now committed itself to providing financial assistance to local school districts for a wide variety of subjects and projects. For many years there was a fear on the part of many citizens that federal assistance to education would lead to control of educational policies by the national government. The legislation passed in 1965 indicated that Congressmen believed this fear to be subsiding. In any case we now have the opportunity to see whether large-scale federal aid will lead to excessive federal control.

"Slums and Suburbs"

James B. Conant says that the most serious crisis facing urban schools today grows out of the dichotomy implied in the title of his book *Slums and Suburbs*.[2] In the central cities of most of our metropolitan areas the school system is burdened with the problem of providing education in the urban slums. In these areas buildings and facilities are usually old, the adults are not interested in supporting education, and the students are not motivated and see little relationship between schools and the needs of later life. In too many cases, according to Conant, the slum schools have been the orphans of the school system. These schools are often staffed with the youngest and most inexperienced teachers because as soon as a teacher has enough seniority to choose where he wants to teach he asks to be moved to a more desirable location.

Conant suggests that it may be necessary to pay premium salaries in slum area schools to induce some of the best teachers to serve there. He also urges that special emphasis be given to providing *better* than average education for minority groups in the early grades, that vocational programs in fields such as auto mechanics be expanded, and that particular

---

[2] James B. Conant, *Slums and Suburbs* (New York: McGraw-Hill Book Company, 1961).

attention be given to developing programs for the slower than average learner. He notes the need to enlist the support of adults in slum areas and the importance of encouraging local business and labor leaders to help provide employment opportunities for high school graduates from these areas. Where employers or unions are reluctant to provide employment for minority groups, federal funds should be used as an incentive in insuring equal employment practices.

In the suburbs, interestingly, the problem is almost the opposite for there the difficulty arises from an overemphasis on certain aspects of education. The suburban dweller has high hopes that his children will be able to attend college, and the curriculum of the suburban school reflects this orientation. The suburban school system usually places heavy emphasis on a college preparatory program to the neglect of vocational training and other programs for the student whose education will end with high school. While it is usually true that the better schools and other advantages which higher family income can provide make it possible for a high percentage of suburban high school graduates to go to college, the school curriculum should not overlook those whose lack of ability or interest prevents their going on. Related to this is the problem of the parent whose ambitions for his children do not reflect their true ability and who pushes them toward college regardless of their aptitudes or inclinations.

Conant points out the need for a balanced curriculum in suburban schools which, while continuing to emphasize college preparatory programs appropriate to the majority of students, does not overlook the importance of providing alternatives for the minority who will not continue in school. He also urges a counseling program beginning in grade school which will give a student and his parents an evaluation of the student's abilities and some indication of what type of institution of higher education (Ivy League school, state university, junior college, vocational school, etc.) he can realistically expect to qualify for.

Schools and Race

In 1954 the United States Supreme Court took action which brought the national government directly into the controversy over racial segregation in the schools. In that year the Court ruled that legal segregation in elementary and secondary education was a violation of constitutional rights,[3] a decision which resulted in a long and continuing struggle to

---

[3] Brown v. Board of Education of Topeka, 347 U.S. 483 (1954).

eliminate racial segregation from the schools. The Court was not specific on how quickly this had to occur, and the efforts to implement the decision have brought heated and sometimes bloody conflict. Opponents of the decision have argued that it attempted to push school districts into action that could only be successfully accomplished through a slow and evolutionary process. Civil rights advocates, while supporting the decision, believe that implementation has been far too slow. Regardless of one's point of view on the decision itself, it would be hard to contend that desegregation has been pushed at a rapid rate. It is estimated that of the three million Negro students in eleven southern states in 1964, ten years after the decision, fewer than thirty thousand were attending classes with white students.

Civil rights groups have long urged that federal aid to education bills require schools to eliminate segregation in order to qualify for funds, but Congressmen supporting the bills were reluctant to include such a requirement for fear of killing the entire program. The desegregation requirement finally became law when Article VI of the Civil Rights Act of 1965 provided that all facilities (including schools) receiving federal funds must eliminate segregation. As with the court decision, implementation met difficulty. In the first major confrontation the Office of Education in 1965 dramatically attempted to cut off thirty million dollars in aid to the Chicago school system, but after much negotiation the Office of Education reconsidered its position and Chicago received its money. The government has since moved more carefully but still with firmness, guidelines for desegregation have been established, and progress is being made. At the close of 1966 only thirty-four of five thousand affected districts had been declared ineligible for aid after hearings by the Commissioner of Education.

Even where desegregation has been established in law, segregated housing patterns mean that the schools in fact often remain segregated. School officials are then faced with the question of whether their responsibility is merely to remove the legal barriers that have kept schools segregated or whether they should take positive steps to insure that actual integration will occur. In a few cities plans have been adopted to bus students in order to provide racial balance in each school. Such plans incite great controversy not only because of the racial issues involved but also because they strike against the concept of the neighborhood school which many citizens consider to be a vital part of our educational system. In 1965 the question of bussing was a major issue in the school board elections in Boston, and an ardent opponent of bussing emerged as victor. Plans for bussing will continue to cause heated controversy for some time to come.

PUBLIC HEALTH

Although the role of the government in public health activities has occasionally provoked controversy, some governmental responsibility for protecting the public health has long been accepted as proper. A century ago this consisted mainly of quarantine regulations, the isolating of those with a highly contagious disease. The concentration of population in urban areas made it necessary for local governments to undertake more extensive activities in the public health area, and the advances in medical research made it possible for them to do so.

Public Health Functions

Today public health responsibilities can be grouped into the following general categories: (1) collection of vital statistics; (2) communicable disease control; (3) promotion of community sanitation; (4) maternal and child health care; (5) provision of laboratory services; (6) health and hygiene education; (7) operation of hospitals.

Public health officials play a big part in the collecting and analyzing of statistics on births, deaths, frequency of disease, and related matters. Local health departments are often responsible for the collection of data and forwarding of it to the state agency responsible for administration of vital statistics. Control of communicable disease is one of the oldest public health functions, and many diseases which once were serious threats to society—such as typhoid fever, yellow fever, small pox and diphtheria—are well controlled and seldom heard of today. Much of the current effort of communicable disease control agencies is directed toward tuberculosis and venereal disease. Community sanitation is another function of health departments and includes such activities as inspection of milk and food and the regular checking of dairies, restaurants, public restrooms, water supplies, swimming pools,. and other facilities where sanitation is vital to public health.

While public health agencies do not ordinarily provide medical services for the general public, they often offer special service relating to maternal and child care. The services include lectures and educational material for parents and prospective parents as well as prenatal and postnatal clinics and home visits by a public health nurse. Special effort is made to provide these services for the indigent and to encourage those in this situation to take advantage of them. In many areas where medical laboratories are not available through other channels, these services are provided by the local public health department, making it possible for physicians to get analyses of tests and other materials necessary for the proper diagnosis and care of patients.

One of the best known activities of public health agencies is hygiene education. Through presentations at schools, churches and civic groups, press announcements, programs on radio and television, and distribution of printed material, efforts are made to acquaint the public with good health habits and alert them to possible dangers. The wide familarity with slogans like "Brush your teeth twice a day, see your dentist twice a year" is evidence of at least partial success.

Municipal and county hospitals and hospitals operated by special public health or hospital districts are a common public health function today. In many places these facilities are the main source of medical care for the poor, and the financial burden placed on the facility because of this is often a heavy one. There is a general tendency for public hospitals in smaller cities to be self-sufficient while those in larger cities operate at a deficit, and one reason for this is the concentration of people unable to pay for medical services in large urban areas. It should not be thought that the municipal hospitals exist only as charity institutions to serve the indigent. In many cities public hospitals serve citizens of all economic levels and much of the best medical care and medical research available is to be found in these county and municipal hospitals.

Most local governments engage in many activities that are closely related to public health even though they are not administered by a public health department. Garbage collection, trash collection, the establishment of sewage disposal systems, and water purification would be examples. There are also other services which, while not dating back as far as the more traditional services, are becoming accepted in many communities as legitimate components of a complete public health program. Mental health facilities, for example, are becoming increasingly common. These make the services of psychiatrists, psychologists, and counselors available to those with mental and emotional problems. Industrial hygiene is another new area. A very important new function, one that we shall discuss below, is air pollution control.

Governmental Organization

The pattern of governmental organization for the administration of public health functions has developed in a manner parallel to that for planning, libraries, and certain other functions. There was in an earlier period a fear of letting political officials at city hall get too closely involved in public health, and the responsibility for this function was consequently placed in an independent commission. The public health board or commission often was dominated by physicians, dentists, and others who were professionally associated with the function, although there was usually some provision made for lay representation. It was the responsibility of the board to appoint the chief public health officer and establish general policies relevant to public health matters.

The twentieth century trend to administrative integration has affected public health administration as well as other services and it is now common for the chief public health officer to be appointed by the chief executive of the city or county. While the board of health still exists, it is more often advisory and sometimes serves as an appeals board for those who are subject to public health inspection and regulation. Public health departments usually have a highly professional staff and the department director commonly holds either the M.D. or D.P.H. (Doctor of Public Health) degree.

There is also a tendency for public health responsibilities to be shifted to jurisdictions with a larger population base. The costs involved make it difficult for small communities to provide adequate health services and make the avoidance of duplication a practical necessity. As a result many cities have turned over the responsibility for public health services to the county or to a public health district including several counties.

Local public health agencies receive financial and technical assistance from state health departments which have been established in all states beginning with Massachusetts in 1869. These state offices establish state-wide health standards, coordinate the activities of local agencies, provide certain state-wide health services, provide research facilities, and administer a multitude of federal grants-in-aid programs related to health.

The national government has had an interest in public health since the first decade of its existence, the United States Public Health Service having its origins in the establishment of a medical care program for seamen in 1798. Today the Public Health Service is responsible for a vast array of programs involving the operation of hospitals and clinics, medical education, research, and grants-in-aid. A division of the Public Health Service, the National Institute of Health, carries on research on a wide variety of subjects concerned with the causes and cures of disease.

Air Pollution

No health problem is causing urban officials more concern than air pollution, the presence in the air of contaminates that can be both aesthetically displeasing and physically harmful. In varying degrees the problem has been recognized for hundreds of years, but its real seriousness has been recognized primarily since World War II. Sources of air pollution include industrial plants, incinerators, dust from unpaved streets, burning dumps, trucks, buses, and private automobiles. The major source will vary from one area to another. In New York, for example, industrial plants are considered to be an important source of pollutants while it is estimated that over 90 per cent of the air pollution in the Los Angeles area results from motor vehicles, primarily the automobile.

Los Angeles is one of many urban areas that are especially susceptible to pollution conditions because of what are called "air inversion layers." Such inversion layers result from low hanging layers of warm air which keep the lower masses of cooler air from rising. The inability of the low air masses to rise and dissipate holds the pollution in. In addition the generally low wind velocity keeps the pollutants from blowing away. When an area is partially surrounded by mountains, as is Los Angeles, it is even more difficult for pollution to escape.

There are at least four serious problems that result from air pollution. First, there is the aesthetic problem. Phoenix, Arizona, and Denver, Colorado, are examples of beautiful cities which are losing much of their charm and attractiveness to increasingly serious air pollution concentrations. Both of these cities share with Los Angeles the climatic conditions that give them heavy concentrations of pollutants. A second result of air pollution is physical discomfort in the form of burning eyes, nose irritations, and sore throats.

More serious even than physical discomfort is the fact that air pollution can cause lasting damage to health. Nasal, throat, and respiratory diseases and possibly even some forms of cancer have been connected with high levels of air pollution. Finally, air pollution has damaging economic effects in the form of corrosion, damage to paint and building materials, harm to vegetation, and injury to livestock.

Perhaps because California was the first state to face critical problems of this type, it was also the state to move most rapidly to do something about them.[4] In 1947 the state legislature passed the Air Pollution Control Act which enabled counties to form air pollution control districts, and in 1949 the legislature authorized two or more contiguous counties to join together to create such districts. Some districts, such as that in the Los Angeles area, have taken strong action to limit strictly pollution from oil heaters and generators, open dumps, incinerators, refineries, and industry. Such efforts have been sufficiently successful that it is now believed the

---

[4] For a general discussion of different administrative arrangements for the management of air pollution control functions see Kenneth G. Bueche and Morris J. Schur, *Air Pollution Control, Selected Governmental Approaches: Possibilities for Colorado* (Boulder: University of Colorado, Bureau of Governmental Research and Services, 1963).

battle would be won if motor vehicle pollution could be adequately controlled.

Action to cut down on auto pollution has been taken by the state government. Since 1959 the State Board of Public Health has had the responsibility of establishing standards of air quality and allowable amounts of motor vehicle exhaust emissions. Beginning with 1963 models all new automobiles in California were required to be equipped with certain pollution control devices. These devices have been the subject of much criticism —that they are ineffective when cars become older, that they cut down on gas mileage, that many owners remove them immediately after purchase of an automobile—but state officials declared that real progress has been made toward reducing air pollution resulting from automobiles in spite of the annually rising number of cars on the road. The federal government enacted legislation in 1966 requiring air pollution devices on all new automobiles in the country beginning with the 1968 models.

Several states have followed the example of California and enacted legislation designed to reduce air pollution, and the federal government is investing increasing amounts in research to alleviate the problem. The auto industry is constantly trying to improve control equipment, and one long-range possibility being discussed is the development of battery powered cars to be used within urban areas for short trips such as commuting.

In spite of the progress that has been made, air pollution remains one of our most critical problems, and most agree that it is likely to get worse before it gets better. The heavy costs involved for both industry and government, our relative lack of knowledge about how to conquer various aspects of the problem, and the fact that in many areas pollution is not yet bad enough to really arouse the public are all factors which indicate that a solution to air pollution is still rather far in the future.

PUBLIC WELFARE

Few issues have been more controversial historically than public welfare. There has long (at least since the passage of England's Elizabethan Poor Law of 1601) been a general acceptance of the concept that governments had a responsibility to help those in distress, but there is little concensus on the extent of that commitment. The adequacy of unemployment compensation, the justification for paying child support to unwed mothers, and the question of "chislers" on the welfare rolls are examples of the kinds of issues that make welfare a live issue in most legislative chambers.

In the nation's earliest years welfare was primarily a responsibility shared by the family and local governments. A traditional "poor farm" and the "old folks home" represent forms of welfare found in the early 1800's and were the responsibility of local units of government. It was not until the middle of the nineteenth century, beginning in Massachusetts in 1863, that state governments began to establish state welfare boards and become directly involved in welfare programs. In the late 1800's and early 1900's the trend toward state boards and the expansion of state welfare activities increased with rapidity. The belief that welfare could be provided only through institutionalizing recipients began to die out, and new programs such as aid to the blind, aid to dependent children, and assistance for the physically handicapped were adopted. Where the need still existed for institutions, such as for the mentally handicapped, states were beginning to take over this responsibility by the turn of the century, thereby relieving local governments of this financial burden.

One of the broadest welfare programs, old age assistance, began with a few states in the 1920's, but did not really win acceptance nationally until passage of the Social Security Act of 1935. That legislation created the national social insurance system whereby an individual contributes during his working years and then receives monthly payments after retirement. The number of workers covered by the system, the amount of the contributions, and the amount of the benefits received have been regularly increased by Congress in the years since its inception. Members of both political parties in Congress have found it very tempting to support legislation expanding Social Security benefits, and such expansion has become almost an election year ritual.

The establishment of Social Security was significant in another way in that it marked the first large-scale entry of the national government into the welfare field. Since then its support of and participation in welfare programs has increased rapidly, and in 1953 the importance of its responsibilities was officially recognized with the creation of the Department of Health, Education and Welfare as a cabinet level agency. It is probably accurate to say that welfare policy in the United States is established primarily by the national government. Through the creation of extensive national programs like Social Security and large-scale grants-in-aid for state and local welfare programs, the national government has taken the initiative in the policy field, and most state and local welfare programs operate within the general framework established by the national government.

This does not mean, however, that welfare policies are uniform from state to state. Some states have chosen not to establish certain welfare programs even though federal aid is available for them. There are also rather large differences in the amount of money which the states devote to welfare. As a rule the more industrialized and urbanized states—examples would be New York, New Jersey, Illinois, and California—have more extensive welfare programs than others. There is, moreover, no uniformity among the states in the division of welfare responsibilities between the state and local governments. In some states most welfare programs are administered by the state government while others rely heavily on local units of government, particularly the county for administration of welfare programs. The responsibilities of cities for welfare programs likewise follow no pattern. Many cities, especially smaller ones, do not directly administer any activities in this field at all, relying entirely on the county and state administrative apparatus. Larger cities, on the other hand, operate massive programs in their economically depressed areas, some on their own and some in cooperation with state and national agencies or private agencies, and expenditures commonly run into the millions.

Any discussion of the political aspects of public welfare programs should mention the fact that there is a certain amount of natural hostility or skepticism toward the public welfare concept built into the mores and values of many Americans. The Protestant Ethic, with its emphasis on hard work and frugality, is deeply rooted in our society, and it is hard for many to believe that welfare programs do not benefit mainly the lazy and immoral. Many are convinced that "Anyone can find a job if he really wants to," and the natural corollary to that is the belief that unemployment compensation is just a form of payment for laziness. Aid to dependent children is often attacked as being a program to support the immoral, and its more vicious opponents refer to it as "subsidized prostitution." The fact that little evidence exists to support this line of reasoning does not deter those looking for reasons to oppose public welfare programs. There is no way to judge accurately the extent to which such attitudes have affected welfare programs, but a reading of debates in Congress or state legislative chambers will indicate that these types of issues are generally raised when welfare programs are discussed.

On other points it is possible to make some more specific observations about the politics of public welfare. Richard E. Dawson and James A. Robinson have taken several measures of support for public welfare (payments per recipient, percentage of welfare funds coming from the national government, and per capita welfare expenditures both excluding and including federal contributions) and correlated them with certain political and social variables.[5] They found a positive relationship between the proportion of urban population, the amount of industrialization, and the per-

---

[5] Richard E. Dawson and James A. Robinson, "The Politics of Welfare," in Herbert Jacob and Kenneth N. Vines (eds.), *Politics in the American States* (Boston: Little, Brown and Co., 1965), pp. 386–409.

cent of foreign born population (particularly the last) and the degree of effort states put into welfare programs. They also found that wealthier states spend more freely on public welfare than others. In contrast they found a negative relationship between need for welfare programs (as measured by infant mortality, number of children without parents, and percent of young people without a high school education) and support for welfare programs; those states most in need of public welfare spend the least on it. Finally they found a positive relationship between support for public welfare programs and two political variables: political participation as measured by percentage of voter turnout, and inter-party competition. One possible conclusion here is that in areas where the political parties are rather evenly balanced, it becomes politically advantageous to support expansion of public welfare programs.

THE WAR ON POVERTY

In his State of the Union address in January, 1964, President Johnson urged that the federal government wage an all out "war on poverty," and in August of that year Congress took a major step toward implementing the program when it passed the Economic Opportunity Act. The Act created the Office of Economic Opportunity to coordinate the anti-poverty programs, and Sargent Shriver was moved from his position as Peace Corps director to take over direction of the anti-poverty efforts.

The act authorized a series of new programs. A *Job Corps* creates camps and resident education centers to provide job training to young people without sufficient skills to be employable. The *Neighborhood Youth Corps* provides job training and part-time employment to youth in their own communities. The *College Work-Study Program* enables young people in financial need to attend college while working on a part-time basis to help support themselves. One of the most popular of the anti-poverty programs, *Project Head Start,* was designed to give preschool educational experience to children in low income families who had not received the normal education that children in more fortunate families receive at home in their preschool years. Another program that rapidly gained popularity is *Volunteers in Service to America* (VISTA). VISTA, often known as the domestic Peace Corps, offers individuals an opportunity to devote a year or more to serving in urban slums, on Indian reservations, and in other areas of need.

The anti-poverty program has been the center of much political controversy. In addition to the expected opposition to such programs by some in Congress, many state and local officials have complained that these new programs are uncoordinated and that they either ignore or conflict with established welfare programs. Officials of federal departments like Labor and Health, Education and Welfare have said that many of the programs of the Office of Economic Opportunity should appropriately come under their departmental responsibilities, and this has prompted much bureaucratic in-fighting among federal agencies. Much controversy has also revolved around the fact that those involved in the programs have sometimes been accused of attempting to organize the poor into political action groups which would, in turn, work for further expansion of welfare and anti-poverty programs. Some have charged that the political activists in the anti-poverty program are advocates of "radicalism." In spite of such criticism, most of the anti-poverty programs appear to have been accepted by the public and will probably be expanded in the future. There are administrative problems to work out, and some of the programs will undoubtedly be eliminated while other new ones will be established, but the general anti-poverty program appears destined to become a basic part of the welfare activities of the national government.

LAW ENFORCEMENT

One municipal function for which needs and costs seem to increase geometrically rather than arithmetically as population grows is police protection. In almost every large city crime rates are rising even as the size of police forces are increased to provide more adequate protection. "Crime in the streets" has become a political issue and a rallying cry for candidates for office in many cities.

That questions concerning crime and police protection should be involved in political controversy is not, however, a new phenomenon. In the latter half of the nineteenth century and the early years of the twentieth century, city police departments were often ridden with scandal and charged with being dominated by the machine politics of city hall. As was true of some other functions there were those who believed that police administration could best be protected from "politics" by giving it a semi-autonomous status. As a result many departments came to be governed by boards or commissions whose members, while appointed by the mayor or council, had overlapping terms and could not be removed except for special cause. In a few extreme cases, such as Kansas City and St. Louis, the responsibilities were removed even more from local political officials, and power to appoint the local police commission was given to the governor of the state.

The trend today is for the police chief to be responsible directly to the chief administrative officer of the city. In strong mayor cities the police chief is usually appointed by the mayor, in council-manager cities by the city manager, and in weak mayor cities by the council. The internal organization of police departments is commonly based on a semi-military structure with officers holding ranks of captain, lieutenant, sergeant, etc. Until quite recently it was common for municipal government textbooks to discuss (and often to urge) the possible consolidation of police and fire departments into a single administrative unit. The reasoning was that "public safety officers" would be trained in both fire and police protection and could then be used wherever the need occurred, thereby providing both added economy and flexibility. For better or worse, the police-fire consolidation movements never got off the ground. A few cities have taken such action, but for the most part such things as the intense opposition of both police and fire organizations, the lack of interest on the part of local officials and the public, and the absence of state legislation authorizing such consolidation have prevented any widespread trend in this direction.

There is little doubt that the quality of individuals serving on police forces has improved remarkably with time. The day of the large, gruff illiterate in police uniform is passed in most cities. A few cities—Berkeley, California, would be an example—even have police departments made up primarily of college graduates, and most departments in urban areas now place strong emphasis on education. Many junior colleges offer two-year police training programs, and some universities—Michigan State University and City University of New York are among the better known—offer four-year degree programs in police administration.

One force that has necessitated an improvement in the quality of police officers has been Supreme Court decisions demanding much more sophistication in the investigation of crimes and more stringent protection of the constitutional rights of the accused. In a series of recent decisions[6] the court has extended the constitutional protections against unreasonable search and seizure to apply to state cases as well as federal, spelled out additional guarantees to the individual's right to counsel, and established limits on how far police officers may go in interrogating and attempting to secure confessions from those accused of crime. It has been established that those apprehended and accused of a crime must be: (1) immediately informed of their right to counsel; (2) informed of their right to have an attorney provided for them even if they cannot afford to pay the costs; (3) informed of their right to have counsel present while they are questioned; and (4) informed of their right to remain silent. While such pro-

---

[6] See Mapp v. Ohio, 367 U.S. 643 (1960); Escobedo v. Illinois, 378 U.S. 478 (1964); Miranda v. Arizona, 384 U.S. 436 (1966).

visions help assure an accused criminal that his constitutional rights will be protected, they also necessitate a high level of competence on the part of those responsible for preventing and investigating crime.

There are today over forty thousand separate law enforcement agencies operating in the United States, but in spite of this seemingly hopeless maze, police administration is a function where some degree of intergovernmental cooperation has been common for many years. Departments in metropolitan areas regularly exchange information and cooperate in investigations. Larger agencies, such as the State Highway Patrol and the departments of central cities, usually have facilities like crime laboratories or training academies which smaller departments cannot afford, and it is common for them to make the services of such facilities available to smaller departments in the area. The F.B.I. has a reputation for close cooperation with state and local law enforcement agencies. In his State of the Union address of 1967, President Johnson urged that the federal government provide funds to assist local law enforcement agencies with the costs of training, purchase of scientific investigating equipment, and certain other programs. If Congress establishes such a program of financial assistance this will sharply expand the role of the national government in the law enforcement field and mark a new development in the field of intergovernmental relations. There is, nevertheless, much room for improved cooperation, and several studies have suggested that lack of adequate communication has been a significant impediment to effective law enforcement in metropolitan areas.[7] This problem is especially crucial in fighting organized crime and vice which is well coordinated on a national basis while law enforcement responsibilities are dispersed among a multitude of agencies and governmental units.

---

[7] Mitchell Gordon, *Sick Cities* (Baltimore: Penguin Books, 1965), pp. 175–78.

Suggested Readings

Bueche, Kenneth G., and Morris J. Schur, *Air Pollution Control, Selected Governmental Approaches: Possibilities for Colorado* (Boulder: University of Colorado, Bureau of Governmental Research and Services, 1963).

Conant, James B., *The American High School Today* (New York: McGraw-Hill Book Company, 1959).

————, *Slums and Suburbs* (New York: McGraw Hill Book Company, 1961).

James, Charles S., *Police and Fire Integration in the Small City* (Chicago: Public Administration Service, 1955).

Lieberman, Myron, *The Future of Public Education* (Chicago: University of Chicago Press, 1960).

Municipal Police Administration, 3d ed. (Chicago: International City Managers' Association, 1950).

Wilson, O. W., *Police Administration* (New York: McGraw-Hill Book Company, 1950).

chapter 14

Metropolis in
the Future

When it comes to a complex and rapidly changing
subject like urban government and politics, gazing into
crystal balls is a hazardous activity. In this final chapter,
nevertheless, we shall attempt some summary statements and suggest some possible developments that may
lie ahead.

METROPOLITANISM

There is little doubt that the trend toward an urban
society will continue. We are a nation of urban dwellers,
and increasingly the population will be concentrated in
metropolitan areas. Unless our values and preferences
change sharply, which is not likely, we will also be
increasingly a nation of suburbanites. Rising incomes,
shorter working hours, improved transportation systems (especially
freeways), and American preferences for single family homes with yards
and space will accelerate the movement to the suburbs. For some time
to come, suburbia will be the home of the middle income, middle class
American family, while the central city will remain the home of racial
minorities, the unmarried, the elderly, the very poor, and some of the
very rich. The central city will slowly attract some of its former residents
back and may be able to provide attractive accommodations for middle
income families, and minority groups will gradually break the racial
barriers that exist in the suburbs, but current trends indicate that the social
and economic gaps that separate the suburban dweller from his central
city counterpart will continue to exist in the immediate future.

The meaning of this is that the problems of governing widely dispersed,
heavily populated areas will become even more complex. The question of
whether these problems will be dealt with by single metropolitan govern-

ments or by a multitude of governments similar to the present system is not yet answered, but some patterns are beginning to develop. One organization that is urging a drastic reform of our present system of local government is the Committee for Economic Development.

The CED Report

The Committee for Economic Development (CED), a highly respected research group supported by many of the nation's leading businessmen, issued a report in July, 1966, entitled *Modernizing Local Government.* The report included a list of specific recommendations among them the following:[1]

> The number of local governments in the United States, now about eighty thousand, should be reduced by at least eighty per cent.
>
> The number of overlapping layers of local government found in most states should be severely curtailed.
>
> County modernization should be pressed with special vigor, since counties—everywhere except in New England—have high but undeveloped potential for solving the problems of rural, urban and most metropolitan communities.
>
> The fifty state constitutions should be revamped—either by legislative amendment or through constitutional conventions concentrating on local government modernization—to provide for boundary revisions, extensions of legal authority, and elimination of needless overlapping layers.

CED obviously prefers the broad jurisdiction multi-purpose government over the complex of small governments, special districts, and intricate service arrangements now in existence. Some progress, of course, has been made in this direction. The consolidation of school districts has been reducing the total number of governments by eliminating excessively small governmental units for over a quarter of a century. Some modernization of county government has occurred, but CED has touched on a vital point when it emphasizes the need for much more progress in this area. The county government has much potential for meeting the needs of metropolitan areas on an area-wide basis. Counties are part of our traditional system of government; they are familiar to the citizenry and therefore politically acceptable. In many places a single county encompasses the entire

---

[1] *Modernizing Local Government* (New York: Committee for Economic Development, 1966), pp. 17–18.

metropolitan area. The great need is for governmental modernization that will enable the county to function effectively if called upon to serve as the "metropolitan government."

No direct recommendation is made by CED in favor of a single area-wide general purpose government for metropolitan areas. While they urge fewer governments, they also prefer the use of established governmental units—city, county and state—to the creation of new types of governments. This recognizes the political realities involved in undertaking broad scale reform of local government structure. Even the reforms recommended by CED, however, will arouse much political opposition and their implementation will come only through a slow evolutionary process.

The Voluntary Association or Regional Council

The slow evolutionary process of which we just spoke is indeed the way that any governmental reform in metropolitan areas is likely to come. It is for this reason that voluntary associations, or regional councils as they are often called, are possibly the most important new development in the governing of metropolitan areas in recent years. They are the "next logical step" in the evolutionary process. Given the need for cooperation on an area-wide basis at the same time the general reluctance on the part of both local officials and local citizens to create single area-wide governments, it is natural to move toward the voluntary association, which provides a means for at least some communication and coordination without elimination of the existing units of government.

Critics will suggest that this is simply a convenient scheme for appearing to make progress while maintaining the status quo, and there will undoubtedly be cases where this will be true. In general, though, this criticism is not warranted. The associations in operation at present have been quite effective as agents of research, communications and coordination, as persuasive voices in urging cooperation, and as catalysts in the local political process.

The evolutionary nature of the association is its greatest strength. In some areas it may be a step in the direction of the eventual creation of a metropolitan government; in others it may be the step that eliminates the need for a metropolitan government. In either case it is a step that can usually be taken with a minimum of disruption to the political system of a metropolitan area. The voluntary association (along with an expanded role for the county if county governments can be modernized) probably offers the greatest potential in the near future for making effective progress in meeting the governmental needs of the metropolitan complex.

THE NEW FEDERALISM

As important as the relationships among neighboring local governments in the future will be the relationships among the three basic levels of government in our federal system. The position of the national government, in particular, is undergoing rapid change in relation to the problems of metropolitan areas. Whereas it was once accepted that the problems of local governments were primarily the concerns of the states which created those governments, the national government has recently moved forcefully into the problems of urban areas. The creation of HUD is only one indication of this, and there is every reason to believe that this trend will continue and increase. We mention here only two federal programs which potentially may have far-reaching consequences for the governing of metropolitan areas.

Model Cities

The Model Cities[2] program of the national government is designed to provide a comprehensive approach to the needs of the city. The concept of the program is that the city must be seen as a total political, social, and economic system and its problems dealt with on that basis. Emphasis is to be placed on specific areas in a selected group of cities where problems are especially serious. Instead of an uncoordinated series of federal grants —one for education, one for highways, one for slum clearance, etc.—an attempt will be made to identify the various aspects of the existing problems and to develop a comprehensive plan for attacking those problems. Then the resources of the many agents of the national government, along with those of state, local and private agencies, will be brought together in accordance with the plan to provide a coordinated system of implementation.

We must wait to see whether the program will be a success. The concept seems unquestionably sound and appears to be an improvement over the piecemeal approach to urban needs. On the other hand, the problems of the city may be just too complex and the tasks of coordination too great for it to work in actual practice. Let us hope not, for if this concept can work, there is hope for finding solutions to what have seemed to be unsolvable problems.

---

[2] The program was originally called the "Demonstration Cities" program, but, because of the fear that it might be associated with street demonstrations and rioting, the name was changed.

Tax Rebates

We discussed tax rebates, the Heller Plan, in Chapter 9. It is mentioned here again because it is being increasingly discussed in Congress and among other governmental officials and because adoption of some such plan could be one of the most important occurrences in the history of our federal system so far as local governments are concerned.

The national government, and to some extent state governments, have just about preempted the income tax as a source of revenue. Since this is the revenue source that is most progressive and responds most readily to growth in the economic system, local governments are left to rely on more regressive and less productive tax sources. At the same time funds returned to local government (particularly those from the national government) are usually on a specific project basis and must be spent in prescribed ways for prescribed projects. The revenue sharing idea, in contrast, foresees distribution of funds on a no (or few)-strings-attached basis. Enactment of a revenue sharing plan could open up the income tax as a revenue source for local governments, enabling them either to better meet some of their most pressing needs or to relieve the burden of other more regressive taxes, or both. The interest in this idea gives cause for believing that some such plan may be adopted in the not-too-distant future. Whether or not one prefers this approach to the more traditional grant-in-aid approach, it is agreed that revenue sharing could radically alter the local fiscal picture.

A FINAL WORD

There are those who say that local government is on the decline, its powers and functions having been usurped by higher levels of government, but the evidence does not support this conclusion. Local governments today, judged by their activities, their professional staffs, and their budgets, are strong, vigorous, dynamic units of government. Reforms, such as some of those recommended by CED, and certain new programs, such as Model Cities or revenue sharing, may strengthen them even further. For the most part local governments are also made up of honest officials. The day of domination by corrupt interests and inept officials ended several decades ago in most cities even though they are still trying to live down the reputation gained at that time.

This does not mean, however, that democracy as it operates at the local level has no problems. There is real danger that the urban citizen will lose control of his local government not to the national government or the corrupt official but rather to such forces as complexity and apathy. The operations of government may become so complicated and the functions so specialized and technical that the possibilities for effective citizen control will disappear.

We return, therefore, to a point that has been emphasized throughout the book—the process of governing the American metropolis is essentially a *political* process. Politics, as we have said, involves the resolution of conflict over public policy, and that is what constantly occurs in government. There is conflict over whether to annex a new area, whether to create a new metropolitan layer of government, whether to spend additional funds for parks or policemen, and the process by which that conflict is resolved (be it by bargaining, negotiation, compromise, capitulation, or whatever) is the phenomenon called *politics*.

Urban governments consist of many kinds of people including planners, civil engineers, garbage collectors, police officers, educators, and social workers, but standing in the midst of all of them is the *politician* who must act as referee, or arbiter, among their competing demands. The performance of the politician is therefore vital to the role of the citizen, for it is primarily through the political official that the citizen is able to state his choices and preferences on policy issues if he is able to do so at all. For some the words *politics* and *politician* have bad connotations, but they are virtually necessary if urban government is to continue to be a democratic process. We may hope to run local governments in a businesslike fashion, but we must remember that they are not just like private businesses. We may hope to keep bad politics out of City Hall, but we must not keep politics out of City Hall for to do so would be to keep democracy out also. Politics and politicians stand at the heart of the democratic process in urban government and that, the author believes, is as it should be.

Suggested Readings

Elias, C. E., Jr., James Gillies, and Svend Riemer, *Metropolis: Values in Conflict* (Belmont, California: Wadsworth Publishing Co., 1964). A book of readings on the most pressing issues in our urban areas.

"The Future Metropolis," *Daedalus* (Winter, 1961). Entire edition devoted to this subject.

Modernizing Local Government (New York: Committee for Economic Development, 1966).

Vernon, Raymond, *Metropolis: 1985* (Cambridge: Harvard University Press, 1960). The concluding volume in a series resulting from the New York Metropolitan Region Study.

Weaver, Robert C., *The Urban Complex* (Garden City, New York: Doubleday & Company, Inc., 1964). An analysis of urban problems and suggestions for solutions by the Secretary of the Department of Housing and Urban Development.

Index

Dade County, Florida, 64
metropolitan federalism, 108–10
Dahl, Robert A., 51–52
Daley City, California, 199
Daley, Richard, 37
Dallas, Texas, 6, 18, 35, 65, 84, 193
Davidson County, Tennessee
city-county consolidation, 103–105
Dawson, Richard E., 222
Dayton, Ohio, 60
Dearborn, Michigan, 32
Debt limits, 155–56
Democrats, 14, 40, 48, 66, 67, 99, 120–21
Denver, Colorado, 29, 65, 219
DesMoines, Iowa, 59
Detroit, Michigan, 3, 4, 9, 18, 30, 32, 49, 151
Dillon, J. F., 130
Dillon's Law, 73, 130
Dilworth, Richardson, 33
Dormitory suburb, 31
Downtown, problems of, 173–75

Earnings tax, 150–51
Economic interdependence
consequence of urbanization, 8–9
Economic Opportunity, Office of, 223–24
Education, 209–15 (*See also* Schools)
school district organization, 210–211
finances, 212–13
Eichler Homes, Inc., 191
Eisenhower, Dwight D., 139–40
Eisenhower Expressway (in Chicago), 195–96, 198
Elementary and Secondary Education Act of 1965, 213
Elites
in study of community power, 50–54
El Paso, Texas, 3

Employment opportunities, 4–5
Employment patterns, changes in metropolitan areas, 24
Ethics, 20
Evanston, Illinois, 31, 32
Expenditures, local government 153–54
Extraterritorial powers, 86–87

Far reaching approaches to governing metropolitan areas, 97–111
consolidation of similar governmental units, 97–101
city-county consolidation, 101–105
city-county separation, 105–06
metropolitan federalism, 106–10
Federal Aviation Administration, 206
Federal Bureau of Investigation, 136, 226
Federal government
housing programs, 180–86
and metropolitan areas, 129–43
relations with local governments, 136–43
and schools, 212–13
and suburbanization, 23
and urban planning, 168–70
Federal Housing Administration, 23, 180, 185–86, 189
Federal National Mortgage Association, 141
Fees, for government services, 148–149
Finances
local government, 145–59
school, 212–13
transportation, 202–05
Fizer, Webb S., 108
Florida, 98, 108
Fragmentation of government in metropolitan areas, 30–31
Freedgood, Seymour, 35, 41, 46
Fulton County, Georgia, 101